Orla Greevy

Enriching Reverse Engineering with Feature Analysis

Orla Greevy

Enriching Reverse Engineering with Feature Analysis

Introducing the Dynamix Feature Meta-Model

Südwestdeutscher Verlag für Hochschulschriften

Impressum/Imprint (nur für Deutschland/ only for Germany)
Bibliografische Information der Deutschen Nationalbibliothek: Die Deutsche Nationalbibliothek verzeichnet diese Publikation in der Deutschen Nationalbibliografie; detaillierte bibliografische Daten sind im Internet über http://dnb.d-nb.de abrufbar.
Alle in diesem Buch genannten Marken und Produktnamen unterliegen warenzeichen-, marken- oder patentrechtlichem Schutz bzw. sind Warenzeichen oder eingetragene Warenzeichen der jeweiligen Inhaber. Die Wiedergabe von Marken, Produktnamen, Gebrauchsnamen, Handelsnamen, Warenbezeichnungen u.s.w. in diesem Werk berechtigt auch ohne besondere Kennzeichnung nicht zu der Annahme, dass solche Namen im Sinne der Warenzeichen- und Markenschutzgesetzgebung als frei zu betrachten wären und daher von jedermann benutzt werden dürften.

Verlag: Südwestdeutscher Verlag für Hochschulschriften Aktiengesellschaft & Co. KG
Dudweiler Landstr. 99, 66123 Saarbrücken, Deutschland
Telefon +49 681 37 20 271-1, Telefax +49 681 37 20 271-0, Email: info@svh-verlag.de
Zugl.: Berne, University of Berne, Doctoral disseration, 2007

Herstellung in Deutschland:
Schaltungsdienst Lange o.H.G., Berlin
Books on Demand GmbH, Norderstedt
Reha GmbH, Saarbrücken
Amazon Distribution GmbH, Leipzig
ISBN: 978-3-8381-0727-1

Imprint (only for USA, GB)
Bibliographic information published by the Deutsche Nationalbibliothek: The Deutsche Nationalbibliothek lists this publication in the Deutsche Nationalbibliografie; detailed bibliographic data are available in the Internet at http://dnb.d-nb.de.
Any brand names and product names mentioned in this book are subject to trademark, brand or patent protection and are trademarks or registered trademarks of their respective holders. The use of brand names, product names, common names, trade names, product descriptions etc. even without a particular marking in this works is in no way to be construed to mean that such names may be regarded as unrestricted in respect of trademark and brand protection legislation and could thus be used by anyone.

Publisher:
Südwestdeutscher Verlag für Hochschulschriften Aktiengesellschaft & Co. KG
Dudweiler Landstr. 99, 66123 Saarbrücken, Germany
Phone +49 681 37 20 271-1, Fax +49 681 37 20 271-0, Email: info@svh-verlag.de

Copyright © 2009 by the author and Südwestdeutscher Verlag für Hochschulschriften Aktiengesellschaft & Co. KG and licensors
All rights reserved. Saarbrücken 2009

Printed in the U.S.A.
Printed in the U.K. by (see last page)
ISBN: 978-3-8381-0727-1

for Paddy

Abstract

System comprehension is a prerequisite for software maintenance and evolution, but it is a time-consuming and costly activity. In an effort to support system comprehension, researchers have devised many different reverse engineering techniques. Several of these are based on statically analyzing the source code. Purely static analysis techniques, however, overlook valuable end-user knowledge of how a system behaves at runtime.

To address this problem, several researchers have identified the potential of exploiting features in a reverse engineering context. Features are abstractions of a system's problem domain that well-understood by end-users. They encapsulate knowledge of a problem domain and denote units of system behavior. Thus, they represent a valuable resource for reverse engineering a system, The main body of feature-related reverse engineering research is concerned with *feature identification*, a technique to map features to source code. To fully exploit features in reverse engineering, however, we need to extend the focus beyond feature identification and exploit features as primary units of analysis. We formulate our thesis as follows:

> *To exploit the inherent domain knowledge of features for object-oriented system comprehension, we need to explicitly model features, their relationships to source artefacts, and their relationships to each other.*

The contribution of our work is twofold: on the one hand, we enrich reverse engineering analysis of object-oriented systems with semantic knowledge of features, and on the other hand, we introduce new techniques that treat features as the primary entities of analysis. Our key contribution is our definition of Dynamix, a meta-model for expressing feature entities in the context of a structural meta-model of source code entities. Using case studies, we demonstrate how our feature-centric reverse engineering techniques, based on Dynamix, exploit feature knowledge to establish traceability between the problem and solution domains throughout the life-cycle of a system.

Table of Contents

1 Introduction — 1
   1.1 Context — 2
   1.2 The Problem of Object-Oriented System Comprehension — 3
   1.3 Our Proposal: Feature-Centric Analysis — 4
   1.4 Contributions — 6
   1.5 Structure of the Dissertation — 7

2 Towards Feature-Centric Reverse Engineering — 9
   2.1 Context — 10
   2.2 Motivating Feature-Centric Reverse Engineering — 10
   2.3 Related Research: A State of the Art — 11
      2.3.1 Dynamic Analysis for System Comprehension — 12
      2.3.2 Concept Location Approaches — 16
      2.3.3 Feature Identification Approaches — 17
      2.3.4 Feature Modeling in Requirements Engineering — 20
      2.3.5 Analysis Approaches based on Features — 22
   2.4 Summary — 23
   2.5 Elements of Feature-Centric Analysis — 24
   2.6 Outlook — 24

3 Feature-Centric Analysis — 25
   3.1 Motivation — 26
   3.2 Terminology — 27
   3.3 Dynamix — 28
   3.4 Feature Analysis: Complementary Perspectives — 30

TABLE OF CONTENTS

3.5 Feature Affinity of Structural Entities	32
3.6 Feature Properties	33
3.7 The Feature Relationship Properties	37
3.8 Summary and Outlook	40

4 Applying Feature-Centric Analysis: Two Case Studies   **43**

4.1 Introduction	44
4.2 Case Studies	45
4.3 Methodology	45
4.4 Pier Experiment	47
4.5 ArgoUML Experiment	53
4.6 Discussion	57
4.6.1 Strengths of Feature-Centric Analysis	58
4.6.2 Evaluation of Feature Affinity	58
4.6.3 Variations	59
4.6.4 Limitations	60
4.7 Related Work	60
4.7.1 How Dynamix accomodates other Feature Identification Measurements	61
4.7.2 Dynamix Adaptation: Introducing Association Entities	63
4.7.3 Feature Relationship Approaches	63
4.8 Summary	65

5 Evolution Analysis: A Structural Perspective   **67**

5.1 Introduction	68
5.2 Evolution Analysis: an Overview	69
5.3 Extending Dynamix for Evolution Analysis	70
5.4 History and Version Properties	70
5.4.1 Measuring Changes in Feature Affinity (FA)	72
5.4.2 Summarizing Change in Feature Affinity with a History Property	73
5.4.3 A Summary of the Measurements	75
5.5 A Methodology for Analyzing Changing Roles of Classes	76
5.6 Validation	76
5.6.1 Case Study: SmallWiki	77
5.6.2 Analysis of the SmallWiki Results	78
5.6.3 Case Study: Moose	80
5.6.4 Analysis of the MooseResults	80

5.7	Discussion	82
	5.7.1 Variations	83
	5.7.2 Limitations	84
5.8	Related Work	84
5.9	Summary and Outlook	85

6 Evolution Analysis: A Feature Perspective   87

6.1	Motivation	88
6.2	Analysis Strategy	89
	6.2.1 Modeling the History of Feature Entities	89
	6.2.2 History Properties for Features	89
6.3	Visualizing Change	91
	6.3.1 Visualizing *When* Features Change	92
	6.3.2 Visualizing *How* Features Change	92
6.4	Validation	94
	6.4.1 Experiment 1 - Analyzing the Evolution of the Branch	96
	6.4.2 Summary of the Results of Experiment 1	100
	6.4.3 Developer Validation (Experiment 1)	100
	6.4.4 Experiment 2: Analyzing the Evolution of the Main Development Track	101
	6.4.5 Supporting the Merging Changes	102
	6.4.6 Developer validation (Experiment 2 - Main development track)	103
6.5	Discussion	104
6.6	Related Work	105
6.7	Summary	106

7 Visually Reverse Engineering Features   109

7.1	Introduction	110
7.2	Feature Hot Spots	111
7.3	How Dynamix supports Feature Hot Spot Analysis	112
7.4	3D Visualization of Dynamic Behavior	113
7.5	Validation	117
7.6	Discussion	121
7.7	Comparisons with other Related Work	124
7.8	Summary	126

8 Extracting Developer Roles with Feature Analysis   127

TABLE OF CONTENTS

- 8.1 Introduction 128
- 8.2 Extracting Developer Data from Work Artefacts 129
- 8.3 Modeling Developers in Dynamix 130
- 8.4 Structural and Dynamic Views 132
- 8.5 Feature Ownership Analysis 133
  - 8.5.1 A Collaboration View of Developer Teams responsible for Features 133
  - 8.5.2 Developer-focused Features 134
- 8.6 Case Study 1: Student Team Projects 135
  - 8.6.1 Experimental Setup 135
  - 8.6.2 PhoneSimulator-1 - Developer Analysis 136
  - 8.6.3 PhoneSimulator-2 138
- 8.7 Case Study 2: ArgoUML Case Study 140
- 8.8 Discussion 144
- 8.9 Related Work 144
- 8.10 Summary 146

9 Lessons Learned: a Retrospective 147
- 9.1 Definition and Mechanisms 147
- 9.2 Focus of Analysis 150
- 9.3 Aspects of Feature Analysis 151
- 9.4 Summary 152

10 Conclusions 153
- 10.1 Other Feature-Centric Research 155
- 10.2 Future Work 156

A Definitions 159

B Dynamix: Summary and Variations 163
- B.1 Introduction 163
- B.2 Dynamix and Extensions 163
- B.3 Dynamix Variations 163

C DynaMoose: Trace Extraction, Meta-Modelling and Feature Analysis 167
- C.1 Architectural Overview 168
- C.2 Extracting Traces of Features 169
- C.3 Using the Tools of the Moose Reengineering Environment 170

	C.3.1	Visualizing Features and Feature-enriched Structural Views 170
	C.3.2	Evolution Analysis 171
	C.3.3	Developer Analysis 171
C.4	Summary	 171

Bibliography 171

TABLE OF CONTENTS

List of Figures

2.1 Condensed Dynamic Data - Communications Interaction View. 13
2.2 Interaction Diagram showing a repition as a raised part of the diagram. 15
2.3 An example of the Software Reconnaissance method of identifying a call-forwarding feature in the source code. 18
2.4 A FODA Example: A Car Feature Model specifying Features and Feature Relationships. . . . 21

3.1 The Dynamix meta-model defines behavioral and structural entities and their relationships. . . 29
3.2 Feature-Centric Analysis: 3 Complementary Perspectives. 31
3.3 OCL specification of numberOfFeatures and FeatureAffinity properties of a Method Enttity. . 32
3.4 OCL specification of the properties that pertain to participating Classes of a Feature Entity. . . 34
3.5 OCL specification of a Compact Feature View extracted from a Feature Entity. 35
3.6 The Relationships between Classes and Compact Feature Views. 36
3.7 OCL specification of featureSimilarity 38
3.8 Matrix visualization showing the *featureSimilarity* relationships between 3 features. 39
3.9 OCL specification of depends relationship between features. 39
3.10 A Map of the Feature Analyses Techniques presented in the remainder of this dissertation, showing which chapters related to which parts of the Dynamix Meta-Model and Meta-Model Extensions. 42

4.1 Details of the Case Studies to which we applied Feature-Centric Analysis. 45
4.2 Pier Features showing details of Feature Affinity of classes. 46
4.3 Pier Feature Views of Classes showing *singleFeature* classes and *lowGroupFeature* Classes shared between the *addPage* and *edit a page* Features. (Numbers in the feature names indicate the order of execution.) 48
4.4 Pier Features Similarity Matrix. This shows *featureSimilarity* relationships between pairs of features at Class level. 50

LIST OF FIGURES

4.5 Pier Dependency Graph. This shows transitive closure and transitive reduction graphs for *depends* relationships between features. 52

4.6 ArgoUML Feature Views of Classes. 54

4.7 ArgoUML: Distribution of the Feature Affinity values of classes over the package hierarchy highlighting some of the *singlefeature* classes. 56

4.8 ArgoUML: Highlighting the effect of the *startup* feature on the distribution of Feature Affinity levels of the classes. 56

4.9 ArgoUML Features Similarity Matrix similarity relationships between pairs of features at class level. 57

4.10 OCL specification of Software Reconnaissance property for a Method Entity. 61

4.11 The distribution of average values of the *dedication* and *concentration* metrics for each Feature Affinity level of the Pier Case Study. 62

4.12 OCL specification of the Dedication and Cconcentration Metrics in the context of Dynamix. . 63

4.13 Dynamix extended with Association entities to accomodate metrics of *Feature Identification* techniques. 64

5.1 We extend Dynamix with Hismo *ClassVersion* and *ClassHistory* entities to support evolution analysis from a *Structural* perspective. 71

5.2 The Weighted Changes ($changeFA$) to a role (Feature Affinity) of a Class with respect to Features between two versions of a system. 72

5.3 OCL specification of the *activityIndicator* property to characterize changes in the Feature Affinity level of classes. 74

5.4 An Evolution Matrix of classes showing the Measurements we apply to Feature Affinity of Classes to measure changing roles over time. 75

5.5 SmallWiki Versions used for the Evolution Analysis of Changing Roles of Classes.. 77

5.6 A Subset of the Results of the SmallWiki Case Study. We list the classes with changing FA and the *activityIndicator*. (for >, we show only classes with a ChangeFA $>= 3$) 78

5.7 Moose Versions used for the Evolution Analysis of Changing Roles of Classes. 80

5.8 Moose Classes with Changing Roles with respect to our features model. 81

6.1 Dynamix is extended with Hismo entities to model the notion of Feature history. 90

6.2 Version Analysis of the *editPage* Feature (Branch development track) showing the corresponding *Evolution Chart*. 93

6.3 Feature Additions View of the *editPage* feature (Branch development track). 94

6.4 The order of the analyzed versions of Smallwiki. 95

6.5 Evolution charts of 15 SmallWiki features (branch development) revealing *when* changes occurred in feature properties. 97

6.6 Feature Addtions Views (*i.e.,* showing only classes which represent additions to a feature view of the Branch). 98

LIST OF FIGURES

6.7 Additions History measurement applied to *Number of Classes* (CF of a Feature for all features of the branch (dark grey) and main (light grey) development tracks of SmallWiki. 99
6.8 Feature Additions Views of Main Development track shows only added classes. 101
6.9 Feature Intersection View showing only the conflicting additions (*i.e.*, classes that have been added to both main and branch development tracks). 103

7.1 The Focus of our Visual Feature Hot Spot Analysis in Dynamix 111
7.2 How Dynamix models a Feature's Call Graph and Instance Relationships 112
7.3 OCL specification of Feature Hot Spot for an Instance and for a Class of a Feature. 113
7.4 The Elements of our 3D Visualization of Feature Behavior. The ground floor represents a static class hierarchy perspective of a system. The dynamic behavior is represented by nodes above the ground floor (the instances) and the red edges are the message sends between instances. . . 114
7.5 An Overview of the SmallWiki case study after the execution of the Login Feature. 115
7.6 Zooming into the class hierarchy active during the login scenario. 116
7.7 A Detail of the Visualization of the "Edit Page" feature. 118
7.8 A Detail of the Visualization of the "Edit Template" feature. 120
7.9 A Detail of a Visualization of the "Show Page History" feature. 121
7.10 A Detail of a Visualization of the "Search" feature. 122

8.1 We extend Dynamix with Developer and Team and establish *ownership* relationships between developers and classes. 131
8.2 Package Owner of the PhoneSimulator-1 case study showing a package hierarchy view of the source code. We show the classes of each package, colored according to the developer that owns the classes. 132
8.3 Phone Simulator Project: Example of a Package Hierarchy View highlighting packages and classes specific to the *Play Ringtone* Feature, colored by owner (PhoneSimulator-1) 133
8.4 OCL specification for the developerFocused attribute of a Feature Enttity. 134
8.5 Team Collaboration view from the PhoneSimulator-1 System. The small squares represent classes (colored by owner), the medium rectangles represent features and the large rectangle represent teams of developers who collaborated to develop the features. 137
8.6 Package Owner (PhoneSimulator-2) 138
8.7 Developer Collaborations (PhoneSimulator-2) 139
8.8 Package Hierarchy View of the argoUML system showing classes colored by owner 140
8.9 Team Collaboration of ArgoUML showing relationships between Teams 142
8.10 ArgoUML Generate Code For Class Feature 143
8.11 ArgoUML Startup Feature 143

A.1 Explanation of a Polymetric View 160
A.2 A Simple Dendrogram showing two Feature Clusters 161

LIST OF FIGURES

A.3   Applying Transitive Reduction to a Simple Graph.   162

B.1   The Dynamix meta-model showing the main Entities of the Feature, Structure, FeatureHistory, StructureHistory and Developer Packages   164

B.2   Features Package of Dynamix showing Entities to model Multi-Threading (Thread) and One-to-Many Relationships (FeatureTrace) between Features and Execution Paths.   165

C.1   DynaMoose, Moose and the Instrumentation Layer.   168

Chapter 1

Introduction

The goal of the object-oriented paradigm is to achieve an intuitive correspondence between static entities of a problem domain and those of the solution domain. Features denote units of behavior corresponding to well-understood abstractions of the problem domain, but they do not map directly to individual source code artefacts. We center our reverse engineering analyses around the notion of a feature as a dynamic entity. Our motivation is to enrich reverse engineering techniques by taking advantage of the semantic domain knowledge that features represent.

CHAPTER 1. INTRODUCTION

1.1 Context

System comprehension is a prerequisite for software maintenance and evolution, but it is a time-consuming and costly activity. Studies show that 50-60% of software engineering effort is spent trying to understand source code [Basili, 1997]. The task of understanding is complicated by the fact that there is often a discrepancy between the language used to describe the problem and solution domains of a system. Domain analysts and end-users describe a system in terms of features that solve requirements, whereas software engineers tend to focus on implementation details such as architectural layers, interfaces, and source artefacts.

To tackle the task of understanding large and complex systems, people tend to break them down into smaller units [de Bono, 1990]. With object-oriented systems, the class is the unit intended to model a single entity of a problem domain. However, an individual class is typically too small a unit for system comprehension [Zenger, 2002]. Examination of an individual class does not reveal much about the behavior or purpose of a system. Typically, behavior of object-oriented systems is characterized by groups of collaborating classes. Thus, to understand how a system behaves at runtime, a software engineer needs to consider groups of classes. Although many object-oriented languages define a package as a means to statically group classes in the source code, a package does not solve the problem of understanding system behavior, as packages tend to reflect the static structural divisions of a system rather than behavioral groupings [Wong *et al.*, 2000].

From an external perspective, users understand a system as a collection of features that correspond to system behaviors to fulfill requirements. As such, features are well-understood abstractions that encapsulate domain knowledge and denote a system's behavioral units. However, the software engineer cannot identify and manipulate features, as they are not explicitly represented in the source code of object-oriented systems. Typically, feature implementation cross-cuts the structural boundaries (*i.e.,* packages and classes) of an object-oriented system [Wong *et al.*, 2000].

A software engineer is frequently confronted with features. Typically, change requests and bug reports are expressed in a language that reflects the features of a system [Mehta and Heineman, 2002]. Therefore, to perform maintenance tasks, a software engineer needs to maintain a mental map between the features and their implementation as source artefacts. In this dissertation, we propose to support maintenance and evolution of object-oriented systems, by extracting dynamic views that break a system down into groupings that reflect its features.

1.2 The Problem of Object-Oriented System Comprehension

Until the mid 1980's, the procedural paradigm dominated software development. It guided software developers to transform requirements of a problem domain into procedures by a process of *stepwise refinement*. The procedures were structured into modules that typically reflected runtime intent of the system. Thus, by browsing the source code, a software engineer could obtain an impression of how the system behaved at runtime.

A major disadvantage of the procedural paradigm is that it produces systems that hardwire functionality to data, thus hampering their ability to evolve to meet the needs of changing requirements. The object-oriented paradigm revolutionized the way we think about and build software systems. Objects of a problem domain are transformed into software objects in a solution domain. The software objects collaborate by exchanging messages to fulfill requirements or *features* of the system. Object-orientation provides a better paradigm for building flexible systems. However, object-oriented language characteristics such as inheritance, dynamic binding and polymorphism mean that the behavior of a system can best be determined at runtime [Jerding et al., 1996; Demeyer et al., 2003]. Thus, a side-effect of object-oriented systems is that it is difficult to understand their runtime behavior purely by inspecting the source code [Wilde and Huitt, 1992; Dunsmore et al., 2000].

As the flow of control of procedural-based systems is usually explicit in the code, source code browsing and static analysis techniques usually provide sufficient insight into the intent of these systems. In contrast, to gain an understanding of the behavior of object-oriented systems, we need to obtain runtime views. Researchers who analyze runtime data are faced with the challenge of dealing with vast amounts of data produced by dynamic analysis. To address this, they have devised a range of techniques such as filtering and compression [Zaidman and Demeyer, 2004; Hamou-Lhadj et al., 2005], metrics [Ducasse et al., 2004] and visualizations [De Pauw et al., 1993] to reduce the volume of data without loss of information needed to address their research goals. The focus of many of these approaches is to obtain an architectural insight into a program using dynamic analysis [Ball, 1999; Zaidman et al., 2005]. Establishing traceability between problem domain and the solution domain (*i.e.,* source code) is not the primary concern.

In this dissertation, we claim that features are a good starting point for system comprehension, as they not only encapsulate knowledge of a problem domain, but they also denote units of behavior. Many researchers have identified the potential of exploiting features in a reverse engineering context, and a body of research known as *feature identification* has emerged [Wilde and Scully, 1995; Wong et al., 2000; Eisenbarth et al., 2003].

Feature identification techniques offer only one perspective of features in a reverse engineering context: they focus on mapping features to source code to identify starting points for further investigation. Only a few researchers have treated features as explicit entities when reasoning about a system. The main motivation of our work is to capture the notion of a feature as a first-class entity when reverse engineering a system, so that we can enrich high level views of a software system with semantic context of its problem domain. Our goal is to support development and maintenance activities by establishing traceability between feature knowledge of a problem domain and the source artefacts that participate in their runtime behavior throughout a system's life-cycle.

A software system comprises a set of features and relationships between features. Typically relationships between features themselves are specified during requirements analysis, as they express conceptual dependencies and constraints of a system [Riebisch, 2003]. Only few researchers have addressed feature relationships in a reverse engineering context [Salah and Mancoridis, 2004; Kothari et al., 2006]. As these dependencies are not explicit in the source code, modifications often result in unintended side effects such as breaking existing features or leading to behavioral inconsistencies.

We claim that to provide a comprehensive support for object-oriented system comprehension and maintenance activities, we need to extract features and feature relationships from a system and make them explicit. We summarize the motivation of our research with the following question:

Research Question:

How can we exploit the knowledge of an object-oriented system's problem domain to enrich reverse engineering techniques with semantic context?

1.3 Our Proposal: Feature-Centric Analysis

To address our research question, we propose a feature-centric reverse engineering analysis for object-oriented systems. By incorporating the notion of a feature in reverse engineering techniques, we establish links between a problem domain and solution domain of a software system. We propose to extend existing reverse engineering techniques in two ways: (1) by introducing feature-enriched perspectives of a system and, (2) by introducing new techniques that treat features as primary entities of analysis.

As the basis of our analysis, we define a meta-model for features, which we name Dynamix. Dynamix describes a meta-model for features in terms of message send and object instantiation entities in the context of a structural model of the source code. Dynamix underlies all the feature-centric analysis techniques we present in this dissertation.

An underlying principle of our feature-centric analysis techniques, is the idea of looking at the same problem from different perspectives. We extract complementary feature-enriched perspectives of

1.3. OUR PROPOSAL: FEATURE-CENTRIC ANALYSIS

a system. Our goal is to support system comprehension by treating features as first class entities, by considering the roles of structural entities of source code with respect to features, and also by considering relationships between features themselves.

CHAPTER 1. INTRODUCTION

We state our thesis as follows:

> **Thesis:**
>
> *To exploit inherent domain knowledge of features for object-oriented system comprehension, we need to explicitly model features as first class entities, their relationships to source artefacts, and their relationships to each other.*

To obtain an instance of a **Dynamix** model, we first extract and model source code entities. We instrument a system and exercise its features. We adopt the definition of a feature as a *user-triggerable activity* of a system [Eisenbarth *et al.*, 2003]. To exercise features, we adopt various techniques: (1) by manually interacting with the user interface, (2) by simulating the user interactions with scripts, and (3) by executing regression tests. We capture traces of features as a call tree of events that represent message sends between collaborating objects. We process the trace and resolve relationships between features and source artefacts (*i.e.,* classes and methods) referenced by the individual message events of the trace. Each feature is modeled as an explicit entity in **Dynamix**. Moreover, as feature behavior is composed of message sends and object instances, we also model them as explicit entities.

In this dissertation we introduce a variety of reverse engineering analysis techniques that exploit the notion of features. We demonstrate that **Dynamix** supports a wide variety of feature-enriched reverse engineering analyses.

1.4 Contributions

The contributions of this dissertation are:

1. Dynamix, a generic meta-model of runtime behavior of features in the context of a structural model of source entities.

2. A feature-centric analysis comprising of three complementary perspectives: (1) we explicitly model features as semantic groupings of source artefacts, (2) we define new measurement, called *Feature Affinity* to quantify the relationships between a source artefact (*e.g.,* class, method) and a feature, and (3) we introduce a vocabulary to describe relationships between features and describe measurements to quantify these relationships [Greevy and Ducasse, 2005b; Greevy and Ducasse, 2005a].

3. Two novel approaches to analyze evolution of a system: (1) we analyze how the roles of source artefacts change with respect to features [Greevy *et al.*, 2005a] and (2) we analyze how *feature views* (*i.e.,* a grouping of source artefacts) change over time [Greevy *et al.*, 2006a].

4. A novel visual feature analysis approach to detect *feature hot spots* in feature behavior based on analysis of behavioral entities at the level of instances and message sends [Greevy et al., 2005a].

5. An analysis of developer ownership of source artefacts to determine which developers were responsible for the development of which features [Greevy et al., 2007].

1.5 Structure of the Dissertation

Chapter 2 (p.9) elaborates on the problem of system comprehension in an object-oriented context, and surveys the state of the art in dynamic analysis and feature-related reverse engineering techniques. We identify shortcomings of existing approaches in the context of our thesis and identify key elements needed to exploit domain knowledge of features for reverse engineering.

Chapter 3 (p.25) defines Dynamix and presents feature-centric analysis from different and complementary perspectives.

Chapter 4 (p.43) presents an application of three complementary perspectives of feature-centric analysis on two software systems and discusses our findings.

Chapter 5 (p.67) describes a novel approach to evolution analysis of a software system that measures how roles of source artefacts change with respect to features over time. We exploit knowledge of how classes participate in features to understand change intent in source code over time. Our focus in this work is to enrich evolution analysis techniques with knowledge of features. We define extensions to Dynamix to model multiple versions of a system and describe our measurements in the context of these extensions.

Chapter 6 (p.87) complements the analysis approach described in the previous chapter with a *feature perspective* of evolution analysis. We describe a novel approach to analyzing the evolution of a system from the perspective of how its features change over time. Our approach treats features as first class entities. We define extensions to Dynamix to model multiple versions of the feature entities of a system and describe our measurements in the context of these extensions.

Chapter 7 (p.109) presents a 3D visual analysis of features. Once again, this approach treats features as the primary unit of analysis. In contrast to the previous approaches, it takes a more fine-grained view of the runtime data of features, as it focuses on instance and message sends of object-oriented runtime behavior. We apply our approach on a software system and show how our visualizations of features are useful to understand the behavior of a systems features.

CHAPTER 1. INTRODUCTION

Chapter 8 (p.127) presents a technique that explores how software developers address the task of building software systems. This approach extends the focus of existing research work by analyzing developer data from a feature perspective. Our focus is to analyze whether software developers develop on structural code boundaries (*i.e.*, within packages and classes) or on feature boundaries (*i.e.*, cross-cutting).

Chapter 9 (p.147) presents a summary of insights about our experiences and lessons learnt during this research.

Chapter 10 (p.153) presents conclusions, and outlines future work.

Appendix A (p.159) provides a glossary for terms and definitions we use throughout this dissertation.

Appendix B (p.163) summarizes the Dynamix model and describes variations to the model to address modeling features from multi-threading applications and alternative feature definitions.

Appendix C (p.167) describes the analysis environment of our research. Our Dynamix model was implemented in a tool named *DynaMoose*. We elaborate on design issues, an architectural overview, and how DynaMoose is integrated in the reengineering environment of Moose [Nierstrasz and Ducasse, 2004].

Chapter 2

Towards Feature-Centric Reverse Engineering

Our research is directly related to dynamic analysis-based, concept assignment and feature identification approaches to reverse engineering. We survey these approaches to identify current limitations of the state of the art from the perspective of our research goals. Based on this, we establish criteria for a reverse engineering approach that enhances system comprehension by exploiting domain knowledge of features.

CHAPTER 2. TOWARDS FEATURE-CENTRIC REVERSE ENGINEERING

2.1 Context

Traditionally, reverse engineering techniques focused on analyzing the source code of a system [Chikofsky and Cross II, 1990]. In recent years, researchers have recognized the significance of centering reverse engineering and comprehension activities around behavior of a system [Ernst et al., 1999; Richner and Ducasse, 1999; Zaidman and Demeyer, 2004]. They identified that static analysis approaches, though valuable, are incomplete and do not meet reverse engineering goals of today's object-oriented systems. The behavior of object-oriented systems can only be exactly determined at runtime due to language features such as late binding and polymorphism [Jerding et al., 1996; Stroulia and Systä, 2002; Demeyer et al., 2003]. A major shortcoming of purely static approaches to reverse engineering is that they focus primarily on structural aspects of a system rather than inherent domain knowledge embodied in a user's perspective of how a system behaves at runtime.

Our work is directly related to the field of dynamic analysis and a range of techniques known as *concept assignment* and *feature identification*. In this chapter, we review the state of the art, ranging from dynamic analysis reverse engineering approaches to research work incorporating the notion of features. Based on our survey, we establish limitations of related works in the context of our research. This leads us to identify open problems that need to be addressed, if we are to incorporate domain knowledge of features in reverse engineering analysis techniques.

Structure of the chapter. In the next section, we identify criteria of a reverse engineering technique, essential for achieving our research goals. Section 2.3 (p.11) presents a brief overview of research we surveyed to establish limitations of the state of the art. We review a subset of dynamic analysis techniques for system comprehension in Section 2.3.1 (p.12). Section 2.3.2 (p.16) reviews approaches to *Concept Assignment*, as these techniques relate domain concepts with implementation details of a system. Then, Section 2.3.3 (p.17) takes a look at some of the main *Feature Identification* techniques and evaluates them with respect to our research goals. Section 2.3.4 (p.20) provides a brief overview of research in *Feature Modeling* for requirements engineering. We summarize our evaluations of the various research works we reviewed in Section 2.4 (p.23). Based on our evaluations, we summarize fundamental characteristics of a *feature-centric* reverse engineering analysis to meet our reseach goals in Section 2.5 (p.24). Finally, in Section 2.6 (p.24) we provide a brief outlook for the rest of the dissertation.

2.2 Motivating Feature-Centric Reverse Engineering

The main goal of our research is to identify how we can exploit domain knowledge of object-oriented systems that is inherent in a user's perspective of how a system behaves at runtime so that (1) existing reverse engineering analyses can be enriched with semantic context, and (2) we can define reverse engineering analysis techniques that exploit the notion of features as first-class entities. We target our survey of the state of the art, by considering criteria that we consider essential to meet our research goals:

Behavior. Due to language features like polymorphism and late binding of object-oriented systems, behavior of a system cannot be completely automatically determined by analyzing its source code alone.

Exploiting Domain Knowledge. Our research question is centered around the problem of exploiting domain knowledge to enhance system comprehension. We consider features to be units of behavior encapsulating domain knowledge.

Combining Dynamic and Static Views. Two main distinct approaches to system comprehension have dominated reverse-engineering research efforts [Chikofsky and Cross II, 1990]: dynamic analysis approaches and static analysis approaches. Both perspectives are necessary to support the understanding of object-oriented systems [Demeyer *et al.*, 2000].

Features as First-Class Entities. During the lifetime of a system, software engineers are constantly required to modify and adapt application features in response to changing requirements. A reverse engineering analysis needs to support this activity by breaking the system into groupings that reflect its features.

Feature Relationships. Software engineers need to understand relationships between features, as modifications to one feature may inadvertently affect other features. Furthermore, feature relationships reflect constraints and dependencies in a problem domain. Thus, they are important sources of information for system comprehension.

Underlying Model. We identify the importance of defining a unified model of dynamic and static data to accommodate a variety of reverse engineering analyses, so that researchers can reuse techniques and results of their work.

This chapter identifies the environment for our research and establishes the goals of our work.

2.3 Related Research: A State of the Art

In our survey of the state of the art, we identify various research areas relevant to our work. We evaluate these approaches to identify commonalities with our work and open issues in the context of our research perspective.

Dynamic Analysis for System Comprehension. Approaches based on dynamic analysis tend to be complex. The main reason is that it is difficult to design tools to process the huge volume of trace data and present it in an understandable form [Ducasse *et al.*, 2004; Richner and Ducasse, 2002]. As a result, much research effort has been concerned with compression and summarization of large traces [Hamou-Lhadj and Lethbridge, 2004; Hamou-Lhadj *et al.*, 2005]. For our purposes, we restrict our survey to dynamic analysis approaches for system comprehension.

Concept Assignment Approaches. The *Concept Assignment* problem, originally defined by Biggerstaff *et al.*, refers to the problem of discovering human-oriented concepts and relating them to their implementation-oriented counterparts [Biggerstaff *et al.*, 1993; Gold and Mohan, 2003]. We review a subset of *concept assignment* approaches, as features denote concepts of a system's problem domain [Marcus *et al.*, 2004; Kuhn *et al.*, 2005a; Deissenboeck and Ratiu, 2006].

Feature Identification Approaches. The goal of *feature identification* is to establish the relationship between features and source code artefacts [Wong *et al.*, 2000]. Most of these approaches adopt the definition of a *feature* as a user-observable functionality of a system [Eisenbarth *et al.*, 2003]. Typically the approaches include a definition of a measurement to quantify the relevance of a source artefact to a feature. They base their relevance measurement on heuristics and validate their findings with case studies and developer knowledge.

Feature-Based Reverse Engineering Approaches. Recently, researchers have recognized the role of features in the reverse engineering context [Salah and Mancoridis, 2004; Kothari *et al.*, 2006]. We review these feature-related analysis techniques and evaluate them in the context of our work.

Feature Modeling. This research focuses on domain analysis and requirements engineering [Riebisch, 2003]. We include a brief review of feature modeling research in our survey of the state of the art, as it provides a range of definitions for features and feature relationships from the domain perspective. The concepts of this research have not yet been fully exploited by the reverse engineering community.

Based on our survey of the state of the art, we identify the limitations of these works from the perspective of our research. From our survey we extrapolate the elements of a reverse engineering analysis approach that addresses our research goal of exploiting the domain knowledge of features for system comprehension.

2.3.1 Dynamic Analysis for System Comprehension

An extensive amount of research has been dedicated to understanding object-oriented systems using dynamic information [Kleyn and Gingrich, 1988; Korel and Rilling, 1997; De Pauw *et al.*, 1993; Richner and Ducasse, 2002]. For our evaluation, we review a subset of dynamic analysis approaches

2.3. RELATED RESEARCH: A STATE OF THE ART

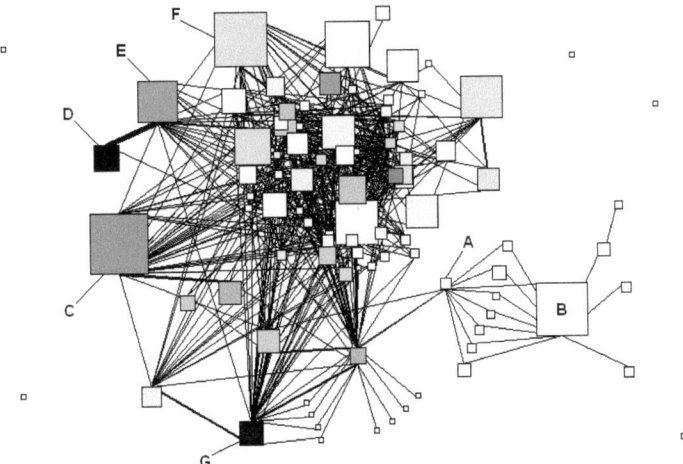

Figure 2.1: Condensed Dynamic Data - Communications Interaction View.

to reverse engineering. As we build on dynamic analysis approaches, the problems of tackling large amounts of data are relevant to our work. Some of the most popular strategies adopted by researchers to analyze dynamic data are: (1) summarization through metrics, (2) filtering and clustering techniques, (3) visualization and (4) query-based approaches. Many of the approaches discussed here apply a combination of these strategies.

Summarization through Metrics. Many researchers have highlighted the importance of metrics for dynamic analysis as good indicators of external runtime behaviors [De Pauw *et al.*, 1993; Walker *et al.*, 1998; Ducasse *et al.*, 2004]. With this strategy, dynamic data is summarized using metrics or some other statistical measure. For example, they compute the frequency of calls or the number of objects created in a trace. The measurements are usually visually rendered.

An example of such an approach is the work of Ducasse *et al.* [Ducasse *et al.*, 2004]. They presented a lightweight metrics-based approach to dynamic analysis and they proposed a polymetric view to visually render the condensed information computed from an execution trace. Figure 2.1 (p.13) shows such a condensed trace generated from one of their case study analyses. In this view, dynamic metrics are mapped to the size and color (grayscale) of the nodes of the graph visualization. The edges represent collaborations between the instances. In this example, a black node represents a class that is heavily used. The research questions they address deal with a software engineer's perspective of the system, such as identifying the most instantiated classes, the class collaborations and the percentage of the methods of a class participating in a trace.

Filtering and Clustering. With this strategy, the amount of dynamic data to be analyzed is reduced using filtering and clustering techniques. Several researchers have incorporated this strategy into their analysis of runtime data [Jerding and Rugaber, 1997; Walker et al., 1998; Ball, 1999; Zaidman and Demeyer, 2004]. One example of this technique, known as *Frequency Spectrum Analysis* (FSA), was pioneered by Ball [Ball, 1999]. He showed how the analysis of frequencies of program entities in a single execution trace can help software engineers decompose a program, identify related computations, and find computations related to specific input and output characteristics of a program. He applied his technique primarily to procedural code.

Zaidman and Demeyer [Zaidman and Demeyer, 2004] based their program comprehension technique on *Frequency Spectrum Analysis*, but adapted it for object-oriented programs. Their approach used a heuristic to divide a trace into recurring event clusters and showed that these recurring event clusters represent interesting starting points for understanding the dynamic behavior of a system.

In another work, Zaidman *et al.* [Zaidman et al., 2005] defined a dynamic analysis approach based on web-mining techniques that identified key classes of a system. They showed that well-designed object-oriented programs typically consist of key classes that work tightly together to provide the bulk of a system's functionality. Their hypothesis was that these key classes represent good starting points for system comprehension.

Visualization Techniques. Substantial research has been conducted on runtime information visualization. Various tools and approaches use dynamic (trace-based) information such as Program Explorer [Lange and Nakamura, 1995a], *Jinsight* and its ancestors [De Pauw et al., 1993], and Graphtrace [Kleyn and Gingrich, 1988]. Vion and Drury [Vion-Dury and Santana, 1994] use 3D to represent the runtime of objects in distributed and concurrent systems. Most of these approaches focus on the analysis of execution patterns as useful abstractions for program comprehension.

De Pauw *et al.* proposed to classify repetitive behavior automatically into high-level execution patterns [De Pauw et al., 1993]. The goal was to reduce the volume of information a software engineer must assimilate, with little loss of insight. They used interaction diagrams to visualize interactions between objects in their tool Jinsight. Figure 2.2 (p.15) shows an example of a visualization of a repetition pattern of an execution trace. In another work, Jerding *et al.* proposed a visual analysis approach where recurring interaction scenarios in program executions can be used as abstractions in the understanding process [Jerding and Rugaber, 1997].

2.3. RELATED RESEARCH: A STATE OF THE ART

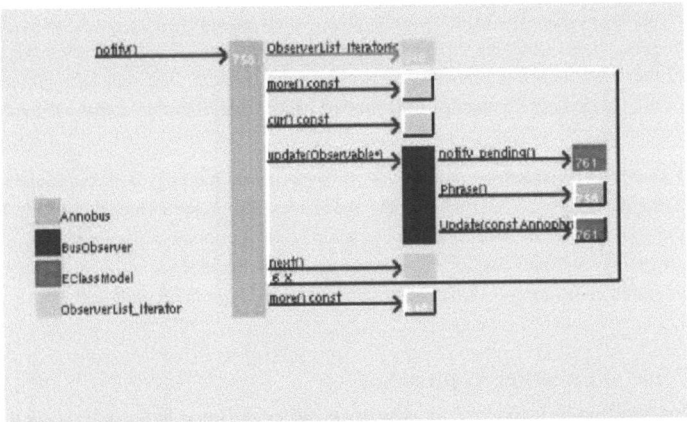

Figure 2.2: Interaction Diagram showing a repition as a raised part of the diagram.

A Query-based Approach. Richner and Ducasse presented a query-based approach to extract collaborations from execution traces, as they provide the software engineer with a larger unit of understanding than classes, and thus are an important aid for maintenance and evolution of a system [Richner and Ducasse, 2002; Richner, 2002]. The technique allows the software engineer to declaratively define perspectives of interest of the system and use these perspectives to recover low-level and high-level views of the system.

Ducasse *et al.* describe an approach that reifies execution traces of program tests and represents them as logical facts about a system's behavior. They use logic programming to express queries to understand the inner structure of a program [Ducasse *et al.*, 2006b]. Their approach also includes a model of the dynamic information to express ordering and containment relationships between events.

Evaluation:

Commonalities.

We have identified the need to adopt a dynamic analysis approach for the analysis of object-oriented runtime behavior. Thus, a key challenge of our work is the problem of large amounts of data.

Variations.

CHAPTER 2. TOWARDS FEATURE-CENTRIC REVERSE ENGINEERING

— *Research Focus.* The primary concern of the above approaches is to obtain architectural insights of a system by analyzing its runtime behavior. Thus, the main research focus of these works differ from the goals of this dissertation. We seek to establish links between the domain knowledge of features and the parts of the trace that correspond to their execution.

— *Underlying Mechanisms and Model.* In some cases, the approaches are purely based on dynamic analysis. Thus, many of the above approaches do not model dynamic behavior in the context of a structural model of source code. In contrast, we emphasize the value of analyzing runtime behavior and relating this behavior to static views of a system. We aim to enrich static analysis-based reverse engineering approaches with semantic context.

2.3.2 Concept Location Approaches

Traditionally, the problem of locating concepts in a program has been an intuitive and informal process. In the context of reverse engineering, several researchers have addressed this problem [Biggerstaff and Perlis, 1989; Rajlich and Gosavi, 2002; Robillard and Murphy, 2002; Čubranić and Murphy, 2003; Marcus et al., 2004]. Marcus *et al.* define concept location as the process of identifying parts of a software system that implement a specific notion or idea that originates from the problem or solution domain [Marcus et al., 2004].

Some researchers have adopted an information retrieval approach based on semantic clustering techniques to tackle the problem of concept location [Marcus *et al.*, 2004; Kuhn *et al.*, 2005a; Kuhn *et al.*, 2005b]. The focus of these works is to analyze identifiers to identify implementation concepts in source code. The goal is to support maintenance tasks in the absence of system documentation.

Deissenboeck and Ratiu present a unified meta-model that extends a structural model of source code with entities that represent concepts of a problem domain. They propose a semi-automatic approach to locating concepts and defining their concept model [Deissenboeck and Ratiu, 2006].

Evaluation:

Commonalities.

— *Concept.* Features and concepts are essentially similar, as they both denote units that encapsulate knowledge about a system.

— *Model.* The work of Deissenboeck and Ratiu emphasizes the role of a unified meta-model to exploit the concepts for reverse engineering [Deissenboeck and Ratiu, 2006]. Similarily,

2.3. RELATED RESEARCH: A STATE OF THE ART

we identify the need to model features in the context of a structural model of source code as the basis of our work.

Variations.

— *Research Focus.* The primary concern of the approaches we reviewed is on assigning concepts to parts of the source code to support comprehension. In contrast to our research perspective, these approaches identify concepts that include both external domain concepts and internal implementation concepts, whereas we consider features to map to real domain concepts that are understood by an end-user.

— *Underlying Mechanisms.* The reviewed approaches considered the program identifiers as a source of information to reveal domain concepts. In contrast to our perspective, the meaning of a concept in the above approaches does not necessarily imply dynamic behavior of a system.

2.3.3 Feature Identification Approaches

Feature identification is a technique to identify subsets of a program source code activated when exercising a feature [Wilde and Scully, 1995; Wong *et al.*, 2000; Eisenbarth *et al.*, 2003; Antoniol and Guéhéneuc, 2005; Koschke and Quante, 2005]. The approaches differ primarily in the mechanisms used to locate the parts of the code relevant to a feature, and in their definition of measurements to quantify the relevancy of a piece of code to a feature. Often, the research effort of these works has focused on the underlying mechanisms used to locate features (*e.g.,* static analysis, dynamic analysis, formal concept analysis, semantic analysis or approaches that combine two or more of these techniques).

Chen and Rajlich proposed a static analysis-based approach to feature identification based on the analysis of a system's call graph [Chen and Rajlich, 2000]. They targeted procedural code, thus their approach did not take object-oriented language features such as polymorphism into consideration. They described their approach as semi-automatic, as it required a software engineer, familiar with the code, to guide the process of feature identification.

In contrast, dynamic analysis approaches to feature identification have typically involved executing the features of a system and analyzing the resulting trace of dynamic data captured. We evaluate a subset of the best-known dynamic analysis-based feature identification approaches, as they are directly relevant to our research perspective.

Wilde and Scully pioneered the use of dynamic analysis to locate features [Wilde and Scully, 1995]. They named their technique *Software Reconnaissance*. Their goal was to support programmers when they modify or extend functionality of legacy systems. The approach is best described using

CHAPTER 2. TOWARDS FEATURE-CENTRIC REVERSE ENGINEERING

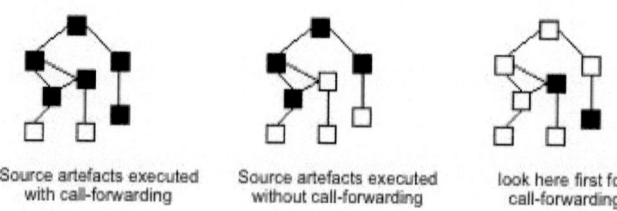

Figure 2.3: An example of the Software Reconnaissance method of identifying a call-forwarding feature in the source code.

the example shown in Figure 2.3 (p.18). Suppose you need to locate the *call forwarding* feature in a telephone switch software system. To achieve this, two sets of test cases are executed, one set that exercises the feature and one set that does not. The execution traces of both sets are compared. Software components that only appear in the first trace are considered good starting points for further investigation of the source code.

Eisenberg and De Volder [Eisenberg and De Volder, 2005] introduced a purely dynamic-analysis technique based on simple heuristics that uses ranking to determine the relevance of a software entity to a feature. They use test suites to generate *dynamic feature traces*. Their technique varied from the Software Reconnaissance technique in that they considered sets of features rather than individual features. They refined the measurement for determining the relevance of a piece of code to a feature by employing heuristics. They base their measurement on: (1) multiplicity of occurrences of a method in a trace and (2) nesting level of a method.

Antoniol and Guéhéneuc proposed an approach to feature identification and feature comparison based on consolidated tools and techniques, such as parsing, processor emulation [Antoniol and Guéhéneuc, 2005]. Their approach combines static and dynamic analysis. They applied their approach to large object-oriented, multi-threaded programs. They exploited process emulation, knowledge filtering and probabilistic ranking to overcome difficulties of collecting dynamic data (imprecision and noise). They showed that their approach is scalable and capable of addressing issues of multi-threading. Furthermore, the authors defined a model, which they refer to as a *micro architecture*, to link the dynamic behavior of features with a model of the program architecture. This approach also refined the relevancy measurement of the Software Reconnaissance approach.

Eisenbarth *et al.* described a semi-automatic feature identification technique which used a combination of dynamic analysis, static analysis of dependency graphs, and formal concept analysis to identify which parts of source code contribute to feature behavior [Eisenbarth *et al.*, 2003]. For the dynamic analysis part of their approach, they extended the Software Reconnaissance approach to

2.3. RELATED RESEARCH: A STATE OF THE ART

consider a set of features rather than one feature. They used formal concept analysis to characterize source artefacts as *general* or *specific* with respect to a feature. They applied formal concept analysis to derive a correspondence between features and code. They invoked scenarios to exercise features and capture execution traces. They used the information gained by formal concept analysis to guide a static analysis technique to identify feature-specific *computational units* (*i.e.,* units of source code).

Wong *et al.* base their analysis on the *Software Reconnaissance* approach and complement the relevancy metric by defining three new metrics to quantify the relationship between a source artefact and a feature [Wong *et al.*, 2000]. Their focus is on measuring the closeness between a feature and a program component. They define three metrics: (1) *disparity* (*i.e.,* it captures the disparity between a source artefact and a feature), (2) *concentration* (*i.e.,* how much of a feature is concentrated in a source artefact), and (3) *dedication* (*i.e.,* how dedicated a source artefact is to a feature).

These metrics show how a feature spreads over an entire system and complements the relevancy measurement of the *Software Reconnaissance* technique [Wilde and Scully, 1995]. As with the Software Reconnaissance approach, each feature is treated individually.

Evaluation:

Commonalities.

— *Feature Definition.* For our research, we adopt the definition of a feature as a *user-triggerable* behavior of a system [Eisenbarth *et al.*, 2003]. We recognize the need to define a relevancy measurement to quantify the closeness of a source code artefact to a feature.

— *Underlying Mechanisms.* Most of the approaches described above are based on applying dynamic analysis. This is necessary to determine the precise behavior of the analysis of object-oriented systems.

— *Model.* Only the approach of Antoniol and Guéhéneuc defines a model of the relationships between features and source code artefacts [Antoniol and Guéhéneuc, 2005].

Variations.

— *Research Focus.* The focus of feature identification is to locate the implementation of a feature in source code. The goal of these approaches was to identify starting points for further investigation of source code. Software Reconnaissance considers one feature at a time, rather than analyzing a set of features. The main variation is in our research focus. We seek extract and model feature entities and establish them as first class entities for analysis of a system from different perspectives.

— *Unit of execution*. In the approaches described above, scenarios and test cases were used to generate execution traces, which were then analyzed to locate the parts of the code relevant to a feature. The execution scenarios also perform other activities. We aim to focus on and extract only the part of an execution that results from triggering one feature.

— *Level of detail in the execution data*. In the approaches described above, the focus of analysis is on method executions. We aim to capture fine-grained dynamic information of object-oriented systems such as instantiation, and to record between which instances messages are sent.

— *Feature Relationships*. We aim to capture and quantify both static and runtime dependencies between features. To detect runtime dependencies, we require that instance information be maintained from one trace of feature execution to the next. None of the feature identification approaches reviewed here provide a means of preserving instance information from one trace to the next. Moreover, they do not focus on explicitly defining and quantifying relationships between features to support program comprehension.

2.3.4 Feature Modeling in Requirements Engineering

Feature modeling is an established technique in the field of requirements engineering. It is used extensively when analyzing requirements for product families. Feature models describe capabilities or functionalities of a system and model the relationships between these features. They group sets of requirements and map them to features. Their approach enables modeling of variability of requirements.

A feature model is a high level description understandable by customers and is located between the requirements model and the design model. It was first described in the *FODA* (Feature Oriented Domain Analysis) paper [Kyo C.Kang *et al.*, 1990]. The goal of feature models is to describe a system according to its features, where a feature is defined as: *A prominant or distinctive user-visible aspect of a software system or systems. Features are any prominent and distinctive aspects or characteristics that are visible to various stakeholders (i.e., end-users, domain experts, developers, etc)* [Kang *et al.*, 2002].

It defines a hierarchical model or feature tree that expresses relationships between features and makes explicit, baseline and optional features. It proposes a simple graphical notation to express these relationships. Features may be defined as mandatory, optional or alternative. Mandatory features represent baseline features and their relationships. The optional and alternative features represent specialization of the more general features. Figure 2.4 (p.21) shows an example of FODA Feature Model notation for a car system used by Kang *et al.*. in their paper [Kang *et al.*, 2002].

2.3. RELATED RESEARCH: A STATE OF THE ART

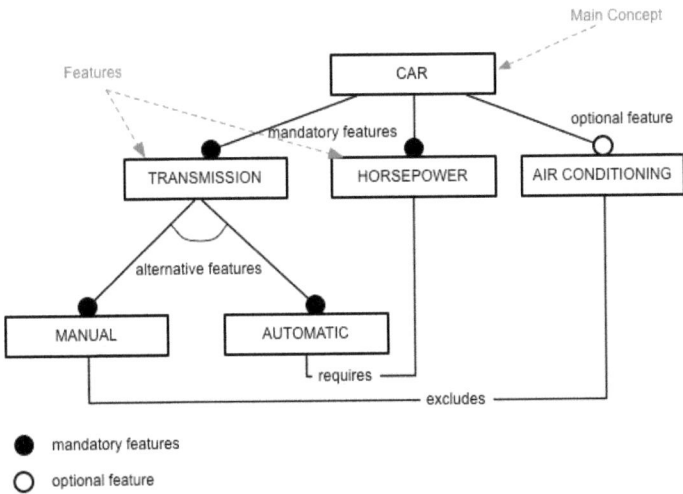

Figure 2.4: A FODA Example: A Car Feature Model specifying Features and Feature Relationships.

Evaluation:

Commonalities.

This work defines both a feature model and relationships between features.

Variations.

— *Research Focus.* Feature modeling limits its focus to requirements analysis. The vocabulary of feature modeling represents a valuable source for knowledge to be exploited in the context feature-centric reverse engineering, in particular when considering reverse engineering the relationships between features. Features are treated as first-class entities but feature modeling makes no provision for traceability of features throughout the life-cycle of a system.

— *Definition of Feature Relationships.* Not all of the relationships between features described by *FODA* (*e.g.*, alternative or excludes) can not be determined automatically by analyzing source code or system behavior. Our focus is to reverse engineer feature relationships to identify dependencies between features (*e.g.*, the *requires* relationship). We aim to quantify shared references to static and dynamic entities in the features.

2.3.5 Analysis Approaches based on Features

Recently, some researchers have addressed feature analyses that extend beyond pure feature identification [Salah and Mancoridis, 2004; Kothari et al., 2006].

Salah and Mancoridis [Salah and Mancoridis, 2004] proposed a hierarchy of dynamic views based on execution traces of feature behavior. Their goal was to describe views that support program understanding by depicting low level interaction between objects of a trace and dependencies between features.

Kothari et al. [Kothari et al., 2006] proposed an approach to system comprehension that considers features as the primary unit of analysis. Their hypothesis is that understanding the similarities between features supports maintenance of a system, as it is helpful to know which features are closely related to a feature being changed. They develop a measure of similarity between pairs of features and they use it to partition features into sets. They define a set of *canonical feature sets* (i.e., a minimum set of features that represent a system). They define a similarity measurement based on computing similarities in call graphs of features.

Evaluation:

Commonalities.

> These works consider features as primary units of analysis. They also consider relationships between features. The approach of Salah et al. analyzes relationships between features based on shared usage of source artefacts and objects [Salah and Mancoridis, 2004].

Variations.

> — *Research Focus.* These works extend their focus beyond feature identification to consider features as first-class entities of their analysis. In contrast to our work, their research perspective does not consider incorporating the notion of a feature into existing reverse engineering analyses to enrich them with semantic context.
>
> — *Underlying Model.* Neither of these approaches provide a definition of a unified model for features and structural source entities. Thus, it is difficult to build on the results of these approaches.

2.4 Summary

We summarize our evaluations of the research work we reviewed as follows:

Dynamic Analysis Approaches. Many dynamic analysis-based system comprehension techniques focused on gaining architectural insights into a system. Thus, the problem of exploiting domain knowledge and establishing links to source code is not a primary concern of these approaches.

Concept Assignment Approaches. The research into concept assignment is motivated by a need to relate external domain knowledge to the internal representation of this knowledge in source code. The approaches we reviewed assume domain knowledge to exist in the source code in the form of program identifiers (*e.g.,* class, method and variable names). They adopt information retrieval approaches to mine domain knowledge. In contrast, from our perspective, domain knowledge lies in a system's features.

Feature Identification Approaches. Our survey of the state of the art revealed that the main body of feature-related research in reverse engineering can be classified as *feature identification.* This research represents a basis for our work. We extend the notion of mapping features to source artefacts to incorporate feature as first class entitiies of reverse engineering analysis techniques. To support this, we define the need for a unified model of features and structural source entities.

Reverse Engineering Features. Despite the wealth of research in feature identification techniques, only few researchers have centered reverse engineering approaches around the notion of features as first class entities. In the case of evolution analysis, for example, researchers typically reason about changes in source code over time [Demeyer *et al.*, 2000; Lanza and Ducasse, 2002; Krajewski, 2003; Gîrba and Lanza, 2004]. By focusing only on source code, such analysis techniques overlook important semantic information about the roles of source artefacts in features.

Feature Modeling in Requirements Engineering. Relationships between features represent another important source of domain knowledge. Feature relationships reflect rules and constraints over a system's problem domain. A *login* feature of an application, for example, must execute before other features are accessible to a user. Such relationships are not necessarily explicit in source code. Therefore, to support maintenance and system evolution activities, it is essential to make feature relationships of a system explicit. Feature relationships have received only sparse attention in a reverse engineering context.

2.5 Elements of Feature-Centric Analysis

By reviewing the state of the art, we identified limitations of existing research work with respect to our research goals. We define key elements of a *feature-centric* analysis that are essential to achieve these goals.

1. *Behavior.* To capture a system's behavior, we need to perform dynamic analysis.

2. *Combining Static and Dynamic Analysis.* To complement structural analysis of a system, roles of source artefacts need to be enriched with feature context (*i.e.,* how they participate in features at runtime).

3. *Features as First-Class Entities.* As a basis of any feature-centric analysis we need to define a meta-model that treats features as first class entities (*i.e.,* primary units) and establishes relationships between features and source artefacts implementing their functionality. Therefore, an underlying model should unify behavioral data of features and structural data of source code such as packages, classes and methods. A unified model would provide a framework for our feature-centric analysis. The model needs to be generic, extensible and should easily accommodate metrics from other feature analysis techniques.

4. *Feature Relevancy Measurements.* Feature identification represents the foundation of our work. Thus, a feature-centric analysis approach needs to provide a measurement to quantify the relevance of a software artefact to a feature, or set of features.

5. *Feature Relationships.* A feature-centric analysis approach needs to identify and quantify relationships and dependencies between features.

2.6 Outlook

In the rest of this dissertation, we outline a feature-centric analysis for reverse engineering object-oriented systems. The key characteristic of our feature-centric approach is that we analyze a system from different complementary perspectives: we enrich static perspectives of a system with domain knowledge of features and define analysis techniques that are centered around features. A unified model of execution entities of features and source code entities underlies our analysis. We validate our feature-centric approach by applying it to a number of object-oriented systems. We demonstrate how our analysis is supported by our unified model. We demonstrate the flexibility and extensibility of our model to support visual analysis techniques, evolution analysis techniques and analysis of developer data related to ownership of source code.

Chapter 3

Feature-Centric Analysis

The basis of our approach is to treat features as first-class entities of analysis. We define a meta-model, which we call Dynamix, *to describe behavioral data of features in the context of a stuctural meta-model of source code. Based on* Dynamix, *we define a feature-centric approach to analyze a software system from three complementary perspectives: (1) a feature perspective relating runtime behavior of features to source artefacts, (2) a structural perspective enriching static views with feature context, and (3) a feature relationship perspective revealing dependencies between features.*

CHAPTER 3. FEATURE-CENTRIC ANALYSIS

3.1 Motivation

In the previous chapter we reviewed different approaches to system comprehension and reverse engineering that analyze a system's behavior or incorporate the notion of features. Our survey revealed that, although there is a growing awareness in the value of features as a key to understanding software systems, little emphasis has been placed on centering analysis techniques around features.

In this chapter, we introduce Dynamix, our meta-model to describe dynamic runtime behavior of features as first-class entities. To motivate our feature-centric approach, we consider the following reverse-engineering questions:

1. *How do features relate to source artefacts (e.g., classes and methods)?* Understanding how a feature is implemented is essential for a software engineer, as maintenance requests are usually expressed in a language that reflects a feature perspective of a system [Mehta and Heineman, 2002].

2. *How do source artefacts relate to features?* It is difficult to determine how classes and methods contribute to the runtime behavior of features just by reading the source code. Control flow is not explicit in classical object-oriented programs. Understanding the role of a class or method in a system's behavior is essential, when a software engineer needs to modify or adapt it.

3. *How are features related to each other?* A software system's behavior is defined by its features. Relationships may exist between features that define dependencies or constraints to ensure correct behavior of a system. At the requirements analysis phase of a system, relationships between features are specified to avoid behavioral conflicts [Gibson, 1997]. Over time, the original requirements specification may no longer reflect the implementation, as new features are added or existing features are modified. Consequently software maintenance activities may result in unintended side effects. Knowing which features could be affected by modifications supports maintenance and evolution activities.

Dynamix provides the basis on which we define a feature-centric analysis. Our approach to reverse engineering a system considers structural and behavioral data of a system from three complementary perspectives. Each perspective addresses one of the above research questions.

Structure of the chapter. In the next section we define feature terminology and the underlying concepts of our approach. In Section 3.3 (p.28) we describe Dynamix, our meta-model to express the behavioral entities of features. We introduce our three perspectives in Section 3.4 (p.30). In Section 3.5 (p.32) we define our Feature Affinity property of source entities. We define different Feature properties in Section 3.6 (p.33) and in Section 3.6 (p.33) we define feature relationship properties. We summarize our contributions and provide a brief outlook on the various feature-centric analyses presented in the subsequent chapters of the dissertation in Section 3.8 (p.40).

3.2 Terminology

Our work is centered around the notion of a feature. As we complement and build on previous feature identification approaches, we adopt the definition of a feature proposed by Eisenbarth *et al.* [Eisenbarth *et al.*, 2003], as it is generally accepted by other researchers in a reverse engineering context [Eisenberg and De Volder, 2005; Antoniol and Guéhéneuc, 2005]:

> A feature is an observable unit of behavior of a system triggered by the user. [Eisenbarth *et al.*, 2003].

A user understands a system in terms of features. To activate a feature, the user typically interacts with a system by means of its user interface. Not all features of an application satisfy this definition. System internal housekeeping tasks, for example, are not triggered directly as a result of user interaction. In our intial experiments, we limited the scope of our investigation to user-initiated features. We focused on the user-interface of an application to determine which user-observable features are most adequate to include in our analysis. With later experiments, we designed test cases to invoke features. This means that feature analysis does not have to be restricted to user-observable features but may include any unit of functionality of a system.

Feature trace. We use the term *feature trace* to refer to an individual execution trace captured as a result of triggering one feature. A feature trace consists of a tree of events, where each node in the tree represents a performed event (*e.g.*, an object instantiation or a message send). The edge between two nodes represents a calling relationship between method events.

A marked trace of features. To preserve object instance information from the execution of one feature to the next, we performed some of the experiments described in this dissertation by marking the start and end of an execution of a feature in one execution trace. To simplify our discussion, we use the term feature trace to refer to either an individually captured trace or to a portion of a marked trace corresponding to one feature.

Source artefacts and source entities We refer to elements of source code (*i.e.*, packages, classes and methods) as source artefacts. To distinguish between source code elements and their corresponding structural entities in a model (*e.g.*, Package, Class and Method entities), we refer to model entities as source entities.

Model. A *model* is a simplification of a system built with an intended goal in mind. The model should be able to answer questions in place of the actual system [Bézivin and Gerbé, 2001].

Meta-Model. A *meta-model* is a specification model for a class of systems under study where each system under study in the class is itself a valid model expressed in a certain modeling language [Seidewitz, 2003].

CHAPTER 3. FEATURE-CENTRIC ANALYSIS

Measurement. A measurement is a mapping from the empirical world to the formal, relational world. Consequently, a measure is the number assigned to an entity by this mapping to characterize an attribute [Fenton and Pfleeger, 1996].

3.3 Dynamix

We introduce Dynamix, our meta-model to specify behavioral entities of feature execution data and their relationships. Dynamix also specifies the relationships between the behavioral entities and the structural entities representing source artefacts. Dynamix is MOF 2.0 compliant [1]. Our OCL specifications comply with OCL 2.0 [2].

To obtain a model of dynamic and static data of a system under study, we first extract a structural model by parsing a system's source code. Then, we extract *feature traces* by exercising a set of features on an instrumented system. We transform the execution data of feature traces into Dynamix entities and establish the relationships between the execution entities and the source entities of the structural model.

In Figure 3.1 (p.29) we show the entities of our model in a UML 2.0 diagram [Fowler, 2003]. The *Features* package represents the dynamic behavioral data of the feature traces. The *Structure* package models the entities of the source code. We model behavioral data of features using three entities: *Feature*, *Activation* and *Instance*.

> *Feature.* Each feature trace we capture during dynamic analysis of a system is modeled as a *Feature* entity. A *Feature* entity is uniquely identified by a name. The *Feature* entity allows us to collectively manipulate all the *Activations* that correspond to the events of the feature trace which it models. It maintains a list (modeled as an ordered collection) of all of its *Activations* for ease of manipulation. The first *Activation* of the list represents the root of a feature trace. We assign properties to *Feature* entities based on the *Activations* and their relationships to other entities (*e.g.,* number of *Activations*, number of *Instances* created, number of *Methods* referenced, and Feature Affinity properties). Relationships between features are shown in the model with a *depends* association. We provide the OCL definition for this relationship between features in Figure 3.9 (p.39) or mathematically in Equation 3.3 (p.40).
>
> *Activation.* An *Activation* in our model represents a method execution. It holds a reference to its sender *Activation*. In this way Dynamix models the tree structure of a feature trace. Thus, the model preserves the sequence of execution of method executions of a feature trace. Time is captured and modeled with two attributes, namely *startTime* (*i.e.,* the timestamp in millisec-

---
[1] http://www.omg.org/docs/ptc/03-10-04.pdf
[2] http://www.omg.org/docs/formal/06-05-01.pdf

3.3. DYNAMIX

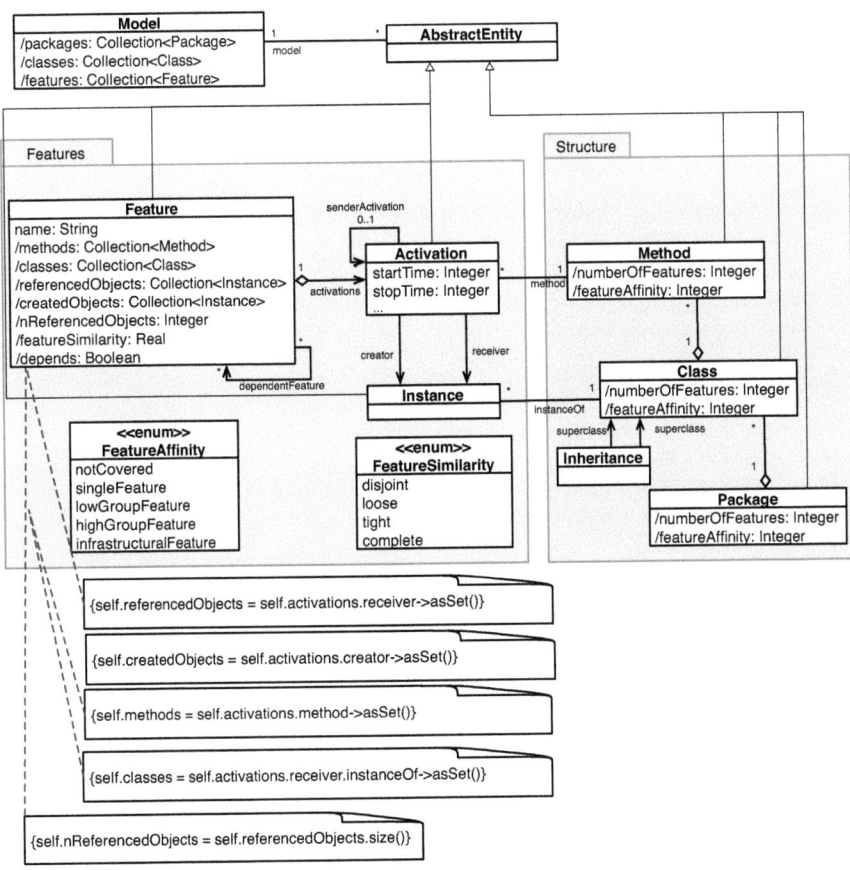

Figure 3.1: The Dynamix meta-model defines behavioral and structural entities and their relationships.

onds, when the method was invoked) and *stopTime* (*i.e.,* the timestamp in milliseconds when it completed execution) of an activation . Each *Activation* is associated with a *Method* entity in the structural model. The *Method* entity of the structural model has a relationship to the *Class* entity where it is defined. In this way, we model relationships between features and source entities. Furthermore, an *Activation* is associated with an *Instance* entity which represents the receiver instance of a message. The sender instance is accessible via its sender *Activation*. Thus, Dynamix models the actual object that invokes a method. This does not necessarily correspond to the static relationship between *Method* and *Class* entities, due to inheritance in object-oriented systems. The return value of a message is also stored as a reference to an *Instance* entity in the *Activation* that models the message send.

Instance. We model every instantiated object of a feature trace as an *Instance* entity. An *Instance* is created by an *Activation* and maintains a list of references to all *Activations* that hold a reference to this object (*i.e.,* Activations reference the receiver instance of a message, *Activations* that hold a reference to the *Instance* in the return value of a message send). The *Instance* is associated with its defining *Class* entity of the structural model.

Dynamix supports feature analysis from different levels of granularity. We exploit relationships between *Feature* entities and source entities to view a system at the package, class or method level of detail. When analyzing large and complex systems, we may need to obtain a *big picture* perspective to locate where features are implemented. In this case, we focus on the relationships between features and packages. For more fine-grained perspectives of feature implementation, we analyze feature-to-class and feature-to-method relationships.

Figure 3.1 (p.29) shows an *AbstractEntity* from which the entities (Structure and Feature entities) of our model, are derived. A *Model* comprises every entity, and every entity is associated with the *Model* entity. For example a *Method* entity obtains a collection of all the *Feature* entities in the model via this association.

Our Dynamix model as shown in Figure 3.1 (p.29) models (1) sequential programs, (2) one path of execution of features. In Appendix B (p.163) we show how Dynamix can be extended to model multi-threaded applications and multiple execution paths of features and discusses how this influences the analysis approaches described in this dissertation.

3.4 Feature Analysis: Complementary Perspectives

We define a feature-centric analysis that exploits feature knowledge of a system from three distinct, but complementary perspectives:

Structural Perspective. From this perspective, we focus on its structural entites (*e.g.,* Package,

3.4. FEATURE ANALYSIS: COMPLEMENTARY PERSPECTIVES

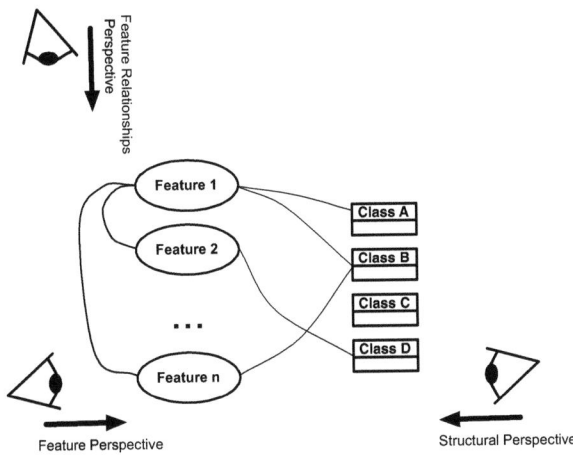

Figure 3.2: Feature-Centric Analysis: 3 Complementary Perspectives.

Class or Method entities). Our goal is to enrich structural analysis of a software system with knowledge of the roles of source artefacts in the features. We apply this analysis on a model of the system described by our Dynamix meta-model.

Feature Perspective. We describe reverse engineering techniques that center analysis and reasoning about a system from the perspective of features. To achieve this we manipulate Feature entities of the model and base our analysis on these entities.

Feature Relationship Perspective. We analyze how features are related to each other by extracting and making the relationships between Feature entities of the model explicit. The relationships are extracted by comparing similarities and runtime dependencies between pairs of features.

Figure 3.2 (p.31) summarizes our three perpectives. The edges represent relationships between classes and features, and between features .

Dynamix combines static and dynamic data, thereby facilitating our three complementary analysis perspectives.

31

```
context Method
  def: numberOfFeatures : Integer = self.model.features
          ->select(f | f.methods->includes(self))->size()

context Method
  def: featureAffinity : FeatureAffinity =
  if self.numberOfFeatures = 0
      then FeatureAffinity::notCovered
    else if self.numberOfFeatures = 1
        then FeatureAffinity::singleFeature
      else if self.numberOfFeatures = self.model.features->size()
          then FeatureAffinity::infrastructuralFeature
        else if self.numberOfFeatures < (self.model.features->size() / 2 )
            then FeatureAffinity::lowGroupFeature
          else FeatureAffinity::highGroupFeature
          endif
        endif
      endif
    endif
```

Figure 3.3: OCL specification of numberOfFeatures and FeatureAffinity properties of a Method Enttity.

3.5 Feature Affinity of Structural Entities

As in other Feature Identification approaches [Wilde and Scully, 1995; Eisenbarth et al., 2003], a fundamental characteristic of our feature-centric analysis is to quantify the relevance of a source entity to a feature. Many approaches compute the relevance of a source entity in the context of one feature. In contrast, we define a Feature Affinity property that quantifies the role of a source entity with respect to a set of features.

The *Feature Affinity* property underlies our *Structural* and *Feature* perspectives. This property defines an ordinal scale corresponding to increasing levels of participation of a source entity in the features of a model. A *Feature Affinity* level is defined to be one of 5 distinct roles, which correspond to 5 mutually exclusive, discrete *Feature Affinity* values. We define this in our model as a UML enumerator called FeatureAffinity (see Figure 3.1 (p.29)).

The values of FeatureAffinity are:

notCovered is a source entity that does not participate in any of the features of a model.

singleFeature is a source entity that participates in only one feature of a model.

lowGroupFeature is a source entity that participates in less than 50% of the features of a model.

highGroupFeature is a source entity that participates in 50% or more of the features of a model.

infrastructuralFeature is a source entity that participates in all of the features in a model.

In Figure 3.3 (p.32) we provide formal OCL definitions for the Feature Affinity property of Method entities of our Dynamix meta-model. (The definitions of these properties for Class and Package entities are of the same format.)

We summarize Feature Affinity property (FA) of an entity e, where e is a Package, Class, or Method entity in our model M, F is the set of features in our model M, and $NOF(e, F)$ is the number of features an entity participates in (appears in its feature trace):

$$(|F| > 1), FA(e, F) = \begin{cases} NOF(e, F) = 0, & \text{notCovered} \\ NOF(e, F) = 1, & \text{singleFeature} \\ (NOF(e, F) > 1) \wedge (NOF(e, F) < \frac{|F|}{2}), & \text{lowGroupFeature} \\ (NOF(e, F) < |F|) \wedge (NOF(e, F) >= \frac{|F|}{2}), & \text{highGroupFeature} \\ NOF(e, F) = |F|, & \text{infrastructuralFeature} \end{cases} \quad (3.1)$$

The Feature Affinity measurement is based on a threshold value. In the above definition, we selected a threshold to be 50% of the features in a model. We chose this value to distinguish between source entities that provide functionality localized in a group of features, and those that provide a more general functionality, used by most of the features of a model.

3.6 Feature Properties

A *Feature Perspective* describes a feature-centric analysis that reasons about a system in terms of its features. We define properties to features so that we can characterize them in the context of a system. For example, we define feature properties that are derived by computing number of participating entities in a feature (*e.g.,* number of participating classes, number of participating activations, number of participating instances).

Furthermore, we define properties for features that exploit the Feature Affinity property of source entities. We use these properties to characterize a *Feature* based on the concentration of types of participating source entities (*e.g.,* number of singleFeature classes participating in a feature). We assume, for example, that a feature with a high number of singleFeature classes or methods is likely to be implemented with functionality that is specific for this feature. If the features have a high number of highGroupFeature or infrastructuralFeature classes, then the features are probably implemented

```
context Feature
  def: nOfClasses : Integer = self.classes->size()
context Feature
  def: nOfSingleFeatureClasses : Integer = self.classes->select
      ( c | c.featureAffinity = FeatureAffinity::singleFeature)->size()
context Feature
  def: nOfLowGroupFeatureClasses : Integer = self.classes->select
      ( c | c.featureAffinity = FeatureAffinity::lowGroupFeature)->size()
context Feature
  def: nOfHighGroupFeatureClasses : Integer = self.classes->select
      ( c | c.featureAffinity = FeatureAffinity:highGroupFeature)->size()
context Feature
  def: nOfInfrastructuralFeatureClasses : Integer = self.classes->select
      ( c | c.featureAffinity = FeatureAffinity::infrastructuralFeature)->size()
```

Figure 3.4: OCL specification of the properties that pertain to participating Classes of a Feature Entity.

using common or generic functionality. For example, our analysis of SmallWiki, a web-based application, revealed that a high percentage of the methods participating in the features have a Feature Affinity level of *infrastructuralFeature* . This is partially due to the http-request-response functionality that is common to all *user triggerable* features of SmallWiki. Closer investigation revealed that the implementation of this application is highly generic.

In Figure 3.4 (p.34) we provide the OCL definition for some of the properties we defined for a Feature entity. The properties pertain to classes participating in features. For Method or Package entities, the definitions are of the same format.

Traces of feature behavior typically consist of many thousands of events [Ducasse et al., 2004]. However, it is difficult to interpret the vast amount of data associated with the feature entity of Dynamix. A single feature trace may consist of tens of thousands of events. This makes it difficult to interpret. To address the question of how features map to classes, it is not necessary to manipulate an entire feature trace. If we are not concerned with sequence of events or frequency of event occurrences, we can base our analysis on compact representations of *Feature* entities. To achieve this, we simply reduce multiple references to source entities to a single element of a sets of participating source entities. We refer to this representation of a feature as a *compact feature view*.

For one of our analysis techniques described later in the dissertation, for example, we manipulate compact feature views consisting of a tuple of sets of source entities, where each set groups entities of a different Feature Affinity level. In Figure 3.5 (p.35) we provide the OCL specification of this type of compact feature view. In addition to the OCL definition, we provide a mathematical definition of a compact feature view V of a feature f, F is the set of all features of our model, e is an entity of

3.6. FEATURE PROPERTIES

```
context Feature
  def: singleFeatureClasses: Set(Class) = (self.classes->
    select( c | c.featureAffinity = FeatureAffinity::singleFeature)
context Feature
  def: lowGroupFeatureClasses: Set(Class) = (self.classes->
    select( c | c.featureAffinity = FeatureAffinity::lowGroupFeature)
context Feature
  def: highGroupFeatureClasses: Set(Class) = (self.classes->
    select( c | c.featureAffinity = FeatureAffinity::highGroupFeature)
context Feature
  def: infrastructuralFeatureClasses: Set(Class) = (self.classes->
    select( c | c.featureAffinity = FeatureAffinity::infrastructuralFeature)

context Feature
  def: compactFeatureView: Set(Set) = {self.singleFeatureClasses,
              self.lowGroupFeatureClasses,
              self.highGroupFeatureClasses,
              self.infrastructuralFeatureClasses}
```

Figure 3.5: OCL specification of a Compact Feature View extracted from a Feature Entity.

our model M, as a tuple of sets of source entities:

$$
\begin{aligned}
SF(f) &\equiv \{e \in M, f \in F | FA(e, F) = \text{singleFeature}\} \\
LGF(f) &\equiv \{e \in M, f \in F | FA(e, F) = \text{lowGroupFeature}\} \\
HGF(f) &\equiv \{e \in M, f \in F | FA(e, F) = \text{highGroupFeature}\} \\
IF(f) &\equiv \{e \in M, f \in F | FA(e, F) = \text{infrastructuralFeature}\} \\
V(f) &= <SF(f), LGF(f), HGF(f), IF(f)>
\end{aligned}
\tag{3.2}
$$

In Figure 3.6 (p.36) we show a representation of classes and compact feature views to illustrate the relationships between features and classes and the assignment of the Feature Affinity property. On the left hand side we show a *Structural Perspective* of a system in terms of its classes. We map colors to values of Feature Affinity of an entity. The colors are mapped to exploit a *heat map* metaphor: the more features that reference a class, the 'hotter' the class. For example, if a class is characterized as having a Feature Affinity level of *infrastructuralFeature*, it is colored red, if it is characterized as having a Feature Affinity level of *singleFeature*, it is colored cyan. Classes that are *notCovered* by our feature analysis are shown in white.

On the right hand side we show a *Features Perspective*. Each feature is visually represented as a large rectangle containing four subgroups of characterized classes represented as small squares

CHAPTER 3. FEATURE-CENTRIC ANALYSIS

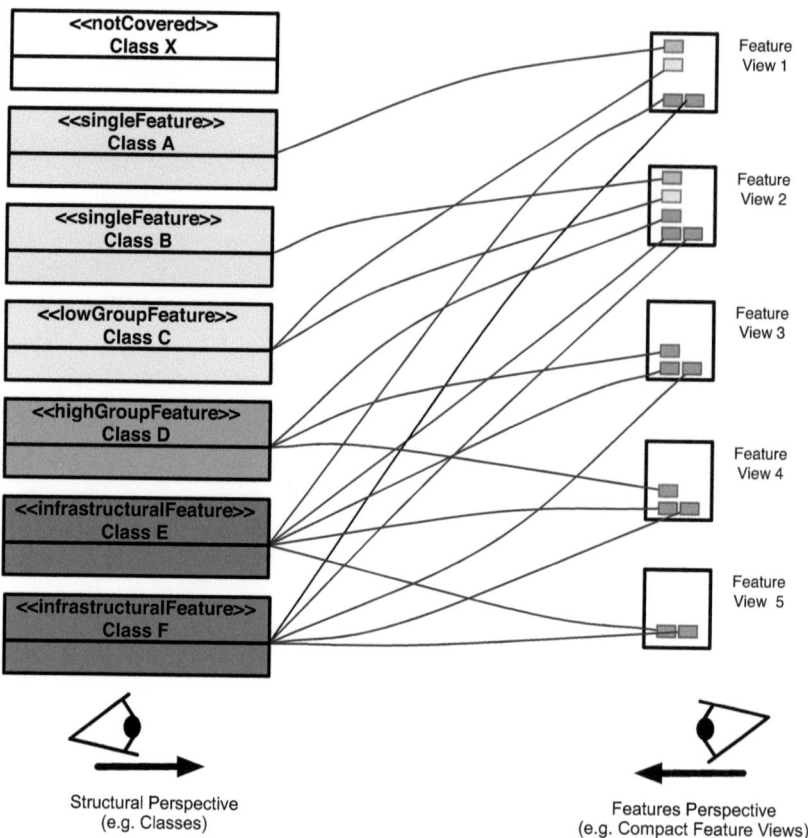

Figure 3.6: The Relationships between Classes and Compact Feature Views.

colored according to their Feature Affinity level. This visualization corresponds to our definition of a compact feature view as specified in Figure 3.5 (p.35). The edges represent a *'is participating in'* relationship between features and classes.

3.7 The Feature Relationship Properties

The third perspective of our feature-centric analysis, the *Feature Relationship Perspective*, focuses on detecting relationships between features. We distinguish between *static* and *dynamic* aspects of feature relationships. We extract *static* relationships based on the shared source entities of two features. The *dynamic* relationships require a more fine-grained view of execution data. We analyze object instantiation and references to objects to detect these dependencies. Thus, a *dynamic* relationship between pairs of features is based on shared usage of objects.

Static Feature Relationships. Typically features of a software system share common code to implement their functionalities. We consider that a static feature relationships exists if two features share usage of source artefacts. Source entities that participate in more than one feature are assigned a Feature Affinity level of lowGroupFeature, highGroupFeature or infrastructuralFeature. However, the Feature Affinity property does not tell us which features share which entities. Our static feature relationship property provides this level of information.

In Figure 3.7 (p.38) we provide the OCL specification of our *featureSimilarity* measure. We apply *featureSimilarity* to pairs of features of a model. We compute the relationship measurement based on a set intersection of source entities of two features. The greater the number of source entities that two feature views share, in proportion to the number of participating source entities, the more similar their implementation. To express the degree of similarity of static feature relationships, our similarity measurement defines an ordinal scale which represents the degree of similarity between two features. This provides us with a vocabulary to characterize relationships between features. We define this in our model as a UML enumerator, **FeatureSimilarity** (see Figure 3.1 (p.29)). We define t to be a threshold value. We use this threshold value to distinguish between different levels of feature relationships (*e.g.,* let $threshold = 0.5$).

Variation: The definition of *featureSimilarity* provided in Figure 3.7 (p.38) includes all source artefacts. However, we could refine this definition to consider only the source artefacts with a Feature Affinity level of *lowGroupFeature* and *highGroupFeature*. This reduces the number and degree of similarity of feature dependencies detected. In particular this refinement avoids the detection of feature relationships that arise from a general shared usage of a *main* class by all features.

CHAPTER 3. FEATURE-CENTRIC ANALYSIS

```
context Feature
  def: simpleFeatureView : Set(Class) = self.classes
context Feature
  def: similarity(aFeature: Feature) : Real = ((self.simpleFeatureView->
    intersection(aFeature.simpleFeatureView)->size()) /
      (self.simpleFeatureView->size()).min(aFeature.simpleFeatureView->size())

context Method
  def: featureSimilarity (aFeature: Feature, threshold: Real ): FeatureSimilarity
  if self.similarity(aFeature)= 0
     then FeatureSimilarity::disjoint
   else if self.similarity(aFeature) = 1
       then FeatureSimilarity::complete
     else if self.similarity(aFeature) < threshold
       then FeatureSimilarity::loose
       else FeatureSimilarity::tight
     endif
   endif
 endif
```

Figure 3.7: OCL specification of featureSimilarity.

$$similarity_e(F_i, F_j) \iff \frac{|V_i \cap V_j|}{min(|V_i|,|V_j|)} \begin{cases} disjoint, & similarity_e(F_i, F_j) = 0 \\ loose, & similarity_e(F_i, F_j) < t \\ tight, & similarity_e(F_i, F_j) \geq t \\ complete, & similarity_e(F_i, F_j) = 1 \end{cases}$$

We use a simple matrix representation to visualize static feature relationships, Figure 3.8 (p.39) shows an example of a *feature relationship matrix* of three features. We use grayscale to represent the degree of similarity of two Feature entities of our model, F_i to F_j. The darker the cell, the more related are the features (black represents *complete*).

Dynamic Feature Relationships. The static relationship measurement does not take the runtime behavioral characteristics of object-oriented systems into consideration. We define a *dynamic* relationship between two features if they reference the same instances at runtime. A refinement of this definition is when a feature requires other features to be executed to establish prerequisite runtime conditions; for example a web application may require a user to execute a *login* feature, thus creating a session instance, which must exist before any other feature of the application can be executed. We call these relationships *depends* relationships.

3.7. THE FEATURE RELATIONSHIP PROPERTIES

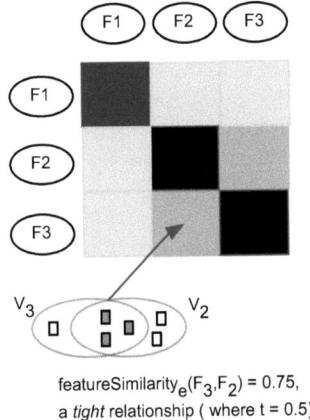

featureSimilarity$_e$(F$_3$,F$_2$) = 0.75,
a *tight* relationship (where t = 0.5)

Figure 3.8: Matrix visualization showing the *featureSimilarity* relationships between 3 features.

```
context Feature
  def: importedObjects : Set(Instance) =
        self.referencedObjects->excluding(self.createdObjects)

context Feature
  def: depends(aFeature: Feature) : Boolean =
  ( self.importedObjects->intersection(aFeature.createdObjects)->size() > 0)
           and not (self = aFeature)
```

Figure 3.9: OCL specification of depends relationship between features.

We consider two features of our model, F_i and F_j. We say that F_i *depends* on F_j if and only if F_j creates objects that are referenced by F_i. Let I_i be a set of objects referenced by F_i, but not created in F_i (*i.e.*, imported objects), and O_j be a set of objects created by F_j, then:

$$depends \equiv \{(F_i, F_j) \mid I_i \cap O_j \neq \emptyset, i \neq j\} \quad (3.3)$$

We use graph visualizations to represent the dynamic relationships between features. The nodes of the graph represent features. We draw an edge between feature nodes if a dependency exists. The width of the edge of the node reflects the strength of the relationship between two features (*i.e.*, the more objects shared between two features, the higher the number of shared objects between two features).

3.8 Summary and Outlook

In this chapter we introduced Dynamix, which explicitly models features as a collection of behavioral entities. Our Feature entity reflects the tree structure of a feature trace. Dynamix establishes links between the behavioral entities and structural entities representing the source code.

We defined our *Feature Affinity* property, which we assign to structural entities to enrich them with feature context. Furthermore, we gave examples of feature properties that we use to analyze a system from a feature perspective. All our definitions relate to our Dynamix meta-model.

In the remainder of the dissertation we present several feature-centric analyses, in different reverse engineering contexts. In the next chapter, we demonstrate how we apply the three perspectives of feature-centric analysis to two case studies. Our goal is to demonstrate how our Dynamix meta-model supports the three analysis perspectives described in this chapter. We aim to show how feature-centric analysis enriches reverse engineering techniques with domain knowledge of a system's features.

A particular focus of research considers software evolution analysis enriched with feature knowledge. We extend feature-centric analysis with a time dimension to reason about the evolution of a system in terms of its features. The feature knowledge of a system provides semantic context for the intent and extent of changes we detect over time. We demonstrate the flexibility of our Dynamix meta-model as we extend it with entities for modeling historical data.

With Figure 3.10 (p.42), we provide a map of the various feature-centric analysis techniques we describe in the subsequent chapters. On the left side we represent the Dynamix meta-model and extensions in terms of UML packages. On the right side, we represent the chapters and briefly summarize the analysis technique they address. Each technique is based on the core Dynamix meta-model. Some of the techniques introduce extensions to the meta-model to facilitate new perspectives such as evolution analysis, or the correlation of developer knowledge and features. We re-use the color scheme of Feature Affinity to represent the level of relevance of each part of the meta-model (*i.e.,* Dynamix and extensions) to a particular technique.

CHAPTER 3. FEATURE-CENTRIC ANALYSIS

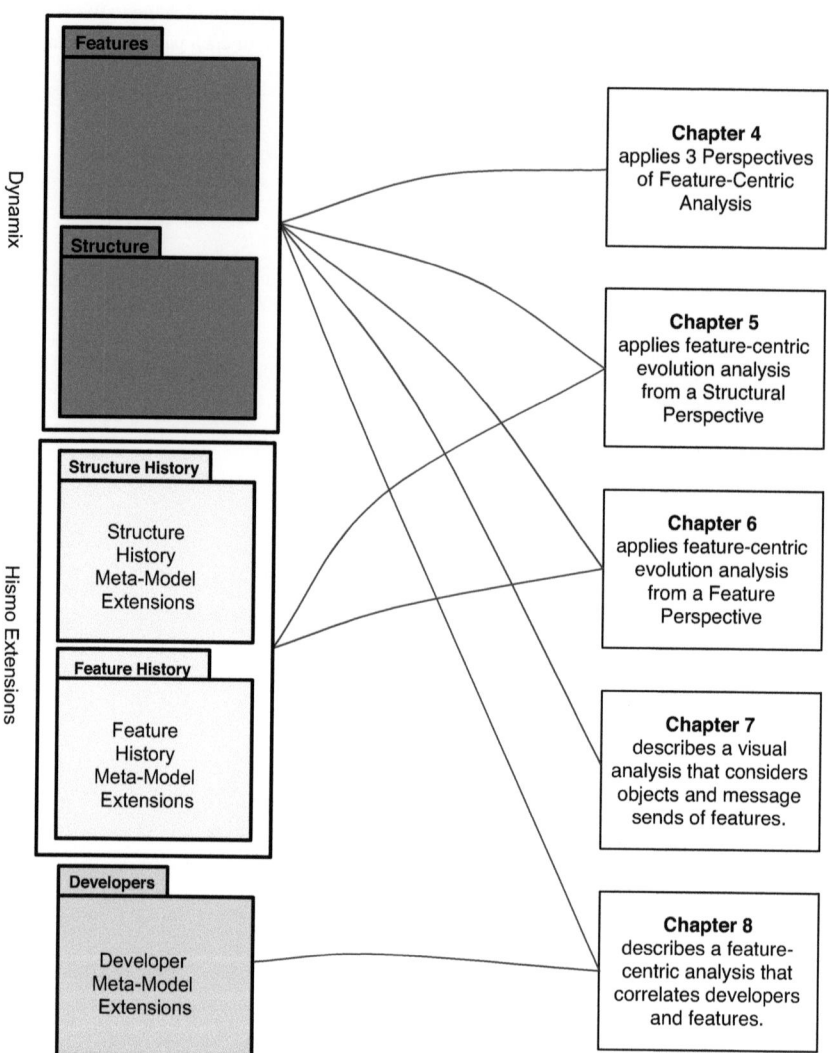

Figure 3.10: A Map of the Feature Analyses Techniques presented in the remainder of this dissertation, showing which chapters related to which parts of the Dynamix Meta-Model and Meta-Model Extensions.

Chapter 4

Applying Feature-Centric Analysis: Two Case Studies

We describe in detail how we applied our feature-centric analysis approach to two software systems. We show how our approach reveals relationships between features and classes and relationships between features. We validate our findings with developer knowledge and system documentation. Furthermore, we compare the results of applying our Feature Affinity measurement with metrics of other Feature Identification approaches.

CHAPTER 4. APPLYING FEATURE-CENTRIC ANALYSIS: TWO CASE STUDIES

4.1 Introduction

In the previous chapter we described our feature-centric approach to analyzing a system from three complementary perspectives. At the core of our analysis is Dynamix, our meta-model of execution data that models features as first class entities and integrates with a structural model of a system's source entities. In this chapter, we perform feature-centric analysis on two object-oriented systems to demonstrate our approach and validate our Dynamix meta-model. We aim to show how our three perspective approach successfully addresses the reverse engineering questions we raised in Chapter 3 : (1) *How do features relate to classes and methods?* (2) *How do classes and methods relate to features?* (3) *How are features related to each other?*

The focus of our feature-centric analysis approach to extract and model a system as described by our Dynamix meta-model. Our emphasis is on describing how we can treat features as first class entites in reverse engineering analyses and thus exploit features for system comprehension.

As each of the above questions directs our focus to one perspective of feature-centric analysis, we structure the presentation of our case study analyses accordingly.

A key characteristic of the approach we describe in this chapter is the use of simple visualizations of features, enriched with the measurements defined in the previous chapter. We support understanding of a system's features and how they are related. We use a clustering technique to sort the features to highlight their similarity. We also extract visualizations of static and dynamic feature relationships.

Our feature-centric analysis is a heuristic approach: we validate our findings of our feature-centric analysis with developer knowledge and available documentation.

Structure of the chapter. In the next section, we introduce the case studies we chose for feature-centric analysis and outline our reasons for selecting them. In Section 4.3 (p.45), we briefly outline the methodology we adopted to obtain our model of a system's source code and behavioral data of features. We describe details of applying feature-centric analysis to the Pier application in Section 4.4 (p.47). Section 4.5 (p.53) describes our analysis of ArgoUML. Subsequently, in Section 4.6 (p.57), we discuss and evaluate our results. We outline variations in our approach and identify strengths, constraints and limitations in Section 4.6 (p.57). We compare our Feature Affinity measurement with other *Feature Identification* metrics in Section 4.7 (p.60). Finally, Section 4.8 (p.65) concludes by summarizing our findings and highlighting the main contributions of our feature-centric analysis.

Application	Size (in classes)	# Features analyzed
Pier	258	11
ArgoUML	2075	11

Figure 4.1: Details of the Case Studies to which we applied Feature-Centric Analysis.

4.2 Case Studies

We chose two object-oriented systems, one medium-sized system ($<$ 300 classes), Pier, and one large open source system ($>$ 1000 classes), ArgoUML to validate our feature-centric approach.

Pier is a reengineered version of SmallWiki [Ducasse et al., 2005b] ported to Squeak [Briffault and Ducasse, 2001], a dialect of Smalltalk. It comprises 258 classes (147 Pier classes, 111 Framework classes). Our choice of Pier was motivated by the following reasons: (1) it is open source, thus its source code is freely available, (2) we are familiar with the predecessor application SmallWiki and have also analyzed this application in previous works [Greevy and Ducasse, 2005b; Greevy et al., 2006b], (3) we are familiar with the features of Pier from the user's perspective, and (4) we have direct access to developer knowledge to verify our findings.

Our second case study, ArgoUML, is an open source UML modelling application implemented in Java. Our choice of ArgoUML was motivated by the following reasons: (1) we have access to developer documentation of ArgoUML to check our findings, (2) we want to illustrate that our technique is language independent in that it is applicable to any object-oriented system (e.g. Java), and (3) ArgoUML has been used by us and other researchers as a reverse engineering case study, in particular for dynamic analysis [Greevy and Ducasse, 2005a; Zaidman and Demeyer, 2005]. To validate the results of ArgoUML, we rely on the documentation and naming conventions used in the source code. Figure 4.1 (p.45) gives an overview of size of the case studies and the number of features we analyzed.

4.3 Methodology

Our first step is to obtain an instance of a Dynamix model for the system under analysis. We extract a structural model of the source entities by parsing the source code. Then, we extract dynamic feature data by exercising a set of features on an instrumented system. In the case of the Pier and ArgoUML applications, we manually exercised features by interacting with the user interface of the application. We captured traces and modeled each feature as a distinct entity in Dynamix. The message events

CHAPTER 4. APPLYING FEATURE-CENTRIC ANALYSIS: TWO CASE STUDIES

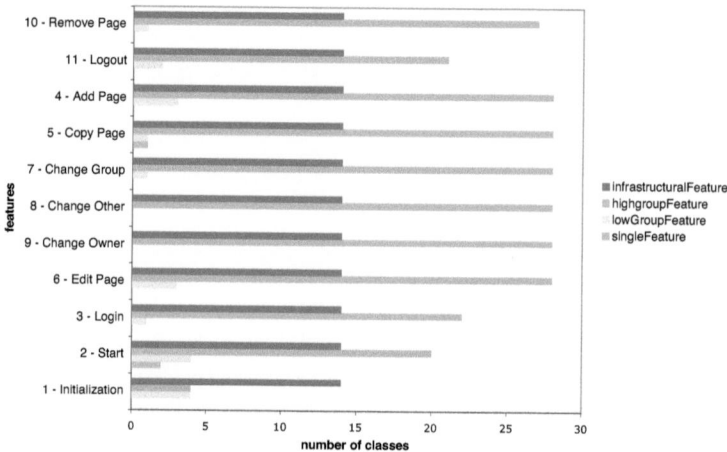

Figure 4.2: Pier Features showing details of Feature Affinity of classes.

of each feature are modeled as a collection of activations and instantiations. For each Activation entity, we resolve reference to a Method entity and for each instantiation we resolve the reference to a Class entity to establish the relationships.

Once we have obtained an instance of a **Dynamix** model, we extract three complementary perspectives: (1) a *Feature Perspective* to reason about a system's features and how they relate to classes by manipulating *compact feature views* (*e.g.,* sets of sets of classes grouped by Feature Affinity level), (2) a *Structural Perspective* to quantify the roles of class in features, and (3) a *Feature Relationship Perspective* to analyze *featureSimilarity* (as described in Figure 3.7 (p.38)) and dynamic *depends* relationships between features (as described in Equation 3.3 (p.40)).

We built simple, interactive visualizations using the Mondrian framework [Meyer *et al.*, 2006] to represent compact feature views and feature relationships. We exploit the interactive characteristics of these visualizations to discover which classes participate in features and which classes and objects are common to features.

4.4 Pier Experiment

In accordance with our definition of a feature as an observable unit of behavior [Eisenbarth et al., 2003], we identify features of Pier by making the assumption that elements of its user interface, namely links, buttons and entry forms of Pier pages, exercise distinct features. Based on this assumption, we selected 11 distinct interactive features (10 typical user interactions with the Pier application such as adding a page, editing a page or deleting a page). In addition, we also selected one non-interactive feature (*Initialization*) that initializes the Pier application at startup.

We extracted one single trace encompassing the execution of 11 distinct features. We implemented markers in the trace to indicate where the execution of each feature was initiated and terminated. The advantage of a single marked trace over individual traces of a previous SmallWiki experiment [Greevy and Ducasse, 2005b] is that we preserve information about which behavioral entities (*i.e.,* instances) are shared between features. This information is essential for the analysis of dynamic feature dependencies.

In Figure 4.2 (p.46) we show the features of Pier that we selected for analysis and the distribution of Feature Affinity over the classes of these features,

How do features relate to classes? We view a system as a set of features, where each feature groups classes that participate in its runtime behavior. Figure 4.3 (p.48) shows feature views of classes. To generate our visualization of feature views, we apply a dendogram seriation algorithm [Morris et al., 2003], a clustering technique to define the order feature views in our visualization according to their static *featureSimilarity* relationship (*i.e.,* the larger the number of classes they share, the closer together they appear in the visualization). We use interactive capabilities of our visualization to discover which classes participate in a feature. To determine the classes that provide *feature-specific* functionality, we focus on *singleFeature* classes ((1) (Figure 4.3 (p.48)) and *lowGroupFeature* classes ((2) (Figure 4.3 (p.48)) of the feature views.

Our analysis reveals *lowGroupFeature* classes PRDocumentScanner, PRDocumentParser and PRDocumentWriter. These classes participate in both the *Add Page* feature and *Edit Page* feature. The developer of Pier confirms that classes which are responsible for page manipulations are conceptually part of these two features. Similarly we detect PUGroup as a *lowGroupFeature* class. This participates in both *Change Owner* and *Change Group* features. Once again, the developer confirms that this class provides a group level security functionality that is exercised by the *Change Owner* and *Change Group* features. The features represent functionality to modify access rights of a user.

How do classes relate to features? Most of the classes of the Pier application are characterized as *highGroupFeature* classes. Only 0.66 % of the classes are *singleFeature*. In Figure 4.3 (p.48) (1) we indicate three *singleFeature* classes we detect, namely PRPierMain, PROutGoingRefer-

CHAPTER 4. APPLYING FEATURE-CENTRIC ANALYSIS: TWO CASE STUDIES

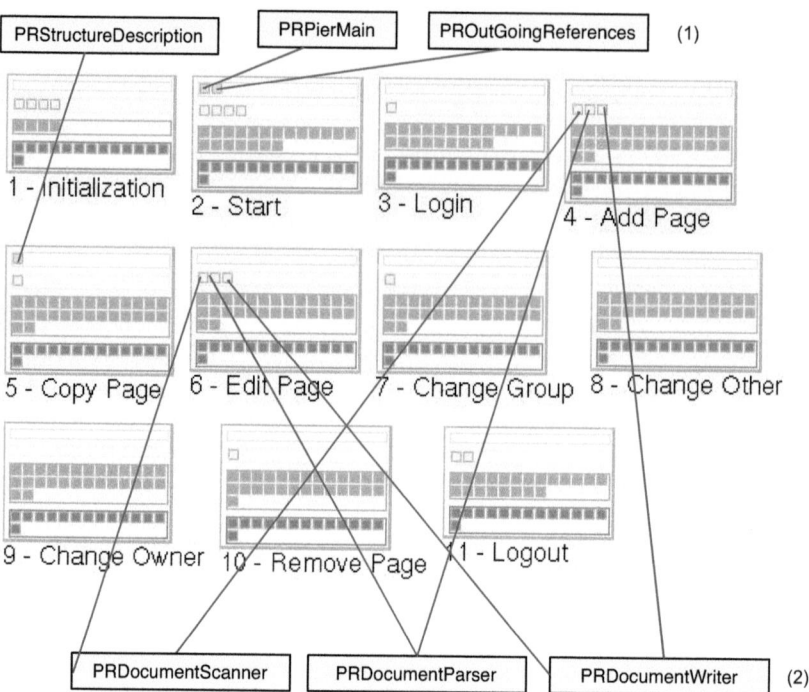

Figure 4.3: Pier Feature Views of Classes showing *singleFeature* classes and *lowGroupFeature* Classes shared between the *addPage* and *edit a page* Features. (Numbers in the feature names indicate the order of execution.)

4.4. PIER EXPERIMENT

ences and PRStructureDescription. The Pier developer confirms that the *singleFeature* classes PRPierMain amd PROutGoingReferences are indeed correctly characterized, as these classes only participate in the *Start* feature of the system. The other *singleFeature* class is correctly characterized in the context of our feature model as only the *Copy Page* feature exercises the functionality of PRStructureDescription. However, the developer of Pier informs us that in the context of the entire application, this is a false positive, as the class PRStructureDescription would also participate in other features which we did not include in our model.

We calculated the average proportional distribution of Feature Affinity over the features. The *highGroupFeature* classes of our analysis account on average for 76% of the classes of a feature. These include classes that implement page rendering functionality and interaction with a web server. The developer confirms our findings: the bulk of Pier's functionality is used by most the features of our analysis.

How do features relate to each other? For our Pier case study, we consider both static and dynamic feature relationships, as our tracing approach preserves instance information between features.

Static Relationships.

We analyze the features to reveal static *featureSimilarity* relationships. We built an interactive visualization which we call the *Feature Similarity Matrix* using Mondrian [Meyer et al., 2006] to show the strength (*i.e.*, number of shared source entities) of *featureSimilarity* relationships.

Figure 4.4 (p.50) shows relationships between pairs of features based on the number of methods they share. The darker the cell of the matrix, the more methods a pair of features has in common. Our visualization reveals that features of Pier share a high proportion of methods. To distinguish between relationships, we configure our threshold t of Equation 3.3 (p.38) with a value of 0.8. In Figure 4.4 (p.50) (1) we highlight the relationship between the *Add Page* feature and the *Edit Page* feature, as they are completely related on a class level. Figure 4.4 (p.50) (2) reveals that feature *Initialization* is the most dissimilar feature to any other feature, and Figure 4.4 (p.50) (3) reveals that features *Change Other* and *Change Group* are tightly related. Both features are conceptually part of the security subsystem of Pier, so we expect these features to reuse a large number of classes. The results of the analysis of the *Feature Similarity Matrix* agree with our analysis of feature views and the developers confirm our findings.

This result agrees with our findings that most of the classes are characterized as *highGroupFeature* or *infrastructuralFeature* by our Feature Affinity measurement.

Dynamic Relationships.

The *featureSimilarity matrix* visualization could be used to represent any of relationships defined for features. Alternatively, we built an interactive graph visualization to represent dynamic relation-

CHAPTER 4. APPLYING FEATURE-CENTRIC ANALYSIS: TWO CASE STUDIES

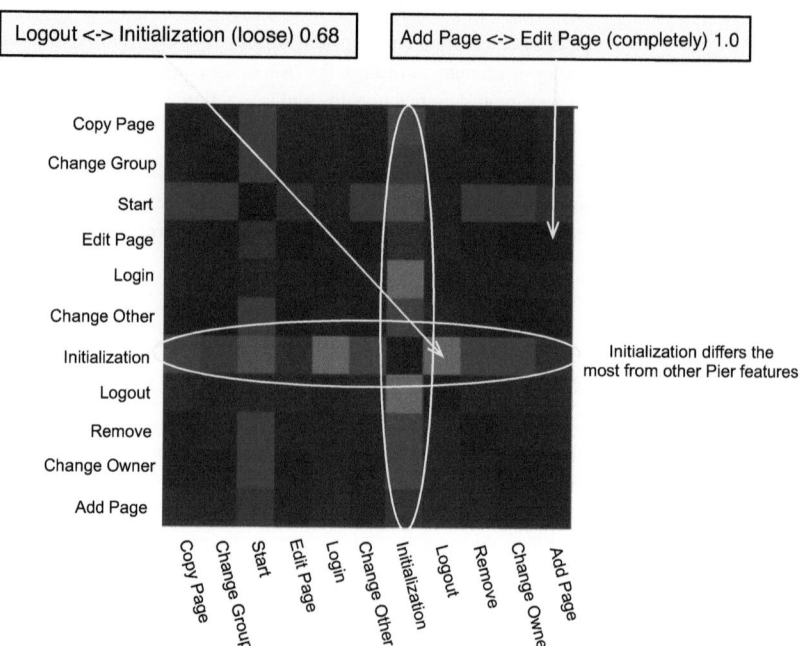

Figure 4.4: Pier Features Similarity Matrix. This shows *featureSimilarity* relationships between pairs of features at Class level.

ships *depends* between features as defined in Equation 3.3 (p.40). Our graph representation exploits the principles of polymetric views described by Lanza [Lanza, 2003]. Each feature is represented as a node of the graph. An edge between nodes represents a dependency relationship between two features and we use an arrow to indicate the direction of the dependency. We map the metric nReferencedObjects as defined in Figure 3.1 (p.29) (*number of referenced objects*) to the width of an edge connecting two features. The wider the edge, the more objects are used by one feature that are created by the other feature.

Our analysis of the *depends* relationships reveals that for our Pier case study, each feature has dependencies with the feature that was executed prior to it in the trace (see Figure 4.5 (p.52)). Between some features, there is a large number of dependencies as the width of the edges reveal: using the *mouse over* interaction on an edge in the graph, a tooltip lists of objects on which a feature depends.

In Figure 4.5 (p.52) we show graph visualizations of feature dependencies we generated for Pier features. In Figure 4.5 (p.52) (1) we show a complete graph of all the dynamic relationships. We mapped a measurement nReferencedObjects (*number of referenced objects*) to the width of an edge. We see that most dependencies exist to the *Start* and *Initialization* features. In Figure 4.5 (p.52) (2) we applied a transitive reduction algorithm to the graph and obtained a hierarchy of relationships. Our transitive reduction algorithm assumes the transitive property holds for all vertices of the dependency graph:

Let R be a relation between to vertices of a graph. Let X be the set of all vertices.

$$\forall a, b, c \in X, aRb \land bRc \rightarrow aRc \tag{4.1}$$

Transitive reduction removes all edges that reflect the transitive property of the graph as it assumes that these relationships are implicit.

This hierarchy corresponds to the order in which we executed the features. Each feature accesses at least one instance created by its predecessor. This result indicates that the order of execution of the features impacts the dynamic relationships. To verify this we traced features with 4 different orders. Each time the result reveals that a feature is dependent on its predecessor. We asked the main developer of Pier to explain this result. He verified that due to the nature of features traced, each feature will access the state of an object representing a user interface element that has been instantiated by the previous feature.

In (3) we show the number of instances of the *Start* feature that the *Remove Page* feature depends on. The *mouse over* tooltip of our graph visualizations also shows details of the relevant instances.

One surprising result we obtained is the strength of the dependency relationship between the *Remove Page* and *Initialization* features. The developer confirms our finding and explains that this depen-

CHAPTER 4. APPLYING FEATURE-CENTRIC ANALYSIS: TWO CASE STUDIES

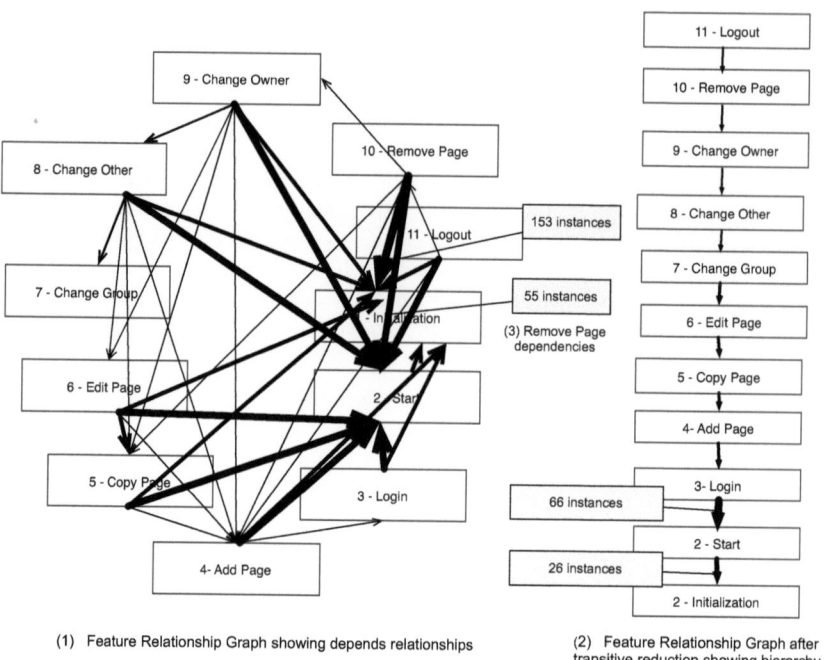

Figure 4.5: Pier Dependency Graph. This shows transitive closure and transitive reduction graphs for *depends* relationships between features.

dency is due to the fact that when a page is removed, the Pier system checks the entire Wiki structure to see if there are any links exist to the page being removed. This results in a lot of accesses to objects that were created during the *Start* and *Initialization* features.

We verified our findings with the developers of Pier. They confirm that the *Start* feature creates instances such as PUSecurity, PRParagraph, PRComponent, PRInternalLink these are then accessed by all the subsequent features. The developers also confirmed that all features depend on the *Initialization* feature, as they all need to access the instance of the PRKernel class which is created during initialization of Pier.

Due to the large number of dependencies detected, we believe that our *depends* definition needs to be refined to distinguish between different types of objects (*e.g.*, low-level objects and objects that represent recurring dependencies between features).

4.5 ArgoUML Experiment

In this case study, we focused on the core of the application, (*i.e.*, we applied selective instrumentation excluding library classes and plugin features from the trace). Our model consisted of 2075 classes. To narrow the scope of our investigation even further, we filtered out classes defined in the library org.tigris consisting of GUI classes and Java library classes. This resulted in 1501 classes.

We consider only packages of the subsystems org::argouml, which consists of 83 packages. Our analysis covers 56 of these packages. We exercised 11 features of ArgoUML. We traced each feature individually, by manually interacting with the user interface of ArgoUML. We achieved a class coverage of 58% of the 1501 classes of the org::argouml packages.

How do features relate to classes? Figure 4.8 (p.56) shows feature views of classes of the 11 features we traced. As with the previous case study, we applied a dendrogram seriation algorithm [Morris *et al.*, 2003] to order the views by their *featureSimilarity* relationship, so that features that share a large number of classes are displayed close together.

ArgoUML startup feature (159853 events). The feature view consists of 521 classes. 208 classes are characterized as *single feature*. Figure 4.8 (p.56) shows that this feature view contains the most *singleFeature* classes of all the features we traced. This feature represents the startup and initialization of the ArgoUML system. According to the ArgoUML documentation, the purpose of this feature is the initialization of the applications main frame, the menu, tool-bar, status bar and the four main areas: navigation pane, editor pane, to do pane and the details pane. By querying the *singleFeature* classes, we discover the main class and ActionAboutArgoUML which is responsible for the splash screen which is displayed at system startup.

CHAPTER 4. APPLYING FEATURE-CENTRIC ANALYSIS: TWO CASE STUDIES

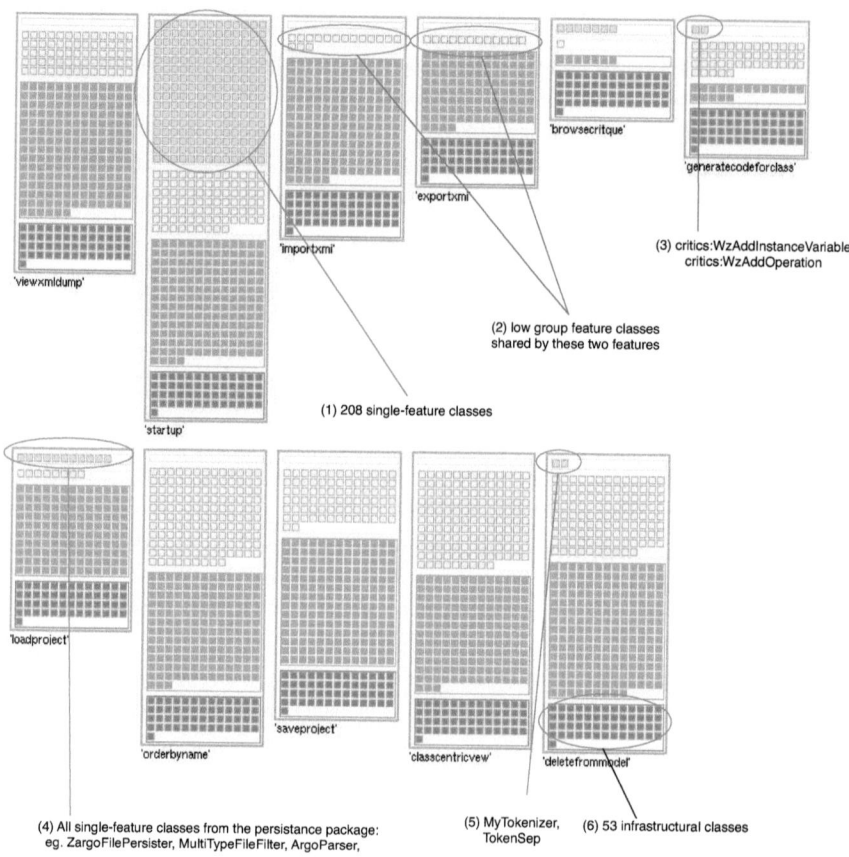

Figure 4.6: ArgoUML Feature Views of Classes.

4.5. ARGOUML EXPERIMENT

According to the documentation, this feature is implemented in the application subsystem of ArgoUML. The classes that provide functionality are: ui.ProjectBrowser, kernel.Project and cognitive support class cognitive.ui.ToDoPane. By querying our visualization, we confirm that these classes have been located for the *startup* feature.

export a model to XMI feature (38611 events). This feature exports a UML model to a file in XMI format. The ArgoUML documentation describes a *peristency subsystem* which provides functionalities that allow the model to be stored persistently in a particular file format or loaded from a persistent storage. Our feature view for the *export model to XMI* feature contains the classes of this subsystem.

import XMI feature (131105 events). We exercised the feature to import a UML model. This feature also exercises the functionalities of the persistency subsystem. In Figure 4.8 (p.56) (2) we highlight the classes that are common to this feature and the *exportxmi* feature. At the class level, both features exercise the functionality of classes such as ActionAddPackage and ActionAddDataType. On closer examination of the source code we discover that the same classes implement export and import functionality. To obtain a more detailed view and to distinguish between import and export functionality we would need to generate feature views at a method level.

load project. We highlight in Figure 4.8 (p.56) (4) the 11 classes that are specific to the *load project* feature. This feature interacts with the *persistence* subsystem of ArgoUML. We discover the following *singlefeature* classes, for example XMLTokenTableBase, ArgoParser and ZargoFilePersister. We verify in the documentation that these classes deal with loading UML models stored in ArgoUML format from persistent store.

new use case feature (270472 events). This feature exercises this functionality to create a new use case diagram in our ArgoUML project. The ArgoUML documentation describes the *Diagram* subsystem that implements draw and manipulate functionalities for UML diagrams.

How do classes relate to features? In Figure 4.8 (p.56) (1) we show the distribution of the Feature Affinity measurement for ArgoUML. This reveals that 34% of the classes that participate in the features, are characterized as *singleFeature*, 32% as *lowGroupFeature*, 27% as *highGroupFeature* and 7 % as *infrastructuralFeature*.

Our feature perspective (Figure 4.8 (p.56)) reveals that a high percentage of the classes that are *singleFeature* (208 classes) were detected in the *startup* feature of ArgoUML. This feature is responsible for system initialization, which typically represents *one-off* functionality. If we treat the *startup* feature as an *outlier* with respect to the features we analyzed and recalculate the distribution of Feature Affinity (as shown in Figure 4.8 (p.56) (2)), we obtain a more representative view of how Feature Affinity levels are distributed over classes for the remaining features we traced (*singleFeature* = 4%, *lowGroupFeature* = 48%, *highGroupFeature* = 39% and *infrastructuralFeature* = 11%).

CHAPTER 4. APPLYING FEATURE-CENTRIC ANALYSIS: TWO CASE STUDIES

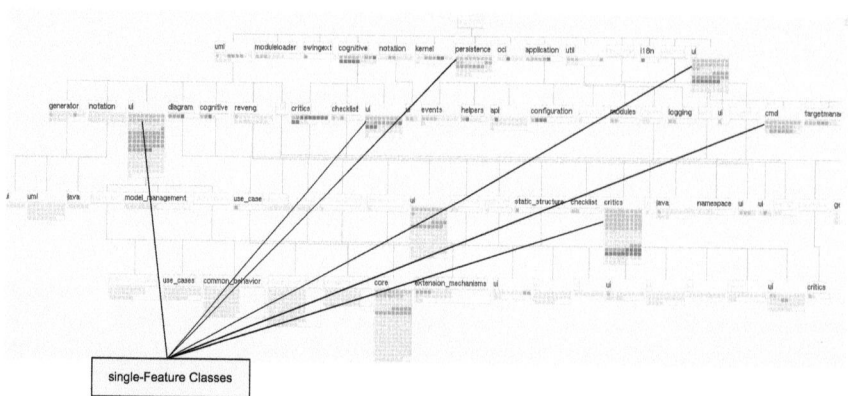

Figure 4.7: ArgoUML: Distribution of the Feature Affinity values of classes over the package hierarchy highlighting some of the *singlefeature* classes.

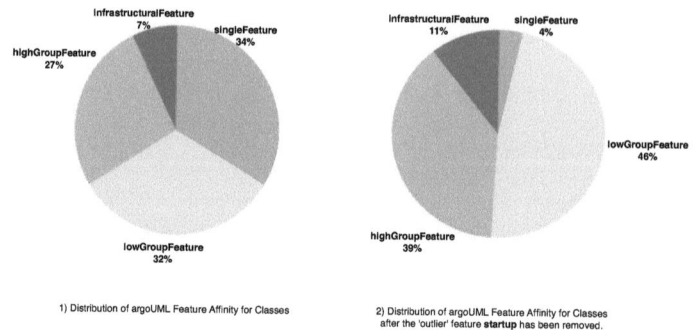

Figure 4.8: ArgoUML: Highlighting the effect of the *startup* feature on the distribution of Feature Affinity levels of the classes.

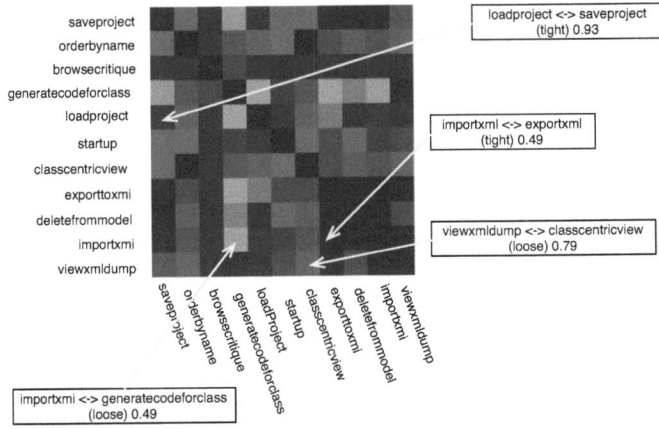

Figure 4.9: ArgoUML Features Similarity Matrix similarity relationships between pairs of features at class level.

In Figure 4.7 (p.56) we show the distribution of the Feature Affinity over the package hierarchy. We highlight some of the single feature classes. This perspective offers an alternative to feature views and the context of the system structure provides the developer with structural information about which parts of the system are related to the features we traced and to which extent.

How do features relate to each other? For the ArgoUML experiment we focus only on the static *featureSimilarity* relationships between features, as the individual traces of features do not preserve instance information needed to analyze the dynamic feature relationships. Figure 4.9 (p.57) reveals that the features *saveproject* and *loadproject* share a large proportion of methods. With a threshold value of $t = 0.8$, this relationship is characterized as *tight*. Similarly we see that the features *importxmi* and *viewxmldump* are tightly related. In contrast the *startup* feature is most dissimilar to the other features. As the *startup* feature performs one-off initialization functionality, this result agrees with our expectations.

4.6 Discussion

In this section we discuss some of the strengths and limitations of our feature-centric analysis approach.

4.6.1 Strengths of Feature-Centric Analysis

As our approach incorporates the goals of *Feature Identification* techniques, we apply it to locate key classes associated with features. Our Feature Affinity property enriches our understanding of classes as it assigns them with a relevance with respect to a set of features. This gives us insights into which parts of the system provide general functionality.

Moreover, the distribution of the Feature Affinity property provides us with an insight into the nature of the system. For example in the case of our Pier case study, we detected that most of the classes are characterized as *highGroupFeature* or *infrastructuralfeature*. This indicates that there is a large propotion of common functionality, used by most of the features we traced. The developers of Pier confirmed this finding. The explained that as Pier is a web application, each user-triggered feature exercises common HTTP request/response and page rendering functionality.

For both case studies, we found that investigating *singlefeature* and *lowgroupfeature* classes were the most revealing to gain an understanding of how the features are implemented.

Our Feature Relationship Perspective provides us with a more precise information about which classes are shared between features. Our feature view perspective does not reveal which features share which classes, whereas our similarity matrix reveals this level of detail. Furthermore, our Feature Relationship Graph provides a means of interactively exploring runtime dependencies between features.

The Feature Affinity level distinguishes between source entities that are common to a small group of features (*lowGroupFeature*) and those that are common to a large group of features (*highGroupFeature*). The *lowgroupfeature* classes are shared by a small number of features. They represent classes that implement functionality that is shared by a small number of features (*i.e.,* less than half of the feature traced). For example, in our Pier case study (see Figure 4.3 (p.48) (2)) we highlight that the features *add page* and *edit the copied page* share the same three classes. Thus, *lowGroupFeature* classes represent good starting points for investigating similarities between features. Moreover, as a result of the applying the dendrogram seriation algorithm, our visualization of feature views orders feature views according to their *featureSimilarity*.

4.6.2 Evaluation of Feature Affinity

Stability of Characterizations. The Feature Affinity of a source entity in our approach is highly dependent on the set of features selected for analysis. The *highGroupFeature* classes represent classes that provide functionality used by most of the features in our model. In the case of our Pier case study, all the features we exercised, except for the *initialization* feature, are initiated by the user. These features exercised classes responsible for handling the HTTP request-response dialog and for

4.6. DISCUSSION

page rendering code of the Pier application. We would expect that classes provide *infrastructural* functionality to the features. However, they are characterized as *highGroupFeature* classes and not as *infrastructuralFeature*. Due to our definition of *infrastructuralFeature* revealing a source entity that participates in all features of our model, the choice of features affects the resulting Feature Affinity level of classes. In this case, we included a feature in our analysis which does not involve user interaction, namely the *initialization* feature.

Precision and Recall. Our feature-centric analysis builds on feature identification techniques. Thus the approach is exploratory in nature. We seek to retrieve relevant classes for a feature. Dynamic analysis is precise in that the feature trace we extract identifies all the classes that are referenced while exercising a feature. It is difficult to determine if for the abstract notion of a feature, if all relevant classes have been identified. We provided the developers of Pier with a list of all the features we traced and the classes we identified for each feature, grouped according to their Feature Affinity level, The developer confirms that all *singlefeature* and *lowgroupfeature* classes are relevant for the features in which they were identified. However, the state that it is difficult to identify which classes are not located by our approach.

We emphasize that our feature-centric analysis is an iterative process, We are in a position to assess our choice of features only after we have performed feature analysis and applied Feature Affinity measurement to the classes.

4.6.3 Variations

Defining Thresholds. In the experiments described in this chapter we defined a threshold value of 50% to distinguish between *lowGroupFeature* and *highGroupFeature* classes. A possible variation of the approach would be to allow a configurable threshold value for Feature Affinity, based on iterative analysis or depending on the type of application to be analyzed. Although we did not experiment with variations in threshold values for Feature Affinity, we did experiment with the threshold values of our *featureSimilarity* measurement. For systems with a high proportion of *infrastructuralFeature* classes (*e.g.,* Pier) the threshold value needs to be set > 0.5. We chose a value of 0.8. Otherwise it is difficult to calibrate the similarities between the features. For ArgoUML we chose a value of 0.5 as the Feature Affinity levels are distributed more evenly than those of Pier over the classes.

Defining Filtering Criteria. Our dynamic feature relationship measurement *depends* yields a large number of object dependencies, making it difficult in some cases to associate semantic context to the relationships. Another variation of our approach would be to define a characterization of objects similar to the Feature Affinity measurement for source entities that reflects if an object is shared by two features, less than half the features, more than half the features and all the features. We believe that this differentiation would help to isolate key feature dependencies. We explore this in more detail in another work [Lienhard et al., 2006].

4.6.4 Limitations

We identify and discuss constraints and limitations of our feature-centric analysis approach, based on the experience we gained from applying it to the case studies.

Mapping Traces to Features. We define a one-to-one mapping between an execution and a feature. Other approaches [Eisenbarth *et al.*, 2003] combine traces from multiple scenario executions to obtain a feature mapping. At present, we do not model multiple execution scenarios for one feature. Our experiments show that by capturing traces for one path of execution, we established a mapping to the parts of the code that implement features. We model features in Dynamix as one thread of execution. However, our model could easily be extended to reflect a one-to-many relationship between features and feature traces and multi-threading or multiple execution paths of a feature into consideration. As our feature analysis approach extracts feature views (*i.e.,* sets of source entities) from Dynamix, we simply need to define how we would extract these sets from a composite feature entity representing either a multiple scenario feature or multiple threads of execution.

Coverage. Coverage of the application by the feature model affects the Feature Affinity level of the source artefacts. If the model contains only one feature, the feature can only be considered in isolation. Only by executing all features of an application, and all possible paths of execution of a feature, would we achieve a stable Feature Affinity level of source artefacts. For example, a class is *singleFeature*, if it participates in one feature. However, its Feature Affinity level may change as soon as we include another feature that references this class in the model. Then the Feature Affinity level would change to *lowGroupFeature*.

Extracting Dynamic Feature Relationships. Our experiments used various techniques to extract traces of features. For our analysis of ArgoUML, we generated a distinct trace for each feature. This approach does not preserve the information about dynamic feature dependencies at the level of objects. For later experiments, we tackled this issue by defining a new tracing approach based on capturing a *marked feature trace* (*i.e.,* one trace containing all feature executions, the start and end of each feature execution is flagged in the generated trace) [Salah and Mancoridis, 2004]. We adopted this approach for the Pier case study so that with a more complete dynamic information, we can analyze dynamic feature relationships as described in Section 3.7 (p.37) of the previous chapter.

4.7 Related Work

Our feature-centric approach is characterized by ease of use and interactive visualizations. Our Feature Affinity measurement is computed by simple set intersection.

```
context Feature
  def: nMethodOccurrencesInFeature ( aMethod: Method ) : Integer =
    self.methods ->select(m | m = aMethod))->size()
context Feature
  def: nMethodOccurrencesInOtherFeatures (aMethod: Method ) : Integer =
    self.model.features->select(f | f.nMethodOccurrences(aMethod) )
      ->reject(self))->size()

context Feature
  def: reconaissenceMetric (aMethod: Method) : Float =
    self.nMethodOccurrencesInFeature
        / self.nMethodOccurrencesInFeature +
          self.nMethodOccurrencesInOtherFeatures
```

Figure 4.10: OCL specification of Software Reconnaissance property for a Method Entity.

4.7.1 How Dynamix accomodates other Feature Identification Measurements

Most dynamic analysis-based feature identification approaches define a relevancy measurement to quantify the relationships between features and source artefacts [Wilde and Scully, 1995; Eisenbarth *et al.*, 2003; Eisenberg and De Volder, 2005; Antoniol and Guéhéneuc, 2005]. They use heuristic approaches to define the degree of relevancy of a source artefact to a feature. The *software reconnaissance* family of approaches determine relevancy of source artefacts by comparing two sets of exhibiting and non-exhibiting traces. Wilde and Scully proposed a relevancy index based on probabilistic ranking to measure the relevancy of a component to a feature [Wilde and Scully, 1995]. Let P(e) be the probability function that assigns a probability to an entity defining the relevancy of an entity to a feature. Their relevancy metric is defined as follows:

$$P(e) = \frac{N(e)}{N(e) + N'(e)} \quad (4.2)$$

where $N(e)$ is the number of times an event e appears in the scenarios exhibiting a feature and $N'(e)$ is the number of times the same event occurs when executing scenarios that do not exhibit the feature. In Dynamix, an event of a trace is represented as an *Activation*, which references a *Method* entity. In Figure 4.10 (p.61) we provide an OCL definition of the Software Reconnaissance metric in the context of Dynamix.

In contrast to Software Reconnaissance, our approach assumes a one-to-one relationship between execution scenarios triggering a feature and the feature itself. We do not compare two types of traces, rather we consider all the features under analysis at once and compute a Feature Affinity, which we assign to each source entity of a model. If we compare the result of our measurement with the Software Reconnaissance relevancy index, we discover that *singleFeature* classes obtain a

CHAPTER 4. APPLYING FEATURE-CENTRIC ANALYSIS: TWO CASE STUDIES

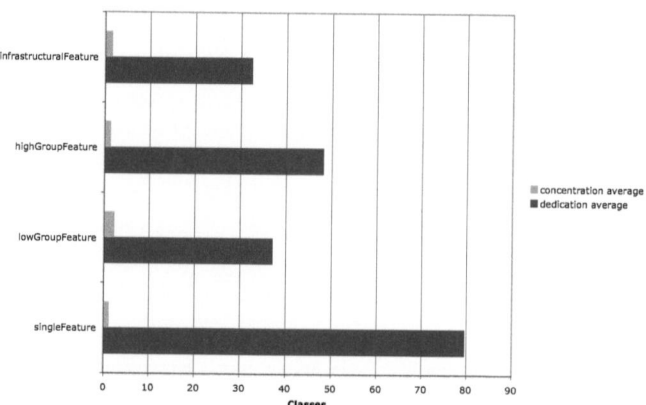

Figure 4.11: The distribution of average values of the *dedication* and *concentration* metrics for each Feature Affinity level of the Pier Case Study.

Software Reconnaissance relevancy index of 1. The main difference between the Software Reconnaissance approach and our Feature Affinity is that Software Reconnaissance assigns relevancy to source entities from the perspective of one feature at a time. Feature Affinity computes relevancy for source entities based on of a set of features.

Feature Affinity also characterizes how source entities provide functionality to groups of related features. Thus, it provides a more general characterization of source entities with respect to a group of features.

Wong *et al.* proposed metrics to complement the Software Reconnaissance metric. They measured the closeness of a feature to a source entity. They originally devised their metrics for procedural code. We implemented the *dedication* and *concentration* metrics they proposed and applied them on our Pier case study to compare them with the results of our Feature Affinity measurement. Figure 4.12 (p.63) specifies the *dedication* metric of a class with respect to one feature. In Dynamix, this value of this metric is assigned to a *FeatureClassAssociation* entity (see Figure 4.13 (p.64)).

In Figure 4.11 (p.62) we show a comparison of Feature Affinity levels and the *dedication* and *concentration* metrics. For each Feature Affinity level, we calculated the average *dedication* and *concentration* values and plotted them as shown. The graph shows that the *singleFeature* classes have a high dedication value and *infrastructural* classes show a low dedication value. For each Feature Affinity level we obtain a low value for the *concentration* metric. This result is due to the nature of

```
context Class
  def: nMethods : Integer =
    self.methods->size()
context Feature
  def: nMethodsOfClassReferenced (aClass: Class) : Integer =
    self.methods->select(m | m in aClass.methods)->size().
context Feature
  def: dedicationMetric (aClass: Class) : Float =
    self.nMethodsOfClassReferenced(aClass) / aClass.nMethods.

context Feature
  def: concentration(aClass: Class): Float =
    self.methods->select ( m | m in aClass.methods)->size() / self.methods.size()
```

Figure 4.12: OCL specification of the Dedication and Cconcentration Metrics in the context of Dynamix.

the Pier application. Most of the functionality of the features is characterized as *infrastructural*, thus yielding a low concentration of any one class. The results of our comparison with these metrics show both our Feature Affinity measurement and the *dedication* and *concentration* metrics reveal similar characteristics for the classes with respect to a set of features.

4.7.2 Dynamix Adaptation: Introducing Association Entities

The Software Reconnaissance metrics [Wilde and Scully, 1995] and the *concentration* and *dedication* metrics [Wong et al., 2000] provide useful insights into the roles of source entities in features. As they focus on source entity-to-feature relationships, we need to extend our Dynamix meta-model with a new kind of entity, an *AbstractFeatureEntityAssociation* entity. This entity models these relationships and allows us to assign properties to them that represent these metrics. The *AbstractFeatureEntityAssociation* entity expresses relationships between a distinct feature and a distinct source entity. Figure 4.13 (p.64) shows the Dynamix extensions, namely a *FeatureClassAssociation* entity and *FeatureMethodAssociation* entity, both inheriting from a *AbstractFeatureEntitiyAssociation* entity.

4.7.3 Feature Relationship Approaches

In a reverse engineering context, only a few researchers have analyzed the relationships between features.

CHAPTER 4. APPLYING FEATURE-CENTRIC ANALYSIS: TWO CASE STUDIES

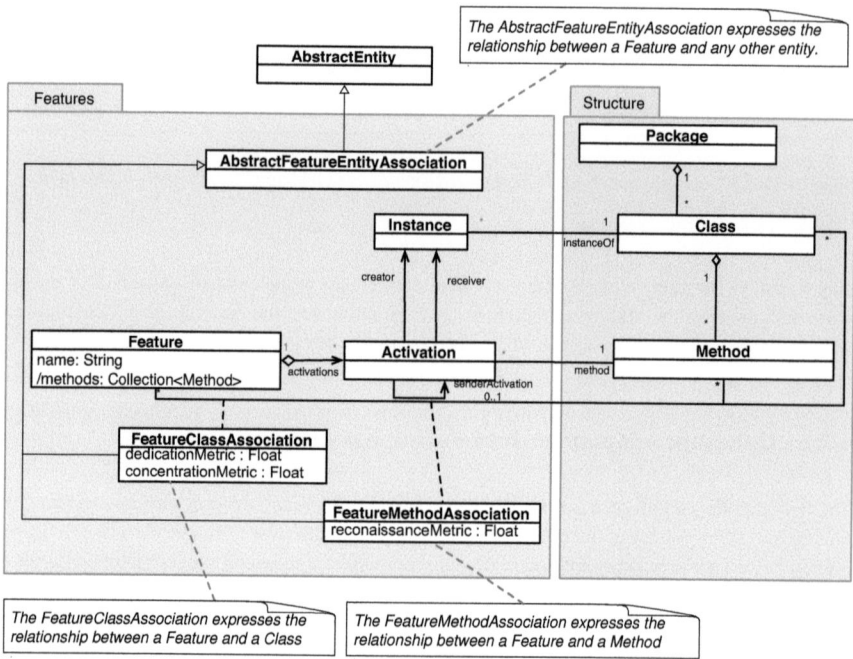

Figure 4.13: Dynamix extended with Association entities to accomodate metrics of *Feature Identification* techniques.

Kothari and Mancoridis [Kothari et al., 2006] described a mechanism to identify similarity relationships between features based on the source entities shared by the feature's implementation. Whereas our measurement considers only the source artefacts shared by two features, their similarity measurement compares entire call graphs. Thus, they also take into account the edges of the call graph (*i.e.,* the message sends between methods). The underlying assumption of their analysis is that similar features are implemented in a similar way and thus share a significant amount of code.

Salah and Mancoridis [Salah and Mancoridis, 2004] described an analysis based on a dynamic analysis based on feature identification technique to define dependencies between features. They define both static and dynamic feature relationships. Their static relationships are based on identifying the common classes referenced by two features. They define a *depends* dynamic relationship between features.

Our contribution is that we formalize the definitions of the different types of relationships. We refine the relationships and introduce a feature relationship taxonomy to distinguish between varying degrees of static relationships,

4.8 Summary

By applying our approach on two case studies, we demonstrate how we discover semantic information about the roles of classes in features, the way features of a system are implemented and relationships between features.

Our approach promotes an understanding of how existing features are implemented. By visually analyzing feature views, a software engineer determines roles that classes play in a set of features. We believe that a positive side affect of our *Feature Perspective* is that it makes it easier for a software engineer to design and implement a new feature and reuse existing functionality. For example, if a software engineer has to add a new feature to the Pier application, he can use his understanding of existing feature implementation to determine which parts of the code can be reused.

The main contributions of this chapter are:

1. Our three perspective analysis builds on the work of feature identification techniques by enrich structural entities with feature context, to define features as first class entities and to describe static and dynamic relationships between feature entities.

2. We focus our approach on object-oriented applications, thus we define Feature Affinity for structural entities of object-oriented software, namely packages, classes and methods.

3. We describe interactive visual representations of the Features of our Dynamix model and the Feature relationships. Our visualziations support high-level and fine-grained feature analysis

CHAPTER 4. APPLYING FEATURE-CENTRIC ANALYSIS: TWO CASE STUDIES

of a software system from three perspectives.

4. **Dynamix** defines a language independent meta-model to relate software entities (*e.g.,* Class, Method) with Feature entities. This renders our approach generally applicable to systems written in any object-oriented programming language.

5. A key characteristic of our approach is *ease-of-use* and simplicity. We compactness of dynamic information. We condense information of feature traces to focus on key information to achieve the Feature Affinity of source artefacts.

6. We compare our Feature Affinity property of source entities with metrics from related works.

7. We provide OCL definitions for the *Software Reconnaissance*, the *dedication* and *concentration* metrics for object-oriented systems in the context of our **Dynamix** meta-model.

The fundamental aspect of our feature-centric analysis approach is that we do not limit our focus to locating features in the source code. Our emphasis is on treating features as first class entites in reverse engineering analyses and to exploit features for system comprehension.

Chapter 5

Evolution Analysis: A Structural Perspective

We present an approach to evolution analysis that focuses on how the roles of source artefacts change with respect to a set of features over time. To support our analysis, we augment Dynamix with entities that model the notion of history explicitly. We demonstrate how semantic knowledge of the role of a class in features supports interpretations of modifications and extensions to a system's source code by applying it to two case studies.

CHAPTER 5. EVOLUTION ANALYSIS: A STRUCTURAL PERSPECTIVE

5.1 Introduction

Most reverse engineering approaches to software evolution analysis focus on static source code entities of a system, such as classes and methods [Demeyer *et al.*, 2000; Krajewski, 2003; Lanza and Ducasse, 2002]. A static perspective considers only structural and implementation details of a system. Thus, key semantic information about the roles of source entities in features of a system is overlooked. Without explicit relationships between features and the source artefacts that implement their functionality, it is xicult for maintainers to discover what motivated changes in source code. Static analysis approaches compare what has changed in a system but does not offer any semantic context for the changes. In this chapter, we extend our feature-centric analysis with a notion of time, so that we can focus on how roles of source artefacts change over a series of versions with respect to a constant set of features.

We aim to support a software engineer to interpret the intent of changes by identifying how roles of classes change with respect to a constant set of features over time. We motivate our analysis with the following questions:

1. *Why did a class change?* When maintaining a system, it is useful not only to detect *what* has changed in a system, but also to understand *why* a change was made [Gîrba *et al.*, 2005b; Demeyer *et al.*, 2002]. We seek to enrich changes of a system with semantic knowledge about the roles of source artefacts in the features of our model.

2. *Are classes becoming more active with respect to features over time?* We consider a class has become more *active* with respect to a set of features if the role of a class changes to indicate that it participates in more features in later versions of a system. Such a change suggests that the class may have been modified, or its functionality is being reused by more of the features in a later version. We assume that the more *active* a class in a set of features, the more generic the functionality it implements.

3. *Are classes becoming less active with respect to features over time, or becoming obsolete?* Classes that are less active with respect to features over time may indicate places in the code that may have been refactored or that functionality within a class has become obsolete. Software maintainers often leave obsolete code in a system if they are unsure which features are using the code. We seek a means of detecting candidate obsolete classes and methods to support software developers during the maintenance.

4. *Are the features of a system resilient to change?* For our experiments, we traced a constant set of features for each version of a system we analyze. We seek to discover if a set of core features of a system are resilient to change.

To address these questions, we focus on how the relationships between classes and features change over time. We limit the scope of this analysis to a constant set of core features of a system over a series of versions. By core features we mean features that represent core or central functionality of a system.

Both evolution analysis and dynamic analysis techniques are faced with the problem of manipulating large amounts of data. We tackle this by (1) computing the *Feature Affinity* property for classes to assign them roles with respect to features, and (2) by applying a *history centered* analysis to summarize changes in the roles of classes over multiple versions.

We apply our evolution analysis approach to two medium size applications: SmallWiki [Renggli, 2003] and Moose [Ducasse *et al.*, 2005a; Nierstrasz *et al.*, 2005]. We extend our Dynamix metamodel with entities that model history and versions of the entities. To measure and summarize change, we define *history* properties in the context of Dynamix. To detect changes between versions, we define how we quantify changes in the roles of classes over time. We validate our results with (1) developer knowledge and (2) we compare the results of our analysis with the the findings of applying a *diff* algorithm [Hunt and McIlroy, 1976] on the first and last versions of the systems we analyze.

We show how our approach reduces the search space to focus only on changes that reflect changes in the roles of classes with respect to features over time.

Structure of the Chapter. In the next section (Section 5.2 (p.69)) we discuss different approaches to evolution analysis. Then, in Section 5.4 (p.70), we present how Dynamix, extended with *History* and *Version* entities of the Hismo model [Gîrba and Lanza, 2004], supports an evolution analysis of changing roles of classes with respect to features. Section 5.4 (p.70) describes how we quantify changes to classes based on *Feature Affinity* and history measurements. In Section 5.5 (p.76) we define an analysis methodology. Then, in Section 5.6 (p.76) we report on two case studies we conducted and present our results. Subsequently, in Section 5.7 (p.82) we discuss our results and outline constraints and limitations of the feature-centric approach we adopt. We list related work in Section 5.8 (p.84) and finally in Section 5.9 (p.85) we summarize our results.

5.2 Evolution Analysis: an Overview

Approaches to analyzing system evolution can be characterized as (1) *version-centered* or (2) *history-centered* [Gîrba and Ducasse, 2006]. Version-centered approaches compare versions of a system with the aim of revealing *when* (*i.e.,* in which version) a particular change occurred. For example, a typical version centered approach would be a comparison analysis that computes the difference between two versions, or a graphic that plots the values of a property in time for a series of versions. History-centered approaches on the other hand, are concerned with revealing *what* changes were made and *where* in the system they occurred, by summarizing evolution according to a particular

CHAPTER 5. EVOLUTION ANALYSIS: A STRUCTURAL PERSPECTIVE

point of view.

In this chapter, we describe an approach that combines both *history-centered* and *version-centered* techniques. As we are dealing with a large volume of information, we first adopt a *history-centered* approach to summarize the changes to the roles of classes. This narrows the scope of investigation to focus only on classes that have changed with respect to the features. Subsequently, to obtain a more fine-grained perspective of the changes, we apply a *version-centered* approach to individual classes to discover in which versions changes occurred.

5.3 Extending Dynamix for Evolution Analysis

Our Dynamix meta-model models one version of a system. To incorporate the notion of multiple versions, we augment Dynamix with *History* and *Version* entities of the Hismo meta-model defined by Girba [Gîrba, 2005]. Hismo is a generic meta-model that treats the notion of *history* as a first class entity [Gîrba, 2005]. A *History* entity summarizes a sequence of versions of an entitiy as one single entity. In the context of our analysis, we extend Dynamix with Hismo entities so that we can manipulate *History* and *Versions* of a Dynamix entity. For a *Structural* perspective of evolution analysis, we focus on the *Class* entity.

Figure 5.1 (p.71) shows Dynamix, extended with History entities of the Hismo model [Gîrba and Lanza, 2004], namely *ClassVersion* and *ClassHistory* entities. A *ClassVersion* extends a class with version information and reflects the fact that multiple versions exist for a *Class*. A *ClassHistory* models a set of *ClassVersion* entities of the same *Class*.

5.4 History and Version Properties

In this section we describe how we apply *version* and *history measurements* [Gîrba and Lanza, 2004] to the Feature Affinity FA property of classes. The history measurements we compute for our analysis are shown as properties of the $ClassHistory$ entity in Figure 5.1 (p.71).

We describe an approach to evolution analysis that focuses on how the roles of classes change with respect to the features of a model over time. We measure changes in class roles using the Feature Affinity property of classes. As outlined in Chapter 3 (p.25), the Feature Affinity property reflects the relevance of a class with respect to a feature.

The interpretation of changes to Feature Affinity depends heavily on the following context of our approach: we do not add new features from one version to the next. We impose this restriction on our technique because the Feature Affinity value of a class is sensitive to the features we trace. If we

5.4. HISTORY AND VERSION PROPERTIES

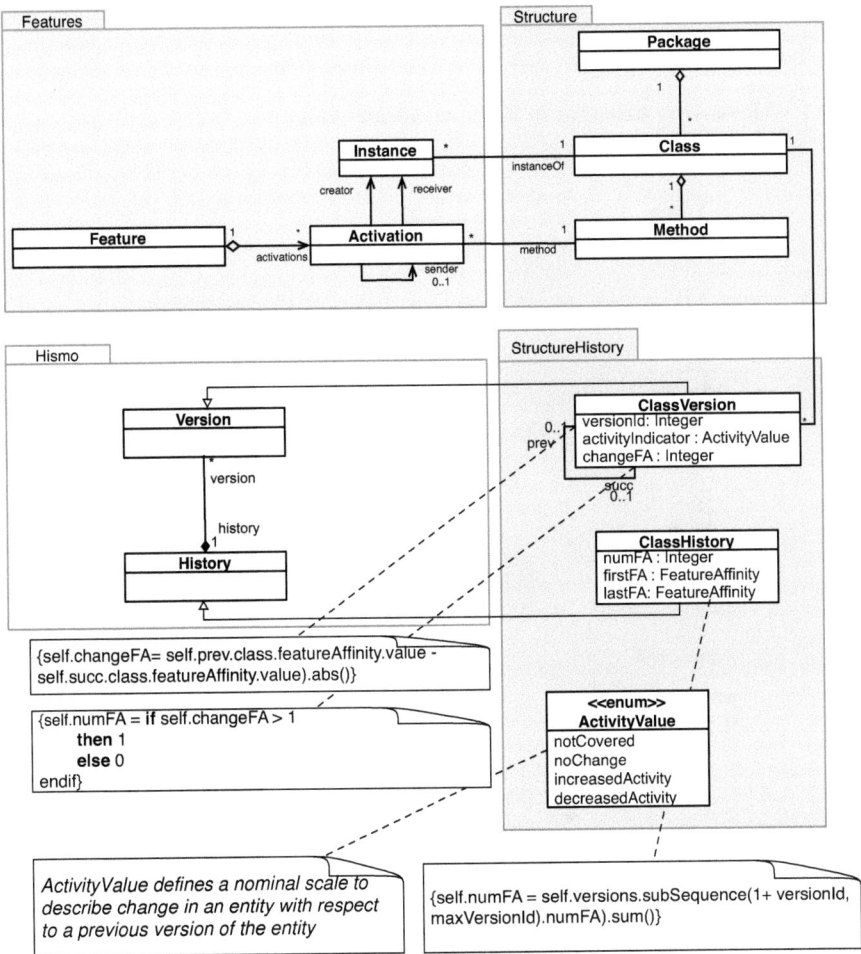

Figure 5.1: We extend Dynamix with Hismo *ClassVersion* and *ClassHistory* entities to support evolution analysis from a *Structural* perspective.

CHAPTER 5. EVOLUTION ANALYSIS: A STRUCTURAL PERSPECTIVE

were to vary the features traced from one version to the next, we would not be able to distinguish between a change in the role of a class due to a change in the code and a change due to including a different feature in our analysis.

5.4.1 Measuring Changes in Feature Affinity (FA)

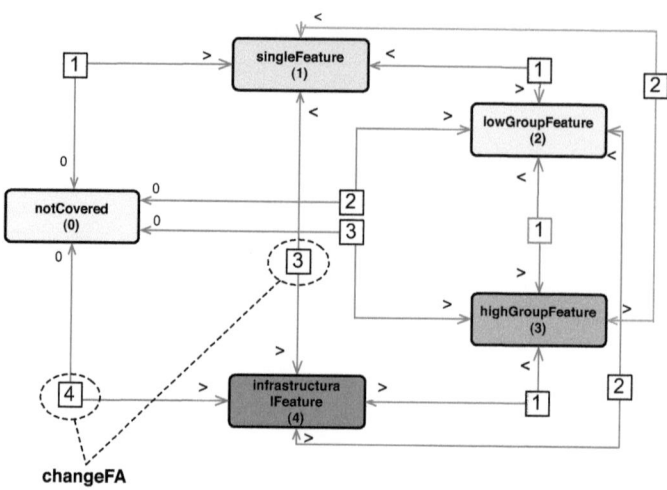

Figure 5.2: The Weighted Changes ($changeFA$) to a role (Feature Affinity) of a Class with respect to Features between two versions of a system.

Figure 5.2 (p.72) we show how the roles of a class of a class change over time as a directed graph. The nodes of the graph represent the Feature Affinity values of a class. The edges represent the changes from one Feature Affinity level to the next. We quantify each change with a numerical value corresponding to the difference between the Feature Affinity levels (their ordinal values) of the two nodes it connects. The diagram also shows if a change of Feature Affinity represents an

5.4. HISTORY AND VERSION PROPERTIES

increase in participation of a class in a set of features (marked as >), a decrease in participation (marked as <), or a change to no participation (marked as 0) on the edge.

To calculate the change to the FA properties, we associate numerical values (0..4) to each value of FA and measure the differences of the property between two versions of a class. Essentially, we quantify the change by measuring the absolute value of the difference of the *Feature Affinity* values of the same class in version i (C_i) with a class in version i + 1 (C_{i+1}).

$$changeFA = |FA(C_i) - FA(C_{i+1})| \tag{5.1}$$

The *changeFA* property quantifies a change. For example, we consider a change from *notCovered* to *infrastructuralFeature* to represent a more significant change than from *singleFeature* to *lowGroupFeature*, as *infrastructuralFeature* classes affect all of the features of our model. In Figure 5.2 (p.72) we show all possible *Feature Affinity* changes of the FA property. The *changeFA* property is associated with the *ClassVersion* entity.

In Figure 5.1 (p.71) we show a UML enumerator, *ActivityValue*, which we define to describe possible types of Feature Affinity changes. We associate an *activityIndicator* property with a *ClassVersion* to reflect the type of change: if a class participates in more features (increasedActivity > symbol), less features (decreasedActivity < symbol), or no features (notCovered 0 symbol) of a model as a result of a Feature Affinity change between two versions. (We use the − symbol to indicate that the Feature Affinity of a class did not change.

In Figure 5.3 (p.74) we provide the OCL definition for the *activityIndicator* property.

5.4.2 Summarizing Change in Feature Affinity with a History Property

The Hismo *History* entity summarizes changes over a series of versions. To summarize changes to the roles of classes, we define a *History Property* for a *ClassHistory* entity which computes the number of times the role of a class changes over time. We refer to this measurement as the *number of changes to FA* ($numFA$). We define $numFA$ measurement applied on Class C for a given property FA as follows:

$$(i > 1)$$
$$numFA_i(C, FA) = \begin{cases} 0, & FA_i(C) - FA_{i-1}(C) = 0 \\ 1, & FA_i(C) - FA_{i-1}(C) \neq 0 \end{cases}$$

```
context FeatureAffinity
  def: value: Integer =
  if self = notCovered
  then 0
    else if self = singleFeature
    then 1
      else if  self = lowGroupFeature
      then 2
        else if self = highGroupFeature
        then 3
        else 4
        endif
      endif
    endif
  endif

context ClassVersion
  def: activityIndicator: ActivityValue =
  if self.succ.class.featureAffinity = FeatureAffinity::notCovered
          then ActivityValue::notCovered
          else if self.succ.class.featureAffinity = prev.class.featureAffinity
          then ActivityValue::noChange
            else if self.succ.class.featureAffinity.value
      > self.prev.class.featureAffinity.value
            then ActivityValue::increasedActivity
              else ActivityValue::descreasedActivity
              endif
    endif
  endif
```

Figure 5.3: OCL specification of the *activityIndicator* property to characterize changes in the Feature Affinity level of classes.

5.4. HISTORY AND VERSION PROPERTIES

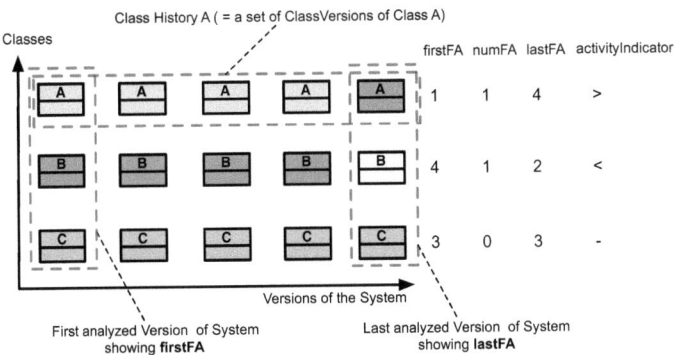

Figure 5.4: An Evolution Matrix of classes showing the Measurements we apply to Feature Affinity of Classes to measure changing roles over time.

$$(n > 2) \qquad numFA_{1..n}(C, FA) = \sum_{i=2}^{n} numFA_i(C, FA) \qquad (5.2)$$

In Figure 5.1 (p.71) we provide the OCL definition of *numFA* in the context of Dynamix.

5.4.3 A Summary of the Measurements

Figure 5.4 (p.75) shows an Evolution Matrix [Lanza, 2003] of a small system consisting of 3 classes (A,B,C) over a series of 5 versions. Each row of the matrix represents a *ClassHistory* (*i.e.*, a set of versions of the same class entity). The classes are colored according to their FA value. We use this simple example to illustrate which history and version measurements we apply to the FA property of classes, and how they characterize the changing roles of a class with respect to a constant feature model.

Measuring the Number of Changes of the FA Property of a class (numFA). This measurement counts in how many versions the FA property has changed with respect to the previous version. We apply the measurement to isolate which classes have changed. For example we see in Figure 5.4 (p.75) that the role of Class A changed once from *singleFeature* to *infrastructuralFeature*, and Class B has changed from *infrastructuralFeature* to *lowGroupFeature*. The role of Class C has remained the same. With this measurement we can filter out classes that do not change with respect to features (*i.e.*, NumFA = 0). In this example, we only need to consider Classes A and C for further analysis.

75

Characterizing Change with the activityIndicator Property. We compute the activityIndicator by comparing the value of FA of the first version a class ($firstFA$) with the value of FA in the last version of a system under analysis ($lastFA$). This measurement is a *version measurement* rather than a *history measurement* as it compares two versions of a system at a time.

In our example system Figure 5.4 (p.75), we see that the Activity Indicator $>$ of the class A reveals that the class is more active in the last version of the system analyzed than the first version. Class B is less active ($<$ activity) and Class C shows $-$ activity (*i.e.*, no change).

5.5 A Methodology for Analyzing Changing Roles of Classes

We outline a methodology to describe how we apply our technique to measure the evolution of classes from a feature perspective.

1. For each version of an application, we parse the source code and extract a model of structural entities.

2. For each version of an application, we exercise the same set of features on the instrumented system and extract feature traces. For the purposes of this experiment, we assume that the external observable behavior of each feature remains unchanged for all versions of our analysis.

3. We compute the Feature Affinity measurements for the classes of our models.

4. We compute history measurement $numFA$ of a *ClassHistory* from the FA property of classes. Then, we narrow our focus to consider only those classes that are affected by change, we define queries to filter out classes that have never undergone any Feature Affinity changes ($numFA$ = 0).

5. We compute the *activityIndicator* between the first and last versions of a system and apply queries to group classes according to *activityIndicator* values.

5.6 Validation

In this section we present the results of applying our approach to two case studies. For our experiments we chose two in-house systems: SmallWiki [Renggli, 2003] and Moose [Ducasse *et al.*, 2005a].

Moose is an environment for reengineering object-oriented systems and is implemented in Visual-Works Smalltalk [Ducasse *et al.*, 2005a]. An important part of the functionality of Moose is the

5.6. VALIDATION

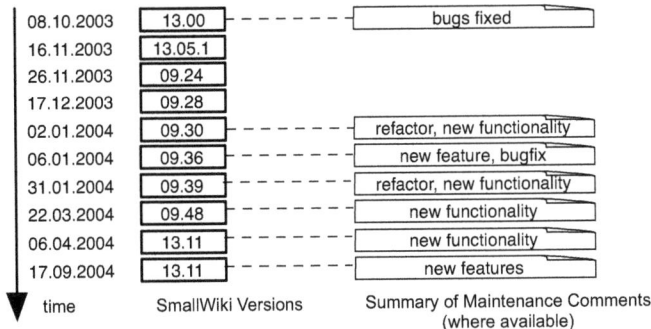

Figure 5.5: SmallWiki Versions used for the Evolution Analysis of Changing Roles of Classes..

import/export framework. This is responsible for parsing source code and representing the data as a structural model of the system. Models are loaded and saved as files.

Our choice of case studies was motivated by the following reasons: (1) they are open source, thus the source code is freely available, (2) we have access to multiple versions of the systems, (3) we are familiar with the features of the application from a user perspective, and (4) we have access to developer knowledge to verify our findings.

5.6.1 Case Study: SmallWiki

We selected the same 6 core features and 10 different versions of SmallWiki from the source code repository that represented a period of development and refactoring of the application. Our selection was guided by the developers. The versions span an 11 month time period *(The two versioning conventions shown in Figure 5.5 (p.77) are due to SmallWiki being released inhouse and to the open source community)*. According to the developers, much of the changes in the code are as a result of iterative development, refactorings and restructuring. Figure 5.5 (p.77) lists the versions we chose. In the third column, we note what type of maintenance activity was reported by the developer at the time a version was checked in to the source code repository for versions where it was available.

Our history model of SmallWiki contains 522 class histories. As a class history is a sequence of versions of a class entity, this metric gives an indication of the size of the application.

Narrowing the Scope with the numFA measurement. We apply a filter to obtain all classes whose

CHAPTER 5. EVOLUTION ANALYSIS: A STRUCTURAL PERSPECTIVE

Activity Indicator	SmallWiki Class	Developer Validation
>	AdminAction	New functionality
>	ErrorUnauthorized_class	New functionality
>	ErrorUnauthorized	New functionality
>	ErrorAction	New functionality
>	FifoCache	New functionality
>	HistoryAction	New functionality
>	SearchAction	New functionality
>	EditAction	New functionality
0	VisitorCollectable	Obsolete
0	VisitorRendererHtml	Refactored, Class split
0	VisitorRendererHtml_class	Refactored, Class split
0	Folder_class	Removed functionality

Figure 5.6: A Subset of the Results of the SmallWiki Case Study. We list the classes with changing FA and the *activityIndicator*. (for >, we show only classes with a ChangeFA $>= 3$)

Feature Affinity levels have changed during the history of a class (numFA > 0) and obtain 63 classes.

Categorizing Changes with the Activity Indicator. We compute the activityIndicator property ($>$, $<$ and 0) and we obtain 40 classes with a $>$ indicator, no classes with an $<$ indicator and 6 classes with a 0 indicator. Our results reveal that 67% of the classes that participate in features are more active and 9% of the classes detected are candidate obsolete classes or may contain candidate obsolete methods as they appear to be no longer participating the features in later versions.

Focusing on Changes. To focus on the changes that indicate introduction of *highGroupFeature* or *infrastructuralfeature* functionality at some point in the evolution of the system, we apply a filter ($lastFA >= 3$). We identify five classes where new or existing functionality is reused by more than half of the features of our analysis.

5.6.2 Analysis of the SmallWiki Results

Why did a class change? For each change we detected, we provided the developers the context in which the change was detected by telling them which features of the system we traced. In the third column of Figure 5.6 (p.78) we list the reason given by the developers as to why the role of a class

5.6. VALIDATION

has changed with respect to the features. We see that in most cases, the developers are adding new functionality to the system. Our analysis reveals that 40 classes are more active in the last version than in the first version of SmallWiki.

Why are classes becoming more active with respect to features over time? In the case of the action classes `AdminAction`, `ErrorAction`, `HistoryAction`, `SearchAction` and `EditAction` the developers of SmallWiki confirm that additional generic functionality was added. This functionality is used by more than half of the features that we traced. In the earlier versions of SmallWiki these classes were characterized as *singleFeature*. Their *changeFA* reveals that some of these classes became either *lowGroupFeature* or *highGroupFeature* over time. In the case of the `ErrorUnauthorized`, `ErrorAction` and `FifoCache` classes, the developers confirmed that they added generic cross-cutting functionality to the features to improve error handling and efficiency with caching mechanisms. We also detect these changes with the *Diff* algorithm. In each of the above cases, the developers confirmed that the changes represent refactorings, and thus they do not affect the observable behavior of the features.

Why are classes becoming less active with respect to features over time? Figure 5.6 (p.78) shows four classes with an activity Indicator of 0. As we do not have 100% coverage of the system, we cannot conclude that these classes are obsolete in the later versions. However, we queried the developers about these classes. They confirmed that in fact the `VisitorCollectable` class was obsolete and could safely be removed from the code base. We used the *Diff* algorithm on a later version of the system and discovered that this class was indeed removed from the code base. In the case of the `VisitorRendererHtml` class, the developers informed us that this class has been refactored. The features we traced are no longer using this class, thus this result represents a false positive. In the case of the `Folder` class, it is still relevant for SmallWiki, but the method that was participating in the features of our model had been removed from the class. This change did not affect the observable behavior of the features.

Are the features resilient to change? In the case of SmallWiki we chose 10 versions of the system that, according to the developers, constitute a period of iterative development. Although the features we traced exhibit no change in their user-observable behavior, the underlying implementation was both extended with generic non-observable functionality (*e.g.*, access control checking) and refactored to improve the design. As most of the changes we detect represent changes to generic functionality, most of the features are affected by change, thus signaling the need for regression testing.

One of the key advantages of our analysis methodology is our ability to tackle large amounts of data. We reduced the study space from 522 *ClassHistory* entities (summarizing 10 versions) to 46 *ClassHistory* entities requiring closer investigation. We applied a more fine-grained version analysis to 12 classes shown in Figure 5.6 (p.78). Here we defined queries that used the *changeFA* property of a *ClassVersion* to focus on classes with a major change in Feature Affinity level from the first to the

CHAPTER 5. EVOLUTION ANALYSIS: A STRUCTURAL PERSPECTIVE

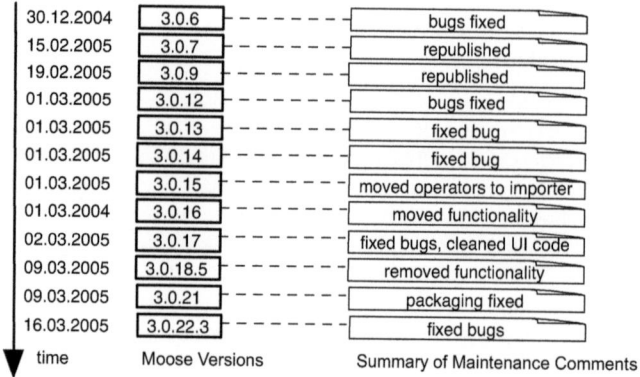

Figure 5.7: Moose Versions used for the Evolution Analysis of Changing Roles of Classes.

last version of our analysis. Furthermore, the *activityIndicator* lets us distinguish between types of changes we detect to help us interpret why a change occurred.

5.6.3 Case Study: Moose

Moose represents an ideal system on which to perform evolution analysis, as it is constantly being refactored, bug-fixed and extended. For our experiment, we selected features of the import/export framework and model navigation features from 12 versions of Moose (696 class histories) spanning a four month time period. We summarize the versions and comments entered by the developers when they commited changed sources to the source code repository in Figure 5.7 (p.80).

5.6.4 Analysis of the MooseResults

Why did a class change? For each change, we provided the developers the context in which a change was detected by telling them which features of the system we traced (the export import subsystem or the navigation). In the third column of Figure 5.8 (p.81), we list the reason that the developers gave, as to why a role of a class has changed with respect to the features.

Why are some classes becoming more active with respect to features over time? In the earlier versions of Moose, the classes shown in Figure 5.8 (p.81) were characterized as *notCovered*. Our

5.6. VALIDATION

Activity Indicator	Moose Class	Developer Validation
>	DelagatorPropertyOperator	New functionality
>	CFCompositionOperator	New functionality
>	CFBlockOperator	New functionality
>	CFAbsoluteProperties	New functionality
>	CFExpressionClass	New functionality
<	AbstractEntity	Removed functionality
0	MSEModelAttributeDescriptor	Removed functionality
0	FileIOFacade	Removed functionality
0	MSEAbstractSchemaSaver	Removed functionality
0	MSEModelAttributeDescriptor	Obsolete
0	CDIFSaver	Removed functionality
0	AbstractTool	Removed functionality

Figure 5.8: Moose Classes with Changing Roles with respect to our features model.

analysis reveals that these classes became *infrastructuralFeature*. The developers confirmed our finding as they reported that they added generic cross-cutting functionality in the classes flagged with the *activityIndicator* >. The changes where general and affected all the features to improve the handling of property and expression functionality in Moose. They did not relate to one particular feature.

To obtain more detailed information, we performed a detailed version analysis on the classes flagged with > to detect *when* (in which version) the roles of these classes changed.

Our analysis reveals a repeating pattern of change for the classes CFCompositionOperator, CFBlockOperator, CFAbsoluteProperties and CFExpression classes.

We discovered that these classes are part of the same hierarchy and that their Feature Affinity change occurred in the Moose version 3.0.15. We verified the finding with the developers. They confirmed that the hierarchy became more important in that version as the system was refactored so that this generic functionality was integrated into all features of the system. This explains our finding that the classes appear to be becoming more active with respect to the same features over time.

Why are classes becoming less active with respect to features over time? Figure 5.8 (p.81) shows that only one class of the system has an activity Indicator of <. The developers confirmed that functionality has been removed from this class due to refactoring. We detected two classes CDIFSaver and AbstractTool that are no longer participating in the featues of our model. The developer explained that the import/export mechanisms of Moose have been completely refactored and that these classes are obsolete. They have been replaced by other classes. Our result proved a useful insight for the developer as it guided him to which classes could be removed from the code base.

Are the features resilient to change? In the case of Moose, we focused our analysis on the import/export subsystem, as the developers indicated that this was reengineered during the time period of our analysis. As with our SmallWiki case study, the features we traced exhibit no change in their user-observable behavior. Our analysis reveals that the underlying implementation was refactored.

Our results of our case studies show that our heuristic approach successfully (1) locates classes where new functionality has been introduced, (2) detects refactoring, and (3) locates candidate obsolete code. Our experiments provided useful insights for the maintainers of the system as to which parts of the system were affected by change, what types of change and how the features were affected.

5.7 Discussion

The large volume of history information and complexity of dynamic information makes it hard to infer higher level of information about the evolution of a system. We adopt a *history-centered* approach to reduce the complexity of the information. We reveal key semantic information about changes to the system by measuring how relationships between classes and features evolve over time.

We limit the scope of our investigation to focus on a constant set of features. Our goal is to apply feature-based evolution analysis to investigate the effects of maintenance on a specific set of features. Our features perspective provides us with feature knowledge to reason about the design intent of the class. Using feature-based evolution analysis we determine the stability of features of a system by monitoring changes in Feature Affinity levels of classes over a series of versions.

> *Comparison with* Diff. We applied the *Diff* algorithm integrated in the Smalltalk Store to the first and last versions of SmallWiki that we analyzed to obtain actual physical changes between the first and last versions of our SmallWiki case study. Diff reveals that 79 physical differences at the class level. Our technique detects 46 classes that have become more, less or inactive with respect to a set of features. However a change in a role of a class may not necessarily mean a physical change in the source code of a class. The change may appear as a result of change in usage of a class. Thus, we cannot compute precision or recall based on the results of *Diff*. Calculating precision in for this experiment is difficult, since by definition all changes we detect are relevant for our question of how classes change with respect to features over time.

5.7. DISCUSSION

History-centered versus version-centered evolution analysis. The advantage of applying a history-centered approach is that it allows us to analyze a large number of versions of a system and to manipulate a large volume of data. Version-centered approaches compare two versions of a system at a time to detect when a change occurs. To obtain a general picture of how roles of classes change with respect to features, a history-centered approach is more appropriate. However, to obtain a more fine-grained view of the evolution of the SmallWiki and Moose systems, we supplemented our analysis with version-centered analysis to obtain information about *when* changes occurred. In this way, our *changeFA* property quantifies the change of a class's role between two versions. Version analysis gives us more precise information about *when* changes occurred. Our approach combines history-centered analysis and version-centered analysis.

5.7.1 Variations

In this chapter, we described one methodology to analyze how the roles of classes vary with respect to features over time. Our goal was to show how the semantic context of features supports interpretation of changes and highlights the extent of these changes on features that have been exercised.

There are many variations to our approach that could be supported by Dynamix. We identify a few of these variations.

Selecting Methods as the unit of granularity. For our experiments we chose the class as a unit of granularity. We detected classes that appear to become less active with respect to the features traced and were flagged with an activity indicator of 0. However, most of these results were false positives, as in most cases the class was not obsolete. In many cases, a method had been removed from a class. To reduce the number of these false positives, we could perform the analysis at the level of methods. We believe that due to the large volume of data, an iterative approach is required, first to reduce the study space and then to perform a more fine-grained analysis at the level of methods.

Combining Feature Affinity properties with other class properties. Our technique is generic and adaptable. For the experiments described in this chapter, we analyzed changing roles of classes. To further enrich our analysis, we could extend our focus to combine and correlate FA changes with other properties of our model, for example properties assigned to Class entites (*e.g.*, NOA, WLOC). This would provide more detailed information about the changes we detect.

Selecting a constant set of features. For our analysis, we extracted and modeled a constant set of features. We did not consider varying the model over time. This is because the Feature Affinity levels of classes is highly dependent of which features we trace. Tracing an additional feature, and including it in our model within one version could affect the Feature Affinity level of a class, even though no change was made to its source code.

5.7.2 Limitations

Coverage. As our focus is on detecting changes over time, we sought to achieve high coverage, so as to obtain a Feature Affinity level or a large proportion of classes. However, as our experiments do not exercise features that have been added in later versions of the system, 100% coverage is difficult to achieve. The results of our experiments show that full coverage is not essential to obtain useful insights into why a system has changed.

Scalability of the approach. Method instrumentation affects the performance of features. For some of the features we traced in our Moose case study, the execution time of the instrumented code made experimentation difficult. To tackle this problem, we applied selective instrumentation for the Moose case study. We selected which packages to instrument. Selective instrumentation of the packages requires prior knowledge of the application and knowledge of the relationships between packages and features. The resulting traces and the values of our measurements are influenced by selective instrumentation. Exploiting knowledge of an application to instrument only the parts of the system required for a specific analysis is referred to by Antoniol *et al.* as *Knowledge Filtering* [Antoniol and Guéhéneuc, 2005].

Detecting new functionality. A limitation of the approach is that it cannot detect new functionality that is added to the system in a generic way, such that no new methods are invoked. Multiple calls to the same method of a class are compacted to one occurrence in a *compact feature view*. This limitation was identified during the validation of Moose case study results. It could easily be overcome by extending our analysis to correlate changes in metrics of structural entities such as classes and methods with FA changes.

5.8 Related Work

Our main focus with this work is to define a reverse engineering approach that exploits history information of a system's features over a series of versions to enrich our understanding of the structural entities (*e.g.*, classes). Other researchers have exploited external information when analyzing the evolution of a system.

Gall *et al.* [Gall *et al.*, 1998] aimed to detect logical couplings by identifying which parts of the system change together. They used this information to define coupling measurements. The more times modules were changed together, the more tightly coupled they are. This approach was based on files and folders of a system, and did not consider the structural units (*e.g.,* classes) of a system.

Fischer *et al.* [Fischer and Gall, 2004; Fischer *et al.*, 2003] modeled bug reports in relation to changes in a system. The purpose is to provide a link between bug reports and parts of a system.

In contrast to these approaches, the focus of our feature-centric analysis is to establish the links between features and classes. Our goal is to enrich existing static evolution analysis approaches with feature knowledge. Our Feature Affinity levels add semantic information to classes and use this semantic information to reason about the evolution of a system in terms of its features.

5.9 Summary and Outlook

In this chapter, our goal was to demonstrate how Dynamix can be extended with *History* entities of the Hismo meta-model to enrich a structural-based evolution analysis with the semantic context of features. We applied our approach to two case studies and showed how our approach successfully interpreted changes in the code. To validate our approach, we verified our findings against developer information. For this analysis we chose a class as the structural unit. Our approach is equally applicable to methods or packages.

The main contributions with this chapter are:

1. we define evolution analysis in the context of Dynamix augmented it with *History* and *Version entities* to represent multiple versions of a system.

2. We describe a novel approach to analyze the evolution of a system based on relationships between structural entities (*i.e.,* classes) and features.

3. We characterize changes in the code in a way that reflects how the roles of classes change.

4. We combine a history and a version analysis approach.

In the next chapter, we complement the structural perspective of evolution analysis with an evolution analysis focusing on changes to *Feature* entities over time.

CHAPTER 5. EVOLUTION ANALYSIS: A STRUCTURAL PERSPECTIVE

Chapter 6

Evolution Analysis: A Feature Perspective

*In contrast to the approach described in the previous chapter, we now present an approach to evolution analysis that focuses on how features change over time. To support our analysis, we augment our **Dynamix** meta-model with entities that model feature history and versions explicitly. Our goal is to exploit domain knowledge of features to understand the intent and extent of changes in a system. To demonstrate the usefulness of our approach, we apply it to a case study, where we address a typical maintenance task of merging parallel development tracks of the same system.*

CHAPTER 6. EVOLUTION ANALYSIS: A FEATURE PERSPECTIVE

6.1 Motivation

In the previous chapter, we presented an evolution analysis technique focusing on how structural entities change over time with respect to a set of features. Now we focus on features as the primary units of analysis, when reasoning about the intent and extent of changes to a system's features.

Our goal is twofold: (1) we want to demonstrate how Dynamix supports the analysis of features over multiple versions, and (2) we aim to support understanding the intent and extent of changes in a system's features supports a software engineer when tackling maintenance tasks. To motivate our analysis we address the following questions:

1. *Which features are affected by changes in the code?* Identifying which features have changed and how they are affected by changes gives us an insight into *change intent*. We analyze changes to determine their *extent* (*i.e.,* if a change affects one or more features). This knowledge helps the software engineer to decide which tests need to be performed after a change has been made.

2. *Do the changes in features indicate an increase in the complexity or refactoring of features over time?* We define complexity of a feature to be a function of the number of software artefacts (*e.g.,* classes) participating in its runtime behavior. We investigate if an increase in the number of classes is indication that new functionality has been added to a system.

3. *Do similar patterns of change indicate relationships between the features?* We investigate if similar patterns of increases or decreases in the number of source entities shared between features is an indication that the functionality or purpose of features are related. By identifying patterns of change, we aim to detect similarities between between features.

In our case study analysis, we address a typical problem of parallel development tracks in the development and maintenance life-cycle of a system. For example, enhancements may be made in one branch in preparation for the next release of a system, whereas bug fixes may be made in a branch that corresponds to the release of the system in production. Inevitably, branches need to be merged to reestablish a coherent code base. Merging branches is a nontrivial task, as changes to one feature may conflict or break other features. Software engineers are faced with the task of understanding what motivated changes in the code and how the changes affect the system as a whole.

We apply feature-centric analysis to four versions of the SmallWiki system [Renggli, 2003] and show how we detect and interpret changes in the context of features. We perform experiments with two distinct development branches of a system, consisting of three and two versions respectively and address problems of merging changes from two development branches. We cross check our results against developer implementation knowledge and the results of applying a *Diff* algorithm [Hunt and McIlroy, 1976] on two versions (*i.e.,* the first and last versions) of both development branches.

Structure of the chapter. In the next Section (Section 6.2 (p.89)), we outline our approach and describe how we measure, characterize and visually represent changes. In Section 6.2.1 (p.89), we describe how we extend our Dynamix meta-model with entities that model the notion of history and versions of features. Section 6.4 (p.94) details the results of our experimentation with a medium size application. We discuss and evaluate the results of our analysis in Section 6.5 (p.104). In Section 6.6 (p.105), we review related work in software evolution analysis approaches.

6.2 Analysis Strategy

As with the structural evolutional analysis approach described in the previous chapter, we adopt an approach combining *history-centered* and *version-centered* evolution analysis [Gîrba, 2005]. We first apply history-centered analysis to gain an overall impression of *which* features are affected by changes and *how*. We summarize changes to focus on *where* (*i.e.*, in which features) changes occurred. Subsequently, we apply a version-centered analysis to obtain a more detailed view of actual changes in features and *when* they occurred.

6.2.1 Modeling the History of Feature Entities

To obtain a *Feature Perspective* of a system's evolution, we define Hismo entities [Gîrba, 2005] to express the history and versions of our Dynamix *Feature* entity.

Figure 6.1 (p.90) shows how we extend our Dynamix meta-model with *FeatureVersion* and *FeatureHistory* entities. The *FeatureVersion* entity extends a *Feature* entity with version and date information. A *FeatureHistory* entity models a set of *FeatureVersion* entities. As *FeatureHistory* is explicitly modeled, we can assign properties to it to summarize how a feature changed over time.

6.2.2 History Properties for Features

In Chapter 3 (p.25) we defined properties for the *Feature* entities of Dynamix. The OCL definitions are provided in Figure 3.4 (p.34)) for the properties *nClasses* (nC) (*i.e.*, the number participating classes in a feature), *nSingleFeatureClasses* (nSFC) (*i.e.*, the number of participating singleFeature classes), *nLowGroupFeatureClasses* (nLGFC) (*i.e.*, the number of participating lowGroupFeature classes), *nHighGroupFeatureClasses* (nHGFC) (*i.e.*, the number of participating highGroupFeature classes) and *nInfrastructuralFeatureClasses* (nIFC) (*i.e.*, the number of participating infrastructuralFeature classes).

CHAPTER 6. EVOLUTION ANALYSIS: A FEATURE PERSPECTIVE

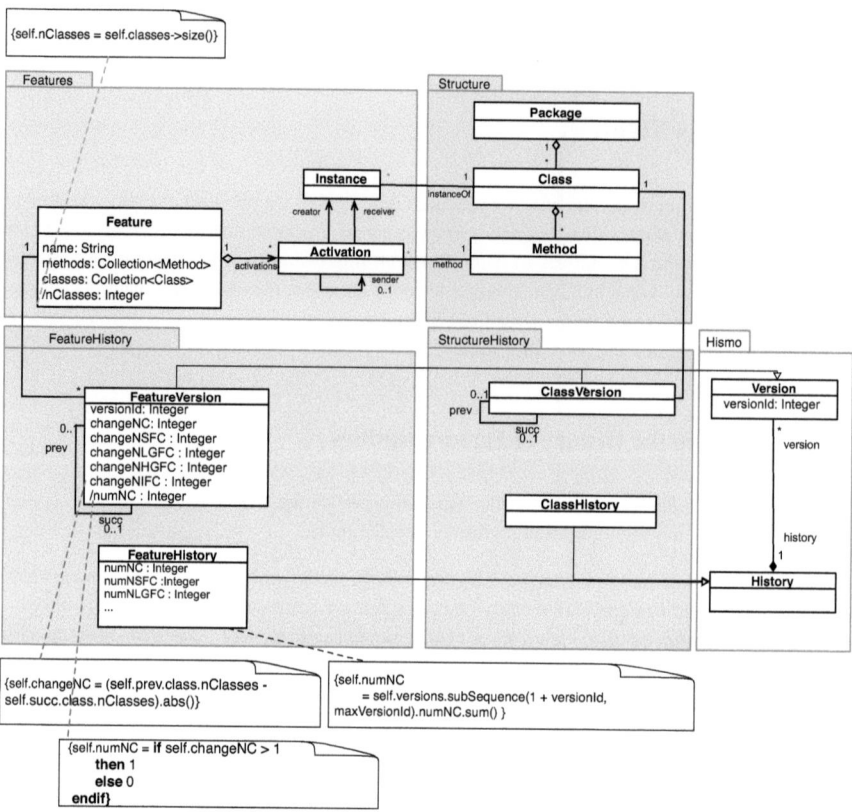

Figure 6.1: Dynamix is extended with Hismo entities to model the notion of Feature history.

To measure changes in features over time, we apply two history measurements defined by the Hismo meta-model [Gîrba, 2005] to the properties of the *Feature* entity.

Number of Changes of a Property (P) - This measurement counts in how many versions a property *P* has changed. We apply this measurement to the *nClasses* (nC) property (*numNC*) to isolate which features have changed with respect to the nC property. The definition of *numNC* is of the same format as *numFA* defined in Equation 5.2 (p.73).

Additions of a Property (P) - This measurement sums increases of a property *P*. We apply this measurement to detect an increase in a feature property (*e.g., addNC* sums the increases to the *nClasses* (nC) property) over time. We interpret increases in the number of classes participating in features to mean one of the following: (1) increased complexity: An increase in the number of classes participating in a feature may indicate the appearance of additional non-observable functionality in a feature, (2) refactorings or design improvements: These activities often lead to an increase in the number of classes to implement a functionality. According to Lehman's second law of evolution, the increase in size of the code is a typical characteristic of an evolving system and effort is required to reduce complexity to ensure the system is still maintainable [Lehman *et al.*, 1997].

$$(i > 1)$$
$$addNC_i(F, nC) = \begin{cases} nC_i(F) - nC_{i-1}(F), & nC_i(F) - nC_{i-1}(F) > 0 \\ 0, & nC_i(F) - nC_{i-1}(F) \leq 0 \end{cases}$$

$$(n > 2) \quad A_{1..n}(F, nC) = \sum_{i=2}^{n} addNC_i(F, nC) \tag{6.1}$$

6.3 Visualizing Change

In Chapter 3 (p.25), we introduced a simple visualization of a *compact feature view* as a grouping of participating software entities (*e.g.*, classes) for one version of a system. To represent changes in features over time, we describe two variations of our *compact feature view* visualization: (1) a *feature additions view* shows feature views showing only source entities that have been added to a feature, and (3) a *features intersection view* showing which source entities have been added in both development tracks of a system (*i.e.*, the intersection of additions). We represent and quantify changes between versions of features using a *feature evolution chart*, consisting of four line graphs plotting how four distinct properties of a feature view change from one version to the next.

The goal of our visualizations is to support the software engineer when reasoning about a system's

CHAPTER 6. EVOLUTION ANALYSIS: A FEATURE PERSPECTIVE

evolution from a feature perspective. A crucial aspect is the interactivity of our visualizations: they allow the software engineer to query the visualization to discover names of participating classes. We built them using Mondrian [Meyer et al., 2006], a framework that provides building blocks to express visualizations of the underlying Dynamix entities.

6.3.1 Visualizing *When* Features Change

Figure 6.2 (p.93) shows how the *editPage* feature of our SmallWiki case study changes over a series of three versions. For each version, we show its corresponding *feature view*. The views group classes by Feature Affinity level and classes are shown in different colors. The chart shown above the feature views is a group of line graphs, each representing the evolution of a different feature property. A horizontal delimiter of leach line graph indicates the maximum value of a feature property, taking all the features of our experiment into consideration (*e.g.*, max $nLGF$ = 36 classes). The values are indicated on the sides of the chart. The actual values of the properties (*i.e.*, the number of classes of each Feature Affinity level) for each version are represented as points on the line graph. We use evolution charts to visually represent *when* (*i.e.*, in which version) a change in a property occurred. With the *editPage* feature, we detect that the value of $nLGF$ (number of lowGroupFeature classes in a feature view) increased from 10 to 36 classes in the second version.

6.3.2 Visualizing *How* Features Change

Our *feature evolution charts* provide the software engineer with a quantitative view of changes to feature properties *nSFC*, *nLGF*, *nHGF* and *nIF*. However, they do not provide information about which classes have been added or removed from a feature.

To address this problem, we introduce the *feature additions view* visualization. Figure 6.3 (p.94) (b) shows only the additional classes participating in the feature.

Figure 6.3 (p.94) (b) shows actual classes that have been added to the *editPage* feature. The Feature Affinity level of the classes is computed with respect to the last version. However, to conclusively determine whether a class has been added to a feature view, we need to apply *numNC* measurement to see if the number of classes has increased. Increases in the individual class groupings may be caused by changes in Feature Affinity levels of individual classes.

6.3. VISUALIZING CHANGE

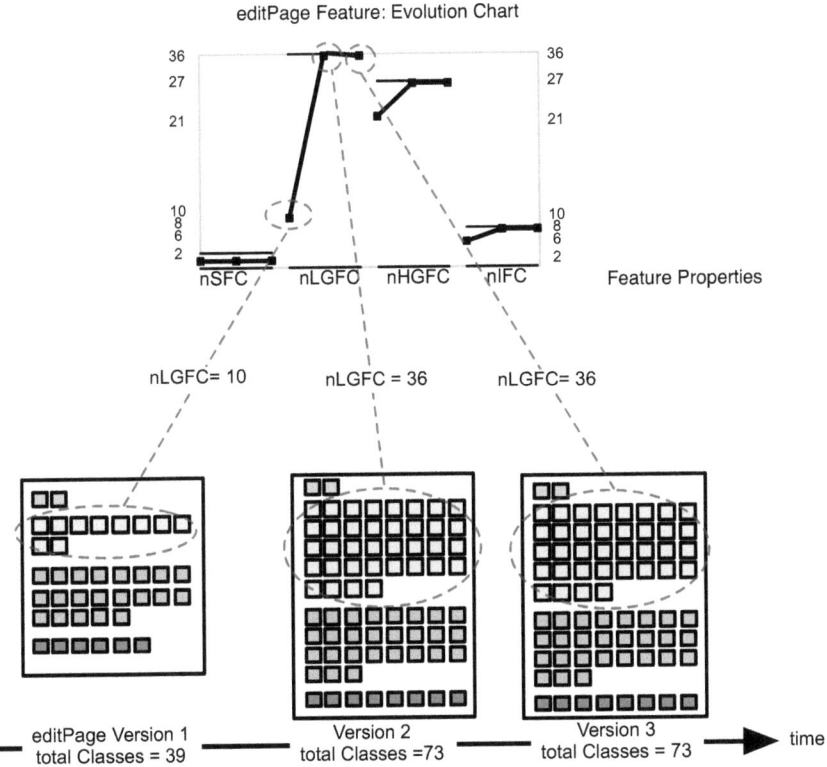

Figure 6.2: Version Analysis of the *editPage* Feature (Branch development track) showing the corresponding *Evolution Chart*.

CHAPTER 6. EVOLUTION ANALYSIS: A FEATURE PERSPECTIVE

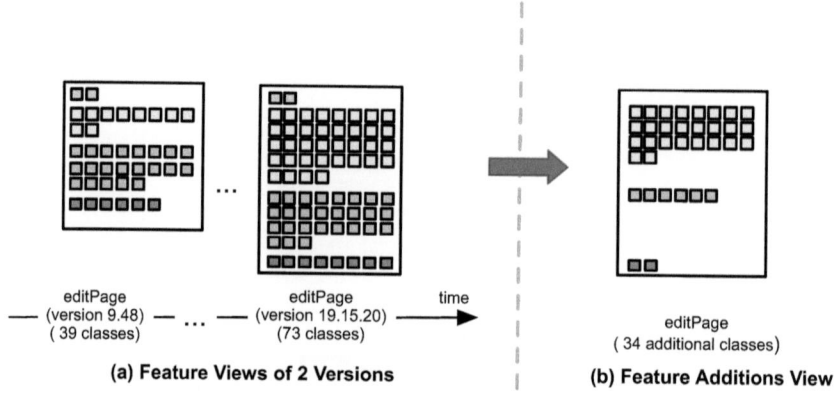

Figure 6.3: Feature Additions View of the *editPage* feature (Branch development track).

6.4 Validation

For our experiments we once again chose the *SmallWiki* application [Ducasse et al., 2005b] as we have access to multiple versions of the system.

Figure 6.4 (p.95) shows the versions of SmallWiki we selected for our feature evolution analysis of two distinct development tracks originating from the same version. These are representative versions that reflect different phases of development in the lifecycle of SmallWiki.

Version 9.48 (22.03.2004). The original SmallWiki was developed predominantly by two people. The results of their work are represented by this version, a major release of the system.

Version 9.52 (17.09.2004). As SmallWiki is an open source project, modifications and extensions are implemented by open source developers. 9.48 and 9.52 represent the main open source development track.

Versions 19.15.6 (30.08.2004) and 19.15.20 (08.09.2004). We selected this series of versions as it represents the work of a developer, who joined the development team at an advanced stage of the project. He undertook the task to refactor and extend SmallWiki with new features and new generic functionality which crosscuts the features of the application. These two versions represent a development branch of the system that is based on version 9.48. Changes to this version were not included in the 9.52 version of the system.

We analyze two distinct development tracks. In our first experiment, we analyze the evolution of the

6.4. VALIDATION

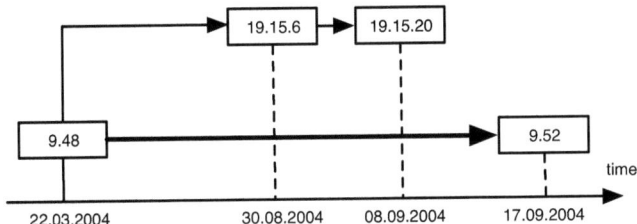

Figure 6.4: The order of the analyzed versions of Smallwiki.

branch development of the system in terms of how the modifications affected the existing features. Then in our second experiment, we analyze the evolution of the same features from version 9.48 to 9.52 (the main open source development track). We want to see what changed in the branch (versions 19.15.6 and 19.15.20) and identify changes that could cause conflicts when merging the branch with the main development track.

As with previous case studies, we identify features of SmallWiki by making the assumption that the elements of the user interface, namely the links, buttons and entry forms of the SmallWiki pages exercise distinct features. We selected 14 distinct features (14 typical user interactions with the SmallWiki application such as login, editing a page or searching a web site). In addition, we also selected one non interactive feature (*start* SmallWiki) that initializes the application at startup. We exercised the features on an instrumented system to capture 15 distinct execution traces.

Our dynamic analysis tool *TraceScraper* [Greevy and Ducasse, 2005b] allows us to define scripts to automate the execution and tracing of features. Thus, we ensure that the features are executed in the same way with the same inputs for each version of the system we analyze. We achieved 84 % coverage of the classes.

The goal of our analysis is to reveal the *extent* and *intent* of changes to a system over time. Our interpretation of the history measurements depends heavily on a key aspect of our approach: we always analyze the *same* set of features, in the same way for each version. Furthermore, from a user perspective, a system appears to behave in the same way in each version. We describe changes we detect in terms of the feature property that revealed that change. Our approach consists of the following steps:

1. We define a model for each version of our evolution analysis. We instrument each version and exercise the same set of features. For each feature we execute, we extract traces of runtime behavior and obtain an instance of our Dynamix model. Our feature views are generated for

each feature trace and we compute our Feature Affinity measurement to partition classes of feature views into four distinct groups.

2. We apply history measurements to (1) feature view properties ($nSFC$, $nLGF$, $nHGF$ and nIF), and (2) a NC (number of classes referenced in a feature view) property.

3. To obtain a more fine-grained view of the changes, we plot the values of the feature view properties over the root version of our analysis (9.48) and the two versions of the SmallWiki branch development track (19.15.6 and 19.15.20) as simple line graphs, as shown in Figure 6.5 (p.97). This visualization reveals when (*i.e.*, in which version) the changes occurred. This visualization supports a *version-centered* approach to analyzing the evolution of feature views. We quantify the changes in properties of feature views.

4. We drive the analysis with the questions we asked at the beginning of this chapter (see Section 6.1 (p.88)).

5. We summarize our results and check them with the developers. Based on the developer knowledge, we document the context of the changes revealed by our feature analysis.

6.4.1 Experiment 1 - Analyzing the Evolution of the Branch

The branch development code base of SmallWiki consists of the evolution of the versions on the main axis as shown in Figure 6.4 (p.95). We apply history measurements described in Section 6.2.2 (p.89) to *FeatureHistory* entities to detect *what* has changed in the system in the context of the features of our model.

Which features are affected by changes in the code? As a first step, we isolate features that have changed. Then we group changes by applying the *number of changes* history measurement to each of the four *Feature* properties ($nSFC$, $nLGF$, $nHGF$ and nIF).

Single Feature Changes. The extent of this type of change is limited to one feature. We compute *numNSFC* to detect for which features, and how often this property changed. Our result reveals that none of the features of our analysis exhibit *singleFeature changes*. Figure 6.5 (p.97) reflect this result as the plot for the *singleFeature* classes (($nSFC$) column) remains unchanged for each version of a Feature.

Low Group Feature Changes. By definition, *lowGroupFeature* change affects a subset of features (< 50% of the features of our model). Most of the features are affected by this type of change. In Figure 6.5 (p.97) we see that the only four features *not* affected by this type of change, namely *properties*, *stylesheets*, *resolveURL* and *comps* do not contain *lowGroupFeature* classes.

6.4. VALIDATION

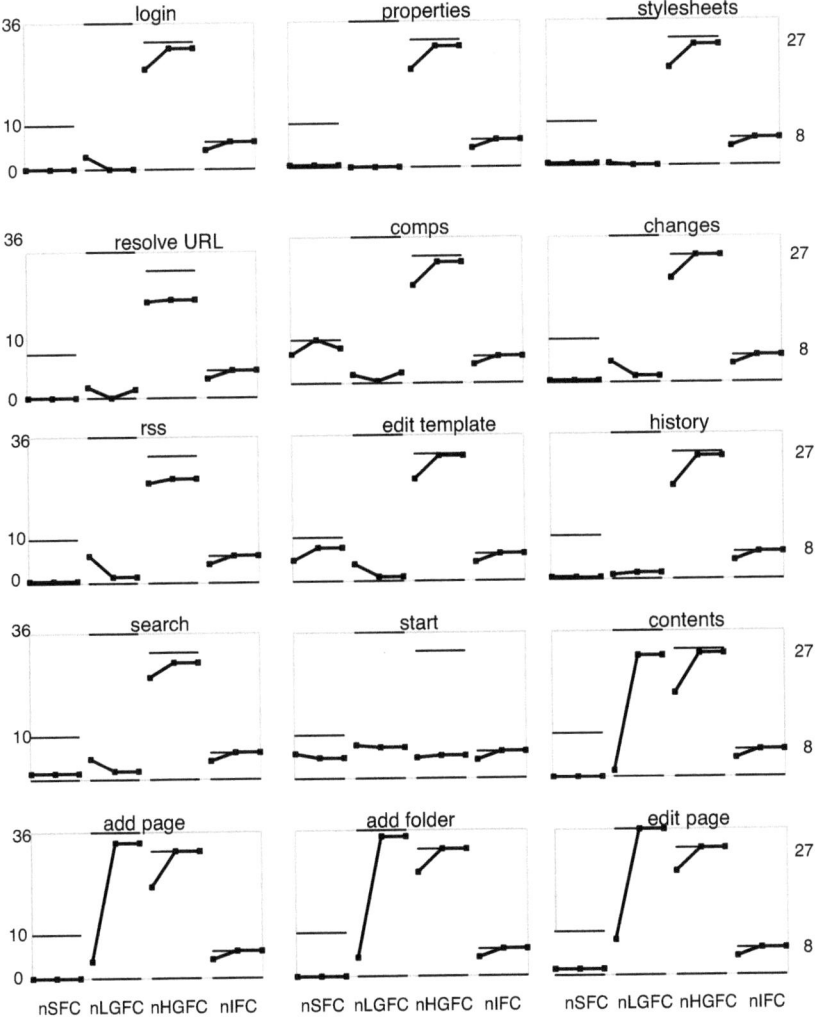

Figure 6.5: Evolution charts of 15 SmallWiki features (branch development) revealing *when* changes occurred in feature properties.

CHAPTER 6. EVOLUTION ANALYSIS: A FEATURE PERSPECTIVE

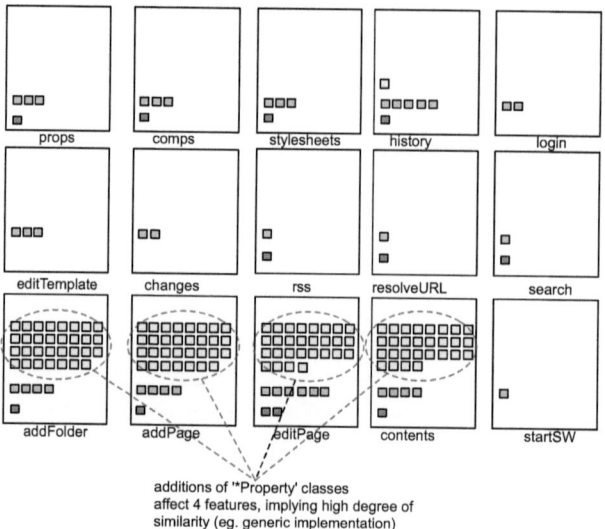

Figure 6.6: Feature Addtions Views (*i.e.*, showing only classes which represent additions to a feature view of the Branch).

High Group and Infrastructural Feature Changes. Once again in Figure 6.5 (p.97) we see that all of the features of our model have been affected by these types of changes. Both *highGroupFeature* change and *infrastructuralFeature* change imply changes to generic functionality of an application.

Another important result of our analysis is that we detected *when* all of the changes were made, namely in the second version of our analysis (*i.e.*, in version 19.15.6 of the branch development track we analyzed (see Figure 6.5 (p.97)). Our technique does not detect any changes in the Features between the versions 19.15.6 and 19.15.20.

Are features becoming more complex over time? We apply the *numNC* history measurement to the features and plot the results from both development tracks in Figure 6.7 (p.99). The light colored bars represent additions to the features in the branch, revealing that all features show an increase in *NC*. Our graph shows that most of the additions occur in 4 features *contents, addPage, addFolder* and *editPage*.

To distinguish between types of additions and determine the extent of their influence on the features, we then compute the Feature Affinity level for added classes with respect to the last version. We

6.4. VALIDATION

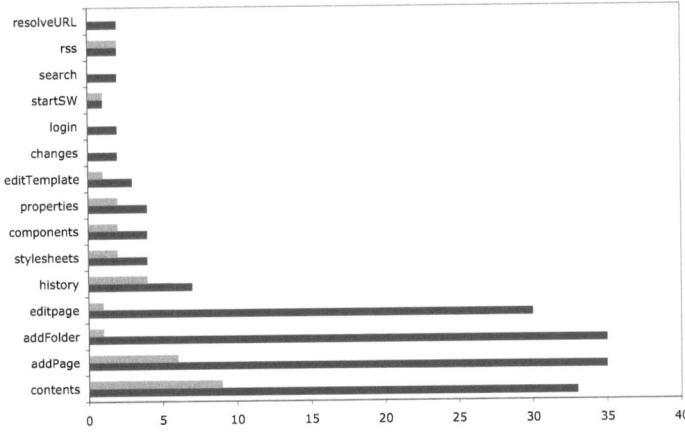

Figure 6.7: Additions History measurement applied to *Number of Classes* (CF of a Feature for all features of the branch (dark grey) and main (light grey) development tracks of SmallWiki.

discover as shown in Figure ?? (p.??) that most of the changes are in the $nLGF$ (number of low-GroupFeature classes in a feature view). Our results reveal that features that are most affected by change are *contents, addPage, addFolder* and *editPage*.

Detailed analysis of the *feature additions visualization* reveals that the changes to these features are as a result of the same added classes participating in the later version of the features. Furthermore, the added classes are named in a similar way *Property (*e.g.,* AccessEditProperty, AccessRemoveProperty, AccessViewProperty, BrokenProperty).

The result is particularly interesting, because although we do not trace any new features, our approach reveals the appearance of new classes indicating new functionality in the system. The developer responsible for this branch confirms that he added generic functionality to manage properties of a Wiki page. This functionality is common to these three features and is exercised by them without affecting their observable behavior.

Do similar patterns of change indicate relationships between the features? An increase in the number of software entities shared between features suggests that these features may be related. For example, the implementation of these features may be realized using generic functionality. We see from the feature views, that a large number of classes participating in feature views are characterized as *highGroupFeature* classes or *infrastructuralFeature* classes. This is because SmallWiki is a web application and all user-initialed features deal with the HTTP request/response communication and page rendering.

Our *Feature Evolution Charts* (see Figure 6.5 (p.97)) reveal interesting patterns of evolution. We ordered the evolution charts to emphasize patterns of change in features.

6.4.2 Summary of the Results of Experiment 1

Although we chose features that appear to behave in the same way for each version, when we apply our history measurements to the classes, we reveal that there is an increase in the number of participating classes in each feature of our model. We obtain a contextual perspective of the additional classes appearing in the feature views by applying *Additions* history measurements to each of the four feature properties nSFC, nLGFC, nHGFC and nIFC. The results of our experimentation are shown in Figure 6.7 (p.99) and Figure 6.5 (p.97). Our analysis reveals two main results:

1. There are similar patterns of change (addition of *lowGroupFeature* classes) detected in the features *addPage* (31 classes), *addFolder* (31 classes), *Contents* (28 classes) and *editPage* (27 classes).

2. There is a small increase in *highGroupFeature* classes and *infrastructuralFeature* classes (3 classes per feature on average), thus indicating addition of functionality affecting most, or all the features under analysis.

6.4.3 Developer Validation (Experiment 1)

To verify our hypothesis that our feature views support understanding of the extent and intent of change, we asked the developers to state the purpose of the changes with respect to the results of our analysis. The developers confirmed our first main result ((1) Section 6.4.2 (p.100)) by stating that a large proportion of the changes were made to reengineer the manipulation and internal representation of elements of the application (*e.g.,* form fields, labels, pages, folders). This reengineering effort accounts for the appearance of new classes, not specific to one feature, but to this group of features concerned with page and folder manipulation.

The reengineering effort accounts for the appearance of new classes in the feature views over the versions of the branch, which our feature analysis characterized as *Low group additions*. Using the interactive capability of our feature view visualizations, we query to reveal the names of the additional classes. The new classes, for example AccessEditProperty, AccessRemoveProperty, AccessViewProperty, BrokenProperty participated in the features of the last two versions of the branch. Once again, the developers confirm that these classes implement a generic mechanism to

6.4. VALIDATION

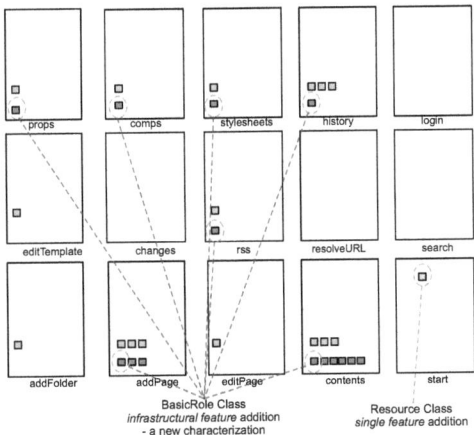

Figure 6.8: Feature Additions Views of Main Development track shows only added classes.

define and add properties to SmallWiki pages. The classes participate in all features that manipulate pages and folders. Furthermore, the developers confirmed that adding these classes does not affect their external observable behavior of the features.

The results of applying the *Diff* algorithm also confirms the addition of 26 new classes in a new `PropertyDescription` package. The *Diff* algorithm also reveals 19 classes exhibiting physical changes to the source code. These changes however do not affect the roles of the classes with respect to the features traced.

The High group and Infrastructural Changes. The small increase in this grouping was also explained by the developers. This reveals an extension of user and role authentication functionality. The classes **BasicRole** and **AdminRole** are responsible for limiting access to administrator functionality. The developers confirm the integration of role-based authentication for all features was one of the defined goals of this development track.

6.4.4 Experiment 2: Analyzing the Evolution of the Main Development Track

The main development code base of SmallWiki consists of the evolution of the two versions on the main axis as shown in Figure 6.4 (p.95). The focus of our second experiment was to apply our analysis technique to identify changes in the main development track that conflict with, or duplicate effort of changes in the branch. We extract feature views for the main development track to provide us with the context of changes.

The most striking result we obtained by comparing the results of applying the *numNC* history measurement to both development tracks (Figure 6.7 (p.99)). There are additional classes participating in only five features of the main development track (at most seven additional classes), whereas in the branch we see that all features have additional participating classes. Computing the *number of changes* history measurement for the nSFC, nLGFC, nHGFC and nIFC yields the following results:

— Only the *startSW* (SmallWiki initialization) exhibits *singleFeature* change.

— The *login* and *changes* features exhibit *lowGroupFeature* change.

— All features exhibit *highGroupFeature* and *infrastructuralFeature* change.

We apply the *Additions* history measurement to the NC property and compute *Feature Affinity* for the classes with respect to version 9.52. Figure 6.8 (p.101) shows the resulting *Feature addition views*. Querying the view (Figure 6.8 (p.101)) reveals that one additional class, **ResourceStore**, participates in the *startSW* feature in version 9.52.

We also discover that the class **BasicRole** has a Feature Affinity level of *infrastructuralFeature*. As we also detected exactly the same change in the branch development track, this suggests duplicated effort in both development tracks. The change is due to the incorporation of role checking functionality in all features of the system.

6.4.5 Supporting the Merging Changes

One of the goals of our experiments is to show how our technique supports developers when merging changes from two distinct development tracks. Our approach isolates and characterizes the types of changes, reducing the volume of information to be analyzed. For example, we assume that a *singleFeature* change is localized in one feature. We also need to distinguish between classes that have been added to a feature view and those whose functional role has changed with respect to the feature model.

Another important factor when merging two distinct development branches is to identify which source artefacts have changed in both development tracks, and check if these changes affect the same features. These changes may be more difficult to merge as the two distinct development tracks may reveal conflicting changes.

Furthermore, classes which have changed in both development tracks may indicate duplication of

6.4. VALIDATION

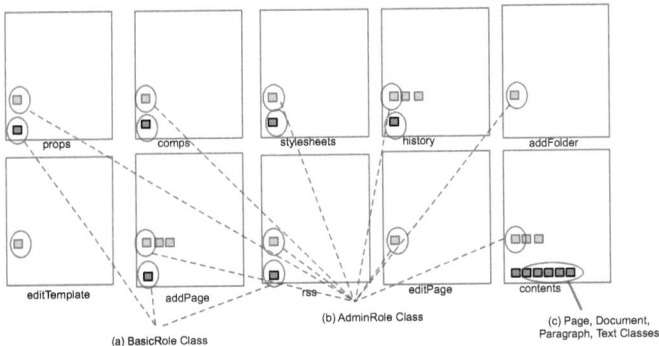

Figure 6.9: Feature Intersection View showing only the conflicting additions (*i.e.*, classes that have been added to both main and branch development tracks).

effort. Our analysis of SmallWiki reveals an example of this. The BasicRole class appears to have changed in the same way in both development tracks (*i.e.*, it changed from being a *singleFeature* class to an *infrastructuralFeature* class. This is due to the fact that this functionality was reused by all features in the later versions of the system. The *singleFeature* addition changes that we detected in our second experiment affected only one feature. The changes we detected in the *startSW* feature of the branch version represent new functionality. These changes could therefore be merged back in the original development track without affecting other features.

6.4.6 Developer validation (Experiment 2 - Main development track)

Two major findings of our feature analysis of the main development track are:

1. We discover the addition of a class named Resource as an addition to the *startSW* feature. As its Feature Affinity level is *singleFeature*, this suggests that this class provides specific functionality to the system only at initialization.

2. We detect that the Feature Affinity level of the classes BasicRole and AdminRole changes in the main development branch. In the initial version of our analysis, these classes have a Feature Affinity level of *singleFeature*, whereas in the last version of our analysis, their Feature Affinity level is *infrastructuralFeature*.

3. We detect additions of *infrastructuralFeature* classes, namely Page, Content, Text, Document in the *contents* feature.

CHAPTER 6. EVOLUTION ANALYSIS: A FEATURE PERSPECTIVE

The developers of the main development track confirm our first finding. They reveal that the class Resource provides SmallWiki with a cache implementation that has been added in the version 9.52. It is instantiated and populated by SmallWiki at startup. Our analysis with *Diff* also reveals that this class has been added in version 9.52.

Our second finding, namely the change of Feature Affinity of the BasicRole class, is confirmed by the developers of both main and branch developments. The integration of role-based authentication for all features was a goal of both development tracks. The developers undertook to extend the authentication mechanism of SmallWiki. The BasicRole class and the AdminRole class are responsible for role-based authentication. Typically access control functionality crosscuts all features, as it is checked before each feature execution. The developers confirm that in version 9.48 (the first version of our analysis) that this class was already present but was only being checked in the *login* feature, explaining why its Feature Affinity value was *singleFeature*. Our analysis of the changes in the branch development also revealed that the BasicRole class has changed Feature Affinity level. However, these classes do not exhibit physical changes in source code and are therefore not detected by the *Diff* algorithm. The changes are due to change of usage by the features.

The developers explain our third finding. New functionality has been added that results in the *content* feature registering all possible page contents. Once again the classes did not exhibit physical changes. Thus the changes are due to increased usage of the classes by the feature.

We use the *Feature Intersection View* as shown in Figure 6.9 (p.103) to isolate and analyze such conflicting changes.

6.5 Discussion

On the changing roles of classes. From our experimentation with the SmallWiki case study, we see that some of the changes we detect in features are due to changes in the Feature Affinity levels of classes. When our technique detects a change in a participating class of a feature, this may not necessarily imply that the feature where the change was detected is directly affected by this change. For example, in the case of the *components* feature, we detected that *singleFeature* classes were removed in the third version of our analysis. However, when we applied the *Additions* history measurement to the *lowGroupFeature* classes (*numNLGFC*), we discovered that the number of *lowGroupFeature* classes had increased. We discovered that the classes had not really been removed from the feature. Their roles (*i.e.*, Feature Affinity) with respect to the features of our model changed in the later version. We interpret this change to mean that the functionality provided by these classes is being used by other features in the later version. We refer to these changes as *false* changes in a feature.

On the increase and decrease in the number of participating classes. As our features appear to behave the same way from a user's perspective in each of the versions we analyzed, changes imply the addition or removal of non observable behavior to the features. Complexity of the features adversely affects the maintainability and comprehensibility of the system [Lehman *et al.*, 1997]. On the other hand, an increase or decrease in feature complexity may indicate that the developers have refactored the code to improve its design [Fowler *et al.*, 1999].

On detecting new features. Our case study is a typical open source system that is constantly being maintained and extended with new functionality and features. Although we do not trace any new features in our experiments, our results revealed the appearance of classes in the system that indicate the addition of new functionalities, perhaps indicating the addition of new features.

On combining evolution analysis techniques. The features perspective considers changes in features over time. However, as we do not achieve full coverage, our analysis is incomplete. Thus, we could overcome a shortcoming of this approach by applying it in conjunction with the structural evolution perspective described in the previous chapter. With a combination of both perspectives, we could take advantage of both the features and the feature enriched structural perspective to understand the changes that we detect.

6.6 Related Work

Hsi *et al.* [Hsi and Potts, 2000] described an approach to studying the evolution of features by deriving three views of an application, a morphological, a functional and an object view, based on the domain knowledge of an application. Their models were derived from the user interface of an application. They compare models of an application while they evolve. The purpose of their approach is to depict the feature architecture of an application independently of the underlying software. They highlight the importance of studying the evolution of a feature perspective of a system.

In another context, Ebraert *et al.* highlight the importance of reasoning about features when considering the problem of dynamic updates to a live system [Ebraert *et al.*, 2006]. They propose to adopt a feature-centric approach to address the problem of runtime updates, as a user of a system could be warned at a feature level, which features would be affected by performing the update. They identified our work as a means of modeling and manipulating features.

Many approaches to evolution analysis are based on comparing two versions of a system to detect changes. The version-centered models allow for the comparison between two versions and they provide insights into when a particular event happened in the evolution. Licata *et al.* assumed that unit tests of a system are partitioned into suites that are roughly aligned with the features of a system [Licata *et al.*, 2003]. The implementation of a feature "cross-cuts" the code base. They emphasized the value to new developers of a system of describing program changes in terms of features. Typically new developers run the program to form a mental model of the user-observable features of a system. Test suites describe a vocabulary that roughly corresponds to the user's, and thus the new developer's ontology of the program. Their approach is version-based as they focussed on the identification of differences between two versions of a program.

Xing and Stroulia detected server types of changes between two versions [Xing and Stroulia, 2004]. They represented each version of the system in an XMI format and then applied UML Diff to detect fine-grained changes like: addition/removal/moving and renaming of classes, methods and fields.

In contrast to the above approaches, our approach adopts a *history-centered* approach. Thus, we can tackle a large volume of data of multiple versions of a system as well as the large volume of dynamic data. The main advantage of a *history-centered* approach is that we reduce the problem space to focus only on what has changed in a system.

Furthermore, we define a feature perspective that analyzes a system as a set of features relating to concepts of a system's problem domain. In this way, we analyze changes in the context of domain knowledge. We use this context to interpret the motivation behind the changes and to determine the extent of the changes on the system and its features. Our Dynamix meta-model expresses the notion of *FeatureHistory* explicitly. All our measurements are defined in the context of Dynamix. We also apply version analysis to obtain a more fine-grained analysis of the changes. Our Mondrian visualizations and our *feature evolution charts* [Meyer et al., 2006] support more fine-grained *version-centered* analysis of changes, and help the software engineer to identify when the changes occurred.

6.7 Summary

The main goal of this chapter was to demonstrate how Dynamix is extended with *FeatureHistory* entities so we can analyze the evolution of a system from a *feature perspective*. To illustrate the extensions to Dynamix and the definition of *feature specific* history measurements, we described how we applied our *feature perspective* to reason about the evolution of two parallel development branches of SmallWiki. We exploit the feature perspective to define the intent and extent of the changes. In particular, we highlighted changes that may cause conflict when merging the two branches. We focused our experiments on the following questions:

1. *Which features are affected by changes in the code?* Our *feature view* visualizations support fine-grained analysis to detect which classes participate in which feature and to which extent

they are participating in the features of the model. Our *feature additions view* helps to narrow the scope of analysis to isolate only the classes that represent a change in a feature. The *feature evolution charts* provide us with a detailed perspective of which feature properties change from one version to the next.

2. *Are features becoming more complex over time?* Our analysis of the SmallWiki application reveals that for both development tracks, the number of classes participating in features increases over time. This evolution is typical for a system undergoing iterative development, which is the case with SmallWiki. The two parallel development tracks we analyzed represent phases where new functionality was added or existing functionality was incorporated into more of the features.

3. *Do similar patterns of changes in features indicate relationships between features?* Due to the generic nature of SmallWiki, our analysis reveals that most of the classes participate in most of the features. As a result, more features are affected by change to these classes. Our *feature evolution charts* and *feature view visualizations* proved to be useful for detecting similar patterns of changes in the features that represent tightly related features.

The main contributions of this chapter are:

— We described a novel approach to analyze the evolution of a system based on how features change over time. Our evolution analysis of features is defined in the context of our Dynamix meta-model, augmented with Hismo *FeatureHistory* and *FeatureVersion* entities.

— We defined *feature specific* history measurements to summarize changes to *FeatureHistory* properties over a series of versions.

— We introduced two variations of the feature view visualizations to support reasoning about the evolution of features: (1) the *feature additions view* shows feature views that show only the additional source entities that have been added to a feature (2) the *features intersection view* shows the source artefacts that have been added in both development tracks of the system (i.e., the intersection of additions). To represent a *version-centered* perspective, we used a *feature evolution chart* showing how four distinct properties of a feature change over a series of versions.

CHAPTER 6. EVOLUTION ANALYSIS: A FEATURE PERSPECTIVE

Chapter 7

Visually Reverse Engineering Features

Most feature identification approaches focus on mapping features to source artefacts such as classes and methods referenced in a call graph, but do not focus on object-oriented behavioral entities, namely object instances and message sends between instances. We show how our **Dynamix** *meta-model represents this level of detail and we introduce a feature-centric analysis perspective focusing on behavioral entities. To tackle the large volume of dynamic data, we base our approach on a novel 3D visualization of feature traces. Our goal is to understand feature behavior by identifying areas of high activity during feature execution by analyzing visual representations of the traces. We show how our visualizations reveal information about which parts of the system participate in a feature and to which extent.*

CHAPTER 7. VISUALLY REVERSE ENGINEERING FEATURES

7.1 Introduction

In previous chapters we addressed specific analysis goals to motivate feature-centric analysis. We compacted the large volume of dynamic information to simple sets of classes or methods representing features. However, our compact feature views focus only on static entities of the feature trace, namely classes and methods. If we are to take a broader view of feature behavior of object-oriented systems, we need to consider object instances rather than classes, and message sends rather than methods.

Zaidman *et al.* describe a dynamic analysis technique showing that a well-designed object-oriented program typically consist of a few key classes working tightly together to provide the bulk of functionality [Zaidman *et al.*, 2005]. The approach described in this chapter is based on that hypothesis. Our goal is to detect the key classes associated with a feature by visually identifying areas of high activity in feature traces. We consider two types of high activity: (1) classes that create a high number of instances, and (2) instances of classes that appear as centers of communication (*i.e.,* a high number of ingoing and outgoing messages). We use the term *feature hot spot* to refer to these areas of high activity during feature execution.

We motivate our visual analysis of feature behavior by considering the following reverse engineering questions:

1. *Which parts of the code (classes and objects) are active during the execution of a feature?* By identifying which classes are instantiated more than others, and how they collaborate during feature execution, we aim to identify which classes represent key classes of a feature.

2. *Which patterns of activity are common to features and which activities are specific to one feature?* Similar patterns of activity of feature behavior, such as similar sequences of communications between objects, may give insights into the architectural structure of a system. Recurring hot spots of activity in feature behavior reveal parts of a system providing *infrastructural*, rather than *feature-specific* functionality. This may give a software engineer insights into the architectural structure of a system.

To address these issues, we devised a novel 3D visualization based on polymetric views [Lanza and Ducasse, 2003] extended to 3D. We render both a structural perspective of a system and dynamic perspective of feature behavior in one visualization. We apply our approach to the SmallWiki application and show the effectiveness of our visual analysis to understand and identify key parts of code contributing to run-time behavior of features.

Structure of the chapter. In the next section, we define feature hot spot terminology. In Section 7.4 (p.113), we describe a novel 3D visualization that depicts feature behavior and how we identify *feature hot spots*. We validate our visual analysis approach by applying it to a case study in Section 7.5 (p.117). Section 7.6 (p.121) discusses our findings and outlines limitations and constraints of our

7.2 FEATURE HOT SPOTS

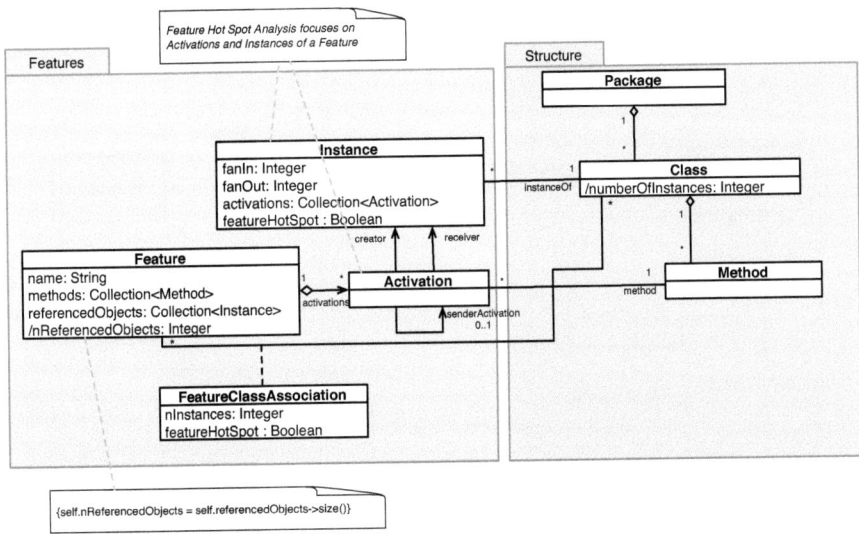

Figure 7.1: The Focus of our Visual Feature Hot Spot Analysis in Dynamix

visualizations. We examine related work in the area of visualization of execution behavior and compare this work with our visualization technique.

7.2 Feature Hot Spots

The term *hot spot* is used in many different contexts. In a geological context for example, it is used to refer to areas of volcanic activity. In the context of dynamic analysis, we use the term *feature hot spot* to refer to areas of high activity in a system during the execution of a feature. We consider two types of feature hot spots:

1. an instance of a class, *i.e.,* an object that acts as a central point of communication of a feature's runtime behavior

2. a class, for which a large number of instances have been created

We visually analyze features to detect feature hot spots. We associate feature hot spots with individual features and identify similar patterns of behavior between features in terms of recurrent feature hot spots. We argue that feature hot spot analysis supports system comprehension.

CHAPTER 7. VISUALLY REVERSE ENGINEERING FEATURES

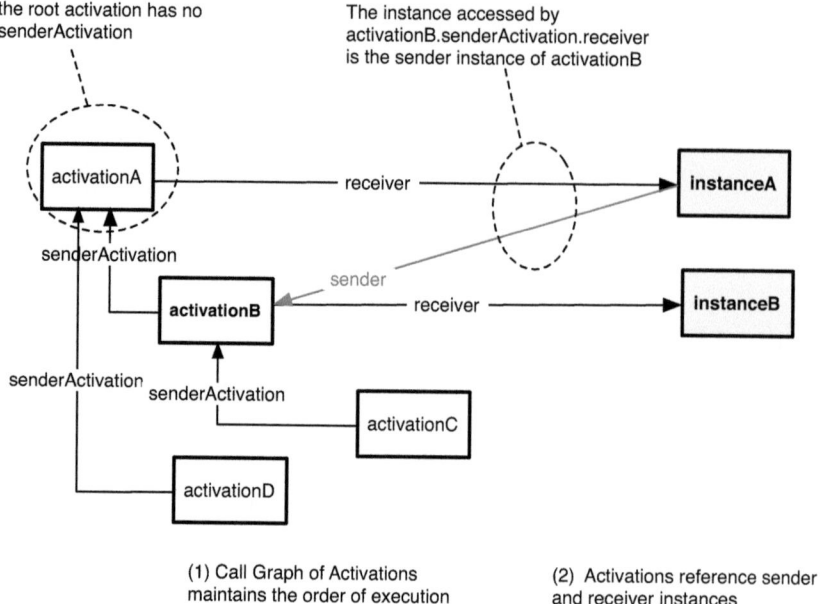

Figure 7.2: How Dynamix models a Feature's Call Graph and Instance Relationships

7.3 How Dynamix supports Feature Hot Spot Analysis

In Chapter 3 we introduced the behavioral entities of our Dynamix meta-model, namely *Feature*, *Activation* and *Instance*. In Figure 7.1 (p.111) we show Dynamix entities and attributes relevant for the feature hot spot analysis approach. We provide the OCL definitions of the two types of feature hot spots defined in Section 7.2 (p.111) in the context of our Dynamix meta-model in Figure 7.3 (p.113).

FeatureClassAssociation. This entity explicitly models the relationship between a *Feature* and a *Class*. We define a *featurehotspot* attribute for this entity which determines if an instance of this class represents a hot spot for the associated feature.

Instance. We define the *fanIn* and *fanOut* attributes of an instance and define the *featureHotspot* attribute as the sum of the number of in-going and out-going activations. Figure 7.2 (p.112) shows how Dynamix models the call graph and relations between activations and sender and

```
context Instance
  def: fanIn : Integer = self.activations
       ->select(a | a.receiver = self )->size()

context Instance
  def: fanOut : Integer = self.activations
       ->select(a | a.senderActivation.receiver = self )->size()

context Instance
  def: featureHotSpot  (aHotspotValue: Integer) : Boolean =
  self.fanIn + self.fanOut  >  aHotspotValue
  endif

context FeatureClassAssociation
  def: featureHotSpot ( aHotspotValue: Integer)  : Boolean =
  self.feature.activations->select(a | a.receiver.instanceOf = self.class )
       ->size() > aHotspotValue
  endif
```

Figure 7.3: OCL specification of Feature Hot Spot for an Instance and for a Class of a Feature.

receiver instances.

7.4 3D Visualization of Dynamic Behavior

To provide a qualitative perspective on the large amount of information produced by traces, we implemented TraceCrawler [Wysseier, 2005], an extension to the CodeCrawler tool [Lanza, 2003]. TraceCrawler provides an interactive 3D visualization, combining both structural information for orientation and dynamic information to support understanding of feature behavior.

Our visualizations represent system behavior of a feature in the context of a static perspective of the system. The static structure of our system is represented using a *System Complexity View* [Lanza and Ducasse, 2003]. It shows classes (nodes) and inheritance relationships (edges) organized as a tree. In Figure 7.4 (p.114) we see a schematic display of our 3D visualization. We display the *System Complexity View* on a plane "floating" above the ground. The white boxes are the classes connected by inheritance edges.

When the trace is interpreted, each instantiation of a class generates a box, like a "floor" of a building, above the ground level of its corresponding class representation. The more boxes are above a class,

CHAPTER 7. VISUALLY REVERSE ENGINEERING FEATURES

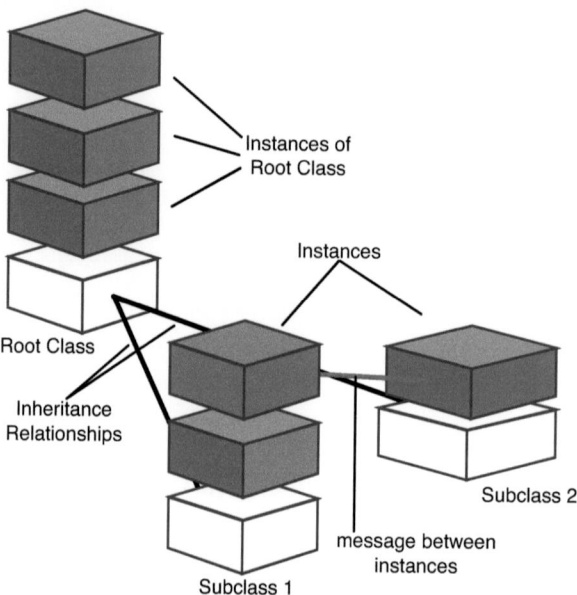

Figure 7.4: The Elements of our 3D Visualization of Feature Behavior. The ground floor represents a static class hierarchy perspective of a system. The dynamic behavior is represented by nodes above the ground floor (the instances) and the red edges are the message sends between instances.

7.4. 3D VISUALIZATION OF DYNAMIC BEHAVIOR

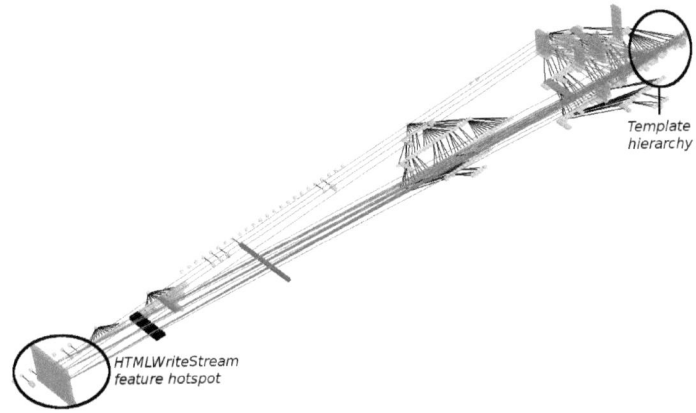

Figure 7.5: An Overview of the SmallWiki case study after the execution of the Login Feature.

the more instances of this class have been created. Each time an object sends a message to another object, a message edge is draw between the two object boxes.

We exploit the visual language of polymetric views [Lanza and Ducasse, 2003]. We map metrics to the width (*NOA = number of attributes*) and to the length (*NOM = number of methods*) of the nodes. Thus, the class hierarchy not only conveys information about the inheritance relationships between the classes, it also reveals information about the sizes of the classes. For example, in Figure 7.5 (p.115), we see that the class `HtmlWriteStream` is represented with a longer box. This means it has a larger number of methods than other classes in the visualization.

We map the *Feature Affinity* measurement to the color of nodes of our visualization. This enriches our visualization with information about the functional roles of classes with respect to features. We use grayscale to indicate the *Feature Affinity* level of a class. The darker the node, the more features it participates in. For example, black nodes represent *infrastructural* classes (*i.e.,* classes that participate in all the features of our analysis) and light grey nodes represent *single-feature* classes (*i.e.,* classes that participate in only one feature of our analysis). In Figure 7.5 (p.115) we show an instance collaboration view of a Login feature from our *SmallWiki* case study. *Feature hot spots* are easily identifiable in this view as nodes of the visualization with a large number of edges or large number of instances.

Crucial to the manipulation of large amounts of data are interactive and navigable capabilities of our visualizations. The software engineer can examine in detail, objects and messages and change his point of view in a 3D space with zooming, panning and rotating capabilities. This provides a closer

CHAPTER 7. VISUALLY REVERSE ENGINEERING FEATURES

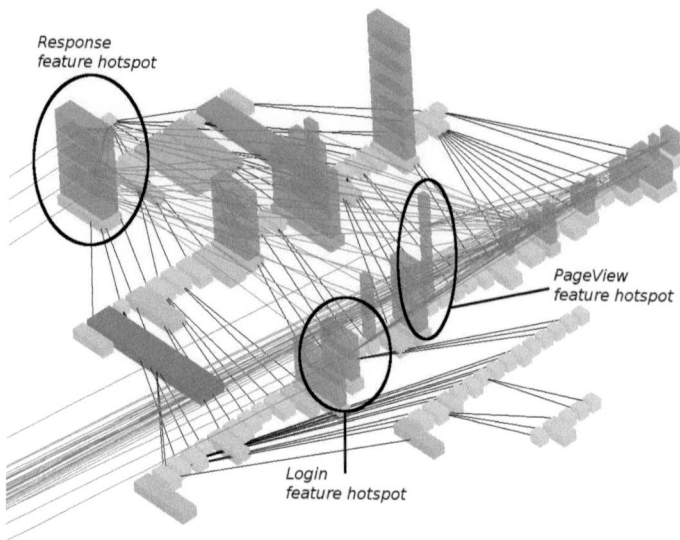

Figure 7.6: Zooming into the class hierarchy active during the login scenario.

look at specific parts of the visualization. At all times, a software engineer has access to the source code of classes represented in the visualization.

The Activations of our Dynamix model maintain information about unique object identifiers of the sender and receiver of a message.

7.5 Validation

In this section, we describe how we apply feature hot spot analysis to features of the SmallWiki system. We verify our findings by checking our results with the developers.

The goals of our analysis are twofold: (1) to identify which classes are most active during the execution of a feature, and (2) to identify patterns of behavior common to the features we analyze. Our visual analysis is a postmortem analysis of feature behavior. We visually analyze an *Instance Collaboration View* [Wysseier, 2005] of each feature to detect hot spots.

For our experiment, we chose 5 features of SmallWiki, representing typical user interactions, namely *Login, Edit Page, Edit Template, Show Page History* and *Search*. In Figure 7.5 (p.115) we show an *Instance Collaboration View* of the **Login Feature Trace** over the entire class hierarchy of SmallWiki. We see which parts of the code actively participate in the behavior of this feature. In particular, we see classes where a number of instances were created and we identify instances with a large number of edges. This implies that they send and receive a large number of messages (*i.e.,* high fan-in and fan-out). These classes act as centers of communication during the runtime behavior of a feature.

The *Instance Collaboration Views* of all the SmallWiki features we analyzed, appear very similar. The developers of SmallWiki confirm that this is due to the generic design of the application. A further reason for this is due to the high proportion of common functionality that is exercised by all the features (*e.g.,* page rendering and server interaction). We look at each feature in more detail. For each feature hot spot we detect in a feature, we validate our findings with developer knowledge to determine if the class associated with that feature hot spot we detect corresponds to a key class for that feature.

Login Feature Trace (5576 events). In Figure 7.5 (p.115), we see a complete visual representation of its dynamic behavior *after* the *Login* feature was exercised. In Figure 7.6 (p.116) we show the same view after we have zoomed in on the right hand side of the visualization. From this perspective, we see some of the feature hot spots in more detail. In general, we discover that the developers of SmallWiki adhered to naming conventions that reflect the functionality and features that they implement.

CHAPTER 7. VISUALLY REVERSE ENGINEERING FEATURES

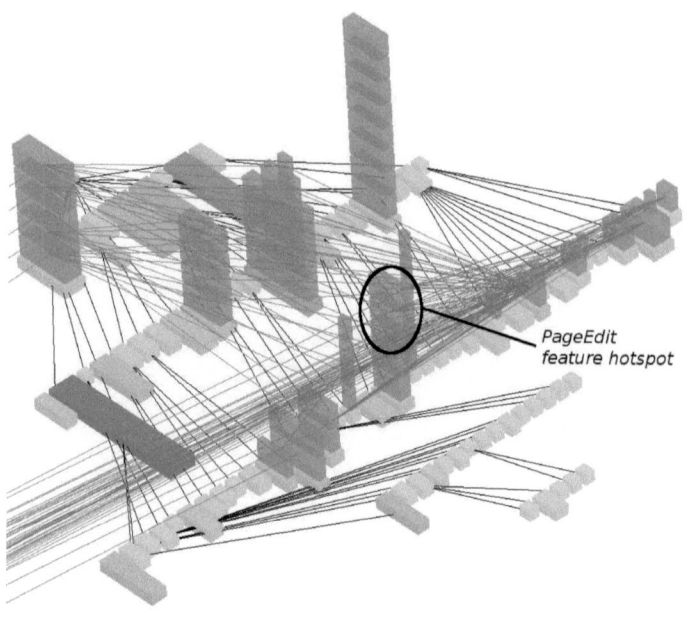

Figure 7.7: A Detail of the Visualization of the "Edit Page" feature.

Our visualization of the *Login* feature reveals four feature hot spots, which we have marked on the visualization:

Login activity feature hot spot. Our visualization reveals that instances of the Login class are created when this feature is exercised. One instance of Login communicates heavily with instances of classes of the Template hierarchy (subclasses of TemplateBody and TemplateHead). We check our findings with the developers. They inform us that they adhered to good naming conventions during the development of SmallWiki, Thus it is not surprising that the Login class is the key class responsible for performing the functionality of the Login feature. They also confirm the participation of classes of the Template Hierarchy. In *SmallWiki*, templates are used for the composition of pages. That is why this instance renders the login entry form and is executed to perform the login functionality.

Response feature hot spot. The developers confirm that the Response class plays a key role, as it is responsible for handling HTTP responses sent to the web browser. Our visualization reveals that during the execution of the login feature, four HTTP responses are sent to the browser. We detect this as the visualization consists of four instances of the `Response` class.

HTMLWriteStream feature hot spot. The functionality to generate HTML code is provided by the **HTMLWriteStream** class. Our visualizations reveal that the **HTMLWriteStream** class participates in all the analyzed features. The nodes are colored black indicating that our feature analysis characterizes this class as *infrastructural*. This reveals that this functionality is generic or common to all features under analysis. This feature hot spot thus represents a recurring behavior or pattern of activity in the features of SmallWiki. The developers confirm our finding.

PageView feature hot spot. Our visualization reveals that the **PageView** class is part of the Action class hierarchy. The developers confirm that this class is responsible for rendering pages. The instance of **PageView** class behaves as a central point of communication. There is a high number of edges between the instance of this class and instances of the **Template** hierarchy. This is due to the fact that SmallWiki pages are composed from templates.

The main part of the computation of the *Login* feature is involved with displaying the login page of SmallWiki. An instance of the class **PageView** provides this functionality by requesting information from other classes that model Templates (subclasses of **TemplateHead** and **TemplateBody**). All five features share the feature hot spots of the Login feature, because these features also require HTTP communication and page rendering functionalities.

Edit Page Feature Trace (12874 events). This feature allows a user to modify a page by entering an editing mode. Once the user is finished editing the page, the new version is saved and displayed in the browser. Figure 7.7 (p.118) shows a part of the visualization of this feature's behavior. We use the zoom capability of our visualization to analyze a new feature hot spot, namely the *PageEdit feature hot spot*. The developers confirm that the **PageEdit** class is the key class responsible for rendering the form to edit a wiki page and to save the submitted content.

Edit Template Feature Trace (15810 events). This feature allows a user to modify the look and feel of pages by changing a template that affects the position, color, etc. of the page elements. This feature-trace is more complicated than the previous ones as there are more events to render. The visualization shown in Figure 7.8 (p.120) reveals one new feature hot spot, namely the *TemplateEditor feature hot spot*. The visualization reveals that an instance of the **TemplateBodyActions** class participates heavily in this feature. There are also two instances of **EditTemplate** communicating with many other objects. Once again we confirm with the developers that these are in fact the key classes that provide functionality to this feature.

Show Page History Feature Trace (8052 events). This feature allows a user to see a list of all pages in SmallWiki which have recently changed. In Figure 7.9 (p.121) we show a part of the visualization of the feature. Here we analyze one new feature hot spot located in the tower of the **PageHis-**

CHAPTER 7. VISUALLY REVERSE ENGINEERING FEATURES

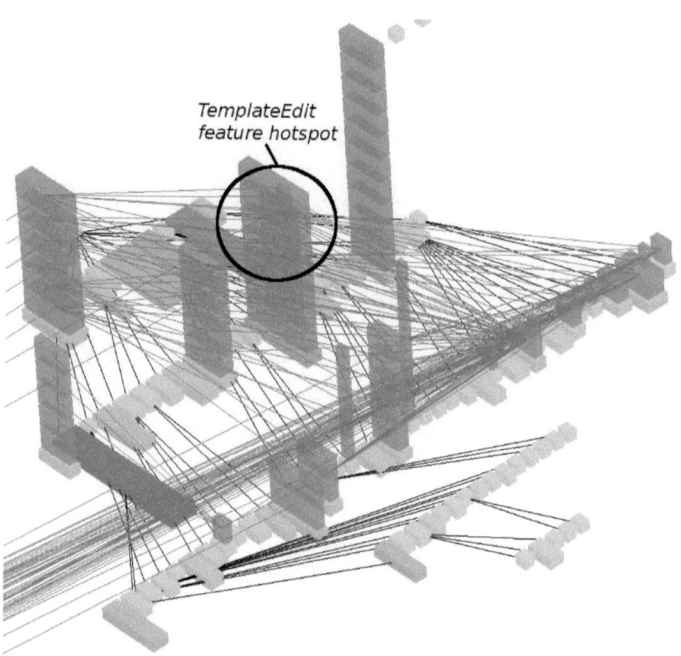

Figure 7.8: A Detail of the Visualization of the "Edit Template" feature.

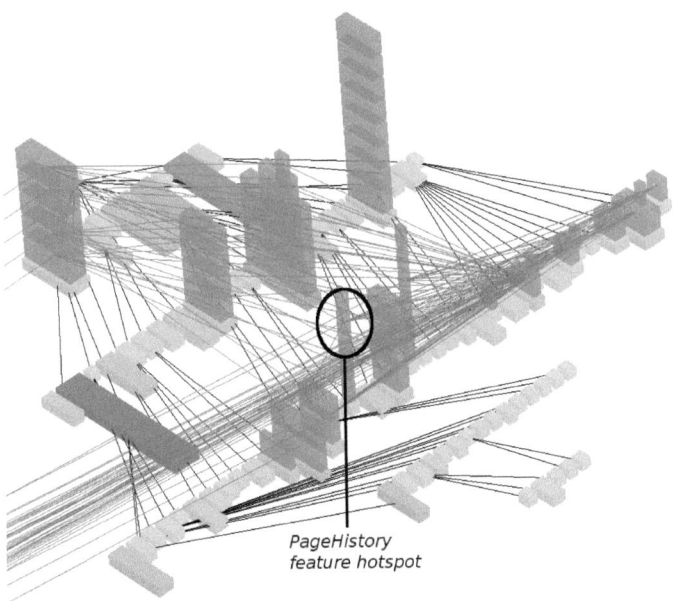

Figure 7.9: A Detail of a Visualization of the "Show Page History" feature.

tory instances, where one specific instance communicates with many other objects. The developers confirms that this is due to the rendering process of the version table of wiki pages.

Search Feature Trace (7554 events). This feature allows the user to search all the pages of the Wiki for a specific string. Figure 7.10 (p.122) reveals a new feature hot spot, namely the *Search feature hot spot*. There is a tower of instances above the Search class. Two of the instances heavily communicate with other objects to perform this task. This is due to the fact that the results of the search request need to be rendered.

7.6 Discussion

The large volume and complexity of dynamic information makes it difficult to infer how a software system implements features. Our visualization metaphor of growing towers of instances represents large amounts of dynamic data effectively, while still maintaining their structural context. By ana-

CHAPTER 7. VISUALLY REVERSE ENGINEERING FEATURES

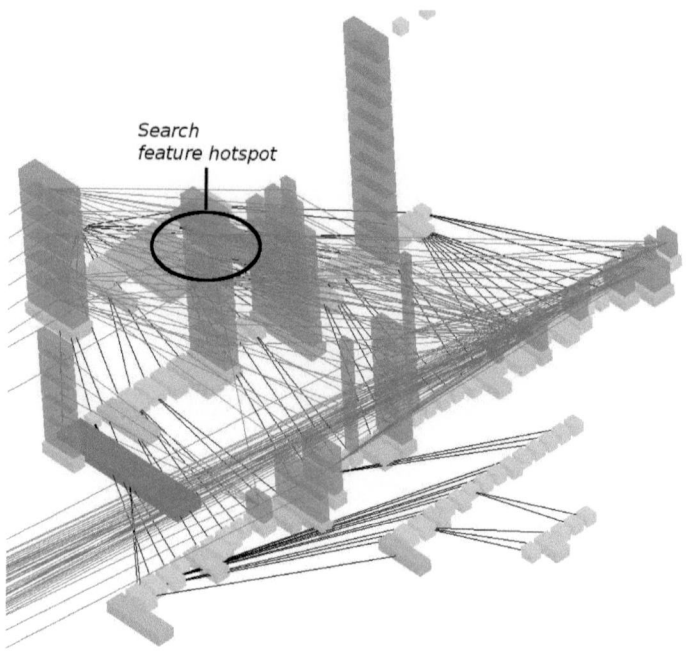

Figure 7.10: A Detail of a Visualization of the "Search" feature.

lyzing our 3D visualizations, the software engineer quickly obtains an overview of runtime behavior of features. The feature hot spots guide a software engineer to identify key classes relevant to feature behavior. Moreover, a visual comparison of the features reveals patterns of recurrent activity that represent *infrastructural* functionality of the system.

The definition of a feature hot spot. For our experiments, we did not define thresholds for feature hot spots. We rely completely on visual identification. However, our approach is easily extensible to incorporate threshold values to explicitly define the number of instances of a class, or a fanIn / fanOut value constituting a class being identified as a feature hot spot. We show in Figure 7.3 (p.113) how we defined these metrics in the context of Dynamix.

Correlating Feature Affinity with feature hot spots. We map Feature Affinity level of the classes to the color of the 3D nodes. This reveals information about the level of participation of each class in the traced features.

7.6. DISCUSSION

Interpreting NOA and NOM. Another kind of information is metric information rendered according to the polymetric view principles [Lanza and Ducasse, 2003]. This is reflected in the width and length of the cuboids and tells us the size of the participating classes.

2D versus 3D. The advantage of using 3D over 2D is that we exploit all three dimensions to render dynamic information. Using only two dimensions would also be possible [Ducasse *et al.*, 2004], however these views typically require that the developer learn the semantics of the visualization. As they map static and dynamic information on two dimensions, the developer cannot intuitively distinguish between the dynamic and static information. Moreover, our approach exploits developer familiarity with UML class diagrams as the static information is displayed as a class hierarchy view. The runtime information is displayed in the context of the static view.

The Interactive Visualization. Our visualizations provide an overview of an entire collection of data that is represented, which may be difficult to interpret in the case of systems with a large number of classes. Therefore, the interactive capabilities of our visualization are an integral part of this discussion. Our visualizations allow zooming, panning and rotation of the view, thus we tackle problems such as occlusion. The interactive capabilities of our visualizations enable us to query a visualization to obtain more fine-grained information about key entities of interest. For example, we query a node of a visualization to obtain a class name and view source code. It is difficult to render such an interactive process on paper media. However, the results of our analysis, namely the detection of feature hot spots are revealed by merely viewing the visualizations. The fine-grained details of a feature hot spot such as browsing source code of the classes are obtained by manipulation and interaction of the visualizations.

Naming. Our analysis of SmallWiki reveals that the developers adhered to sound naming practices. The names of key classes identified by feature hot spot analysis reflect the intention of the corresponding features. We show that, for our SmallWiki case study, semantic analysis or regular expression matching could be applied to the source code to reliably uncover concepts in the code.

Scalability. As discussed above, the expressiveness of the visualization and the interactive capabilities of our technique support the representation and interpretation of large amounts of data. In our SmallWiki case study, we chose five features that generated traces consisting of more than 8000 events. In a previous Moose case study [Greevy *et al.*, 2005b; Wysseier, 2005] we show that we have successfully applied our visualization to feature traces of over 70'000 events. However, the number of classes and instances is a threat to scaleability of the approach. It is difficult to display a large number of classes of a system in a class complexity view on one screen. The zooming and scrolling capabilities of TraceCrawler tool address this issue. The developer can visually identify and zoom in on the relevant areas of the class hierarchy for further investigation.

CHAPTER 7. VISUALLY REVERSE ENGINEERING FEATURES

Coverage. Using dynamic analysis, it is difficult to achieve full coverage of a system. We argue that this is not vital for feature hot spot analysis, as we focus on the traces of individual features.

7.7 Comparisons with other Related Work

Our main focus with this work is the use of 3D visualizations to analyze the dynamic behavior of features and how they interact in terms of the parts of the code that they share.

Zaidmain *et al.* [Zaidman *et al.*, 2005] define a dynamic analysis approach based on webmining techniques that identifies key classes of a system. They argue that well-designed object-oriented programs typically consist of key classes that work tightly together to provide the bulk of a system's functionality. Their definition of key classes corresponds to our notion of a *feature hot spot*. In contrast to our feature-centric approach, they do not partition the dynamic information into individual feature-traces. The advantage of obtaining individual feature traces using our approach is that we exploit feature knowledge and relate this knowledge to the key classes associated with the instances identified in the feature hot spots.

Among the various approaches to support reverse engineering that have been proposed in the literature, graphical representations of software have long been accepted as comprehension aids [Price *et al.*, 1993; Stasko *et al.*, 1998]. The work of Maletic *et al.* has provided important guidelines for our visualizations. We devised our *Instance Collaboration View* visualization and analysis considering the five dimensions of interest of software visualization as defined by Maletic *et al.* [Maletic *et al.*, 2002].

Marcus *et al.* use a 3D metaphor in their sv3D tool to represent a software system [Marcus *et al.*, 2003]. The main difference to their approach is that we exploit 3D to render dynamic information, while they render static information in all 3 dimensions.

De Pauw *et al.* present two visualization techniques. With their tool *Jinsight*, they focus on interaction diagrams [De Pauw *et al.*, 1993]. Thus all interactions between objects are visualized. The focus of our visualizations is to address reverse engineering dynamic behavior of features. Thus we tackle the challenge of obtaining high level views from a large volume of information to support reasoning about the runtime behavior of features.

Walker *et al.* [Walker *et al.*, 1998] use program animation techniques to display the number of objects involved in the execution and the interaction between them through user-defined high-level models. Their tool uses a summary strategy to show live objects using a histogram, and reduces the information space by allowing the user to cluster together code elements to create a high level model. Our *TraceCrawler* tool provides a means of stepping through a trace of a feature and to render each event in the visualization.

7.7. COMPARISONS WITH OTHER RELATED WORK

Jerding et al. propose an approach to visualizing execution traces as Information Murals [Jerding et al., 1997]. They define an *Execution Mural* as a graphical depiction of an entire execution trace of the messages sent during a program's execution. These murals provide a global overview of the behavior, They also define a *Pattern Mural* which visually represents a summary of a trace in terms of recurring execution patterns. Both views are interdependent.

Reiss [Reiss, 2003] developed *Jive* to visualize the runtime activity of Java programs. The focus of this tool was to visually represent runtime activity in real time and to support software development activities such as debugging and performance optimizations. Our focus is feature-centric reverse engineering. Feature trace data is captured from a running system and then modeled in the context of static source code entities. However our technique is non-restrictive and could easily be adapted to interpret real-time trace information.

Kleyn and Gingrich [Kleyn and Gingrich, 1988] and Lange and Nakamura [Lange and Nakamura, 1995b] chose a graph-based approach to visualize dynamic behaviour. Kleyn and Gingrich also animate their views by highlighting and annotating nodes and edges to represent activity in the code.

Pattern detection in dynamic behavior is a research question that has been addressed by many researchers. De Pauw et al. apply pattern extraction algorithms to detect recurring exection behavior in traces [De Pauw et al., 2006]. They state that a fuzzy matching algorithm could classify transactions according to related operations. They apply their algorithm to real examples with traces of up to 40MB. Their analysis reveals that the number of patterns is small, usually about 10 patterns.

Recent work of Nagkpurkar and Krintz [Nagpurkar and Krintz, 2006] describe a technique whereby they characterize the behavior of programs as *phases*. These phases represent repeating patterns in the trace. They decompose a program into fixed-sized intervals of events and combine these according to how similar the intervals are.

In another work, we described a visual analysis approach of traces based on comparing signal representations of entire traces [Kuhn and Greevy, 2006a]. For this work we also chose SmallWiki as a case study. Our analysis reveals patterns in traces. This approach does not compact the information so it preserves the notion of time and frequency. In contrast to our 3D visual analysis approach, it does not represent the dynamic information in the context of a static representation of the source code.

The main focus of our approach is to visualize the dynamic behavior of features to detect *feature hot spots*. Our goal is to guide the attention of the reverse engineer to key classes of a system from a feature perspective. Our visualization metaphor is intuitive as it exploits the developer's familiarity with graph visualizations similar to UML class and sequence diagrams. We emphasize the importance of ease of interpretation of a visualization to gain acceptance by the software developer. Our approach complements the approach of De Pauw et al. [De Pauw et al., 1993] by allowing the developer to

CHAPTER 7. VISUALLY REVERSE ENGINEERING FEATURES

interact with the visualization and control the display of events in a feature trace. Thus the reverse engineer exploits her feature understanding of a system and directly focuses on the parts of dynamic data of interest, in this case the *feature hot spot*. Our visualizations add semantic information to the software entities by showing how they participate in features. The semantic information of feature knowledge supports reasoning about the functional roles of software entities of a system.

7.8 Summary

In this chapter we focus on the behavioral data of object-oriented programs, namely instances and message sends. We show how Dynamix, our unified meta-model of structural and dynamic data supports the visual analysis approach we adopted.

Our *feature perspective* establishes the semantic purpose of a system's source artefacts. The visualizations we presented in this chapter combine a structural view of a system in terms of class hierarchies with a dynamic information of features.

Our goal was to answer the following questions:

1. *Which classes and objects are most active during the execution of a feature?* The feature hot spots we detect in the features of SmallWiki revealed which were the key classes of a feature. The interactive capabilities of the visualization allowed us to query the individual instances to obtain fine-grained information about the classes involved in the feature hot spots.

2. *What are the patterns of activity that are common in feature behavior and which are specific to one feature?* The feature visualizations of our *SmallWiki* case study reveal which classes are active in more than one feature, and recurring collaborations between instances. We also detect behavior that is specific to one feature. Moreover, our *Feature Affinity* measurement of classes reveal classes that are characterized as *infrastructural*. These are shown as black nodes. These classes participate in all features of our model. Thus we identify common functionality.

The main contributions of this chapter are:

— The definition of *feature hot spot* analysis as an approach to understanding the runtime behavior of features.

— A 3D visual analysis of true object-oriented dynamic information, namely instances and message sends between instances.

— Visual analysis to detect behavioral patterns in features.

— OCL definitions for feature hot spots in the context of Dynamix.

Chapter 8

Extracting Developer Roles with Feature Analysis

Software systems are typically developed by teams of developers with responsibilities for different parts of the code. Knowledge of how developers collaborate, and how their responsibilities are distributed over source artefacts is a valuable source of information when reverse engineering a system. Correlating developers with source artefacts reveals a static perspective of the system. We complement this with a dynamic perspective to reveal which features are developed by which developers. We analyze whether developer responsibilities correspond to structural divisions in a system's source code or to features. We apply our technique to two software projects developed by two teams of students as part of their course work, and to one large open source project.

CHAPTER 8. EXTRACTING DEVELOPER ROLES WITH FEATURE ANALYSIS

8.1 Introduction

Many reverse engineering techniques consider source code as the most reliable source of information about a system. Few researchers in the field of reverse engineering have devoted much attention to the roles developers play in implementing a system. We believe that reasoning about how developers build a software system represents a rich source of information for the reverse engineer [Lethbridge et al., 2005]. For example, it is useful to know who is responsible for which part of the system, or who developed which features [Demeyer et al., 2002].

Typically software systems are built by teams of developers. It is a well-known phenomenon that human factors such as collaborations and communication paths are often reflected in the structure of the code. According to Conway's law *"organizations which design systems are constrained to produce designs which are copies of the communication structures of these organizatons"* [Conway, 1968].

The structure of a development team and the division of responsibilities has a major impact on how a software system is structured and implemented. The challenge lies in how to efficiently exploit and access knowledge about which developer developed which parts of the code, and how developers collaborated during implementation.

Often a discrepancy exists between the way developers and domain analysts see a system. Typically the mental model of a developer reflects structural source artefacts such as packages and classes. Domain analysts and users on the other hand, see a system in terms of features (*i.e.,* the capabilities of the system). Thus, understanding which developers are responsible for which source artefacts is useful to support maintenance activities. Understanding which developers are responsible for which features is the key to maintaining traceability between an external perspective of a system and its internal structure.

In this chapter, we focus on a feature perspective of a system and correlate features and developers. We motivate our research by addressing the following questions:

1. *Which developers or groups of developers are responsible for which features?* We seek to extract information that would not only lead to relevant part of the code of a feature, but also reveal which developers are responsible for its implementation and maintenance. From a static perspective, developers who own the most classes in a system represent key developers. From a dynamic perspective, we assume that developers who are responsible for multiple features have a wider domain knowledge of the system than developers who contribute only to specific parts. Knowing which developer is responsible for which feature is useful when faced with the task of assigning bug reports and change requests to developers of large open systems [Anvik et al., 2006; Canfora and Cerulo, 2006].

2. *Do developers develop features or do they develop functional blocks?* We aim to extract a

development strategy of a project, to determine if the division of responsibilities corresponded to structural source artefacts or to features. We seek to reverse engineer which developers best understand parts of a system and whether developers develop on a static architectural boundary or on a feature boundary.

To address these questions, we analyze the correlation between developers of a system in the context of its static groupings of classes (*i.e.*, subsystems and packages) and of dynamic groupings that reflect its features. We obtain relationships between developers and classes by mining data about developers from source code repository of a project. Based on the data, we compute an *ownership* measurement of a class (*i.e.*, the responsible developer) [Gîrba *et al.*, 2005a]. We then build on our feature-centric analysis technique to establish relationships between features and classes, and subsequently we link developers to features.

Structure of the chapter. In Section 8.2 (p.129) we introduce key elements of our analysis technique: (1) a code ownership measurement and, (2) the visualizations we analyze to detect roles of developers from both a structural and a feature perspective. In Section 8.3 (p.130) we describe how we extend our meta-model with entities to model owners (*i.e.*, developers who implement source artefacts) and teams (groups of collaborating developers). In Section 8.4 (p.132) we describe our structural and feature views and briefly explain how we apply our feature analysis technique in the context of developers. In Section 8.6 (p.135) and Section 8.7 (p.140) we report on three case studies conducted using our approach. Subsequently, in Section 8.8 (p.144), we discuss our results and outline the constraints and limitations of our approach, and propose possible variation points. We summarize related work in Section 8.9 (p.144), and finally, we summarize our technique and contributions in Section 8.10 (p.146).

8.2 Extracting Developer Data from Work Artefacts

Recent research in the field of reverse engineering and system comprehension reveals a growing awareness in the role of software developers in a software development process [Lethbridge *et al.*, 2005]. Lethbridge *et al.* define a taxonomy of techniques for collecting data about developers involved in a software project. For our experiments, we adopt what they refer to as a *third degree approach*. In other words, we analyze work artefacts in an attempt to uncover information about responsibilities of software developers of a system. The inputs of our analysis are: (1) source code repository log information (2) source code and (3) execution traces of feature behavior. Our approach makes use of a distribution map-like visualization [Ducasse *et al.*, 2006a] to represent structural and feature perspectives of developer responsibilities.

Girba *et al.* describe a technique to define code ownership based on data extracted from CVS logs

CHAPTER 8. EXTRACTING DEVELOPER ROLES WITH FEATURE ANALYSIS

of a project [Gîrba et al., 2005a]. The technique is based on the assumption that the developer of a line of code is the most knowledgeable about that line of code. We assume that a developer owns a line of code, if he was the last one that committed a change to that line. Based on this assumption, we define the owner of a piece of code as being the developer that owns the most lines of that piece of code.

We adopt the definition of file ownership proposed by Girba et al. as the percentage of lines owned by a developer in a file. And the overall owner of a file is the developer that owns the most lines of code [Gîrba et al., 2005a].

Let $own_{f_n}^\alpha$ be the percentage of lines in revision f_n owned by author α. Given the file size s_{f_n}, and both the author α_{f_n} that committed the change and a_{f_n} the number of lines he added, ownership is defined as:

$$own_{f_0}^\alpha := \begin{cases} 1, & \alpha = \alpha_{f_0} \\ 0, & else \end{cases}$$

$$own_{f_n}^\alpha := own_{f_{n-1}}^\alpha \frac{s_{f_n} - a_{f_n}}{s_{f_n}} + \begin{cases} \frac{a_{f_n}}{s_{f_n}}, & \alpha = \alpha_{f_n} \\ 0, & else \end{cases}$$

In the definition we assume that the removed lines r_{f_n} are evenly distributed over the ownership of the preceding owners of f_{n-1}.

As CVS is a file-based repository, strictly speaking ownership is calculated for files. However, for our experiments, we assume a one-to-one mapping between files and classes. We exploit the fact that the package structure in Java reflects the physical file structure and use this to determine which class maps to which file.

8.3 Modeling Developers in Dynamix

Figure 8.1 (p.131) shows how we extend Dynamix with *Developer* and *Team* (*i.e.*, groups of developers) entities and establish ownership relationships between developers and classes. We exploit existing relationships of Dynamix to determine which developer or team of developers *owns* which features. We model the relationships between *Developer* and *Feature* entities explicitly with the *FeatureDeveloperAssociation* entity. Thus, we enrich Dynamix with knowledge of a system's developers. We reason about the roles of developers in structural groups (subsystems and packages) and dynamic groupings (features) of a system.

8.3. MODELING DEVELOPERS IN DYNAMIX

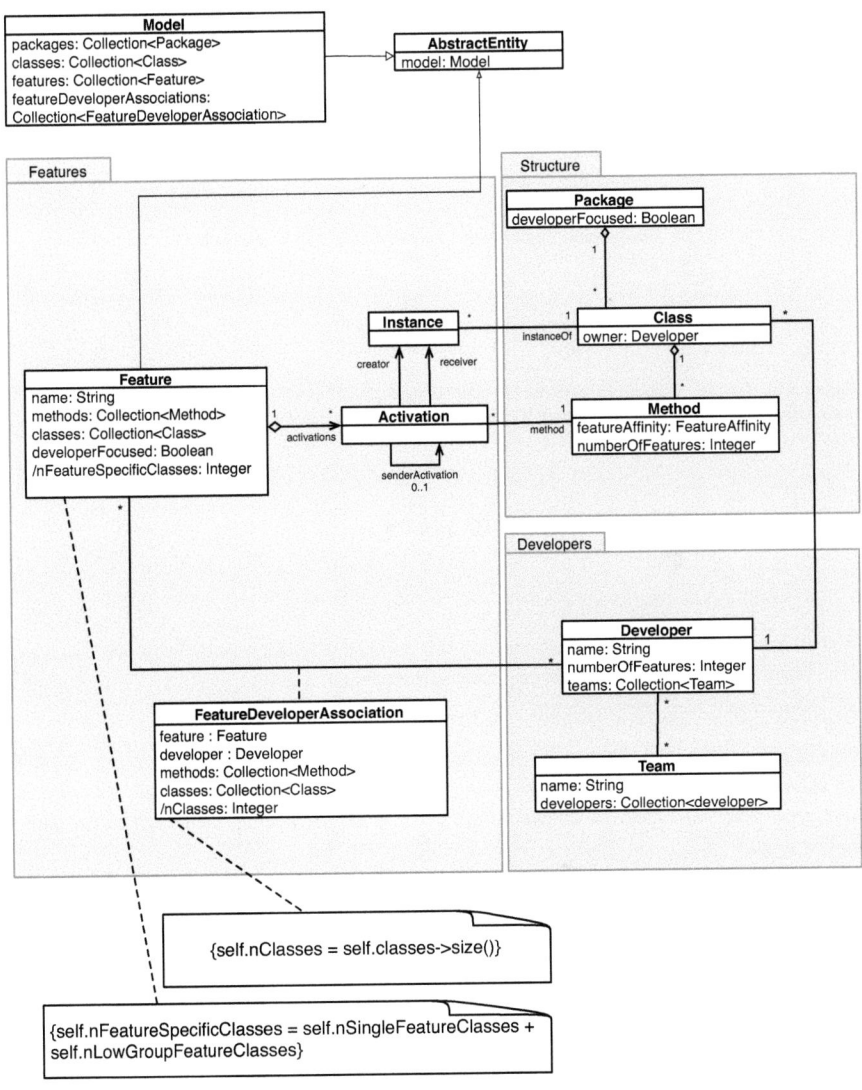

Figure 8.1: We extend Dynamix with Developer and Team and establish *ownership* relationships between developers and classes.

CHAPTER 8. EXTRACTING DEVELOPER ROLES WITH FEATURE ANALYSIS

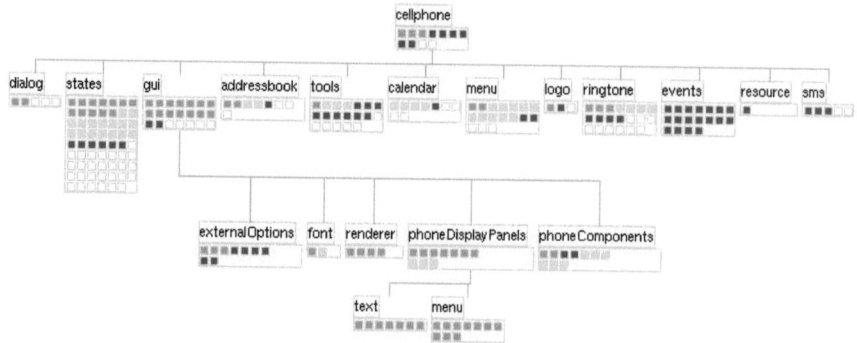

Figure 8.2: Package Owner of the PhoneSimulator-1 case study showing a package hierarchy view of the source code. We show the classes of each package, colored according to the developer that owns the classes.

8.4 Structural and Dynamic Views

We base our analysis on visual representations of a system that reflect roles of developers on classes of a system. We define both static and dynamic perspectives of a system.

We use static analysis to obtain a structural model of the source code of a system and represent the classes as static groupings in terms of the packages in which they are defined. We map the developer ownership which we compute from CVS on classes and represent each owner with a unique color.

Figure 8.2 (p.132) shows the package hierarchy extracted from one of our case studies: the large boxes represent packages and are arranged in a tree, while the small boxes represent classes and are colored by owner. This view reveals a developer's perspective of a system structure. We detect packages, where there is only one responsible developer, or one main responsible developer (*i.e.*, a developer owns most of the classes in a package). We refer to these packages as *developer-focused packages*. On the other hand, there are packages with classes owned by many developers. One goal of our analysis is to determine if the developers adopted a developement strategy reflecting a structural division of responsibilities (on a package boundary) while developing a system.

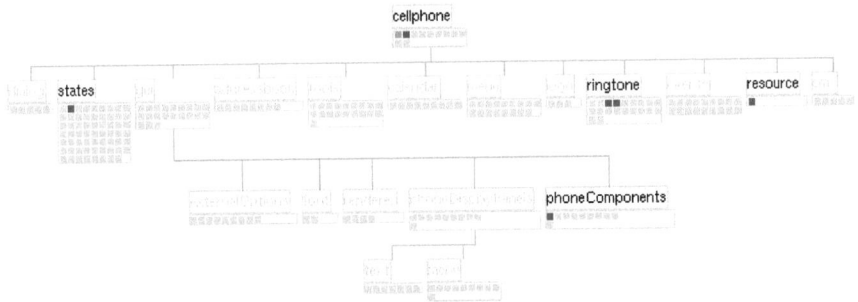

Figure 8.3: Phone Simulator Project: Example of a Package Hierarchy View highlighting packages and classes specific to the *Play Ringtone* Feature, colored by owner (PhoneSimulator-1)

8.5 Feature Ownership Analysis

Our goal is to analyze whether the division of developer responsibilities in a team was influenced directly by *feature* requirements or not. We complement a structural perspective (package hierarchy view), by obtaining feature views of a system. We achieve this by applying our feature-centric analysis to exploit relationships between features and classes. We focus our attention on classes that are either *single-feature* or *low-group-feature*, and refer to them collectively as *feature-specific* functionality.

We establish developer responsibilities with respect to features by identifying which developers own *feature-specific* classes. For example, in Figure 8.3 (p.133), we highlight classes that participate in a feature by the owner of a class. All classes that are not specific to a feature are colored gray.

A high proportion of *developer-focused features* may indicates that developers adopted a developer strategy that reflected a feature perspective of responsibilities (on a feature boundary) while developing a system.

8.5.1 A Collaboration View of Developer Teams responsible for Features

Features are implemented by one or more developers. To understand how developers collaborate to develop features, we extract and model teams of developers and relationships between teams. We define a *feature team* to be a set of owners of classes of a *feature view*. A feature team models collaborations between developers to develop a feature.

Typically developers, or teams of developers are responsible for one or more features in a system.

CHAPTER 8. EXTRACTING DEVELOPER ROLES WITH FEATURE ANALYSIS

```
context Feature
  def: developers: Collection = self.model.featureDeveloperAssociations->
    collect( fd | fd.feature = self)

context Feature
  def: maxNumberOfClassesOwnedByOneOwner : Integer =
    self.developers->sortedBy(self.developers.nClasses).first()

context Feature
  def developerFocused: Boolean =
    self.maxNumberOfClassesOwnedByOneOwned > self.nFeatureSpecificClasses / 2
```

Figure 8.4: OCL specification for the developerFocused attribute of a Feature Enttity.

Once we have extracted which developers are responsible for features as teams, we can represent the relationship between developer teams in a partial order graph. Each node of the graph represents a team (one or more developers) and contains one or more feature views. A team of developers may represent a subset of another team. Our graph models the partial order of teams.

Figure 8.5 (p.137) shows an example from one of our case studies. Each large rectangle represents a team formed by one or more developers. The graph shows responsibilities of a developer and possible collaborations between developers with respect to a set of features we traced. Inside the developer collaboration rectangle, we represent each feature as a grouping of *feature-specific* classes. As with the package view, classes are colored according to owners. For example, the top box represents a team that includes the red, blue, cyan and green developers and the one on the bottom is a team formed by the red and blue developers. The team shown at the bottom of the graph worked on two features, namely the *viewHelp* and *viewAbout* features.

8.5.2 Developer-focused Features

As with our structural perspective, we define a Feature to be *developer-focused* if a high proportion of its *feature specific* classes are owned by one developer (*i.e.*, more than half of the feature specific classes). Thus, we assume that the existence of *developer-focused* features implies a feature-based development strategy was adopted during the development of a system. For this analysis, we define a *developer-focused* feature to be one where more than 50% of the classes are owned by one developer. We provide an OCL definition for the *developerFocused* attribute of our *Feature* entity in Figure 8.4 (p.134).

8.6 Case Study 1: Student Team Projects

To validate our technique, we applied it to five student team projects (each of approximately 200 classes). Each team consisted of four students working over a time span of four months as part of their course work. The applications were developed in Java. CVS [1] was used as a source code repository. The goal of these projects was to implement a cell phone simulator.

In this section, we report on our findings for two of these projects. We refer to the projects as PhoneSimulator-1 and PhoneSimulator-2. In all cases the system requirements for the project were defined in terms of user stories.

Our motivation for choosing these projects was: (1) we have access to the CVS repository to obtain information we need to calculate ownership of files, (2) the resulting systems are the result of team effort, and (3) our approach is a heuristic approach and we require developer knowledge to validate our results.

8.6.1 Experimental Setup

We outline our approach to analyzing team projects.

- For each system, we extract a structural model of source code.
- We identify the features of these systems by associating them with the *user-triggerable* actions accessible via their user interfaces. For each system, we instrumented the application using the JIP profiler [2] and capture individual traces of runtime behavior. We resolve traces and obtain a Dynamix model.
- We process a CVS log information for each application and compute file ownership. We map file ownership to class ownership, and for each system, we generate (1) a *Package Owner* view for the entire system only highlighting feature-specific classes, and (2) a *Team Collaboration* view showing how developers collaborated to develop features (as Figure 8.5).
- We drive our analysis by addressing the questions we identified in the introduction of this chapter (see Section 8.1 (p.128)). We validate our findings with the development team members.

---

[1] http://www.cvshome.org
[2] http://jiprof.sourceforge.net/

8.6.2 PhoneSimulator-1 - Developer Analysis

This system consists of 251 classes and 20 packages and was developed by 4 developers. We traced 14 features and obtained a 70% coverage of classes.

Figure 8.2 (p.132) shows package owner view of a system. The classes are colored by owner (note white classes are those for which our technique did not establish an owner). We see from this view that there are packages with one responsible developer, packages with two responsible developers, and packages with multiple developers.

Our visualization reveals that the *red* developer is solely responsible for the packages gui.renderer, gui.PhoneDisplayPanels.text and gui.PhoneDisplayPanels.menu.dialog. The *blue* developer is solely responsible for the packages events, resource and sms.

We see 5 packages where the same three developers (red, cyan and blue) own classes. This pattern indicates a collaboration between these developers from a structural perspective.

The *green* developer owns only 8 classes in the system, distributed over three packages. Five of these classes are located in the gui::phoneComponents package.

Which developers or groups of developers are responsible for which features? Figure 8.3 (p.133) shows an example of a feature perspective of the system. Here we see feature-specific classes of the *playRingtone* feature in the context of the package hierarchy. The *blue* developer is the main developer of this feature as he owns 60% of the *feature-specific* classes.

In Figure 8.5 (p.137) we show a *collaboration view* based on the features of our model. The view establishes relationships between features and their responsible developers. Our visualization reveals that the *red* developer is the sole responsible for the *feature-specific* classes of three features, namely *selectDateAndTime*, *checkInbox* and *selectNewLogo*. The blue developer is solely responsible for *single-feature* classes of the features *switchOnPhone*, *dialUser* and *hangUpCall*.

Figure 8.5 (p.137) also reveals that both the *red* and *blue* developers are active in all of the features. Thus our analysis suggests that from a domain knowledge perspective, the *blue* and *red* developers have a wider knowledge of the features than the *cyan* and *green* developers.

Do developers develop features or functional blocks? Our analysis of the system indicates that the development strategy corresponds more closely with structural divisions in the system, namely package boundaries rather than a features perspective. We checked our findings with the developers of PhoneSimulator-1. They confirmed that initially they adopted a development strategy based on the model-view-controller pattern. The *red* developer was responsible for the *view* classes and the *cyan* and *blue* developers were responsible for the model and controller classes. The *green* developer

8.6. CASE STUDY 1: STUDENT TEAM PROJECTS

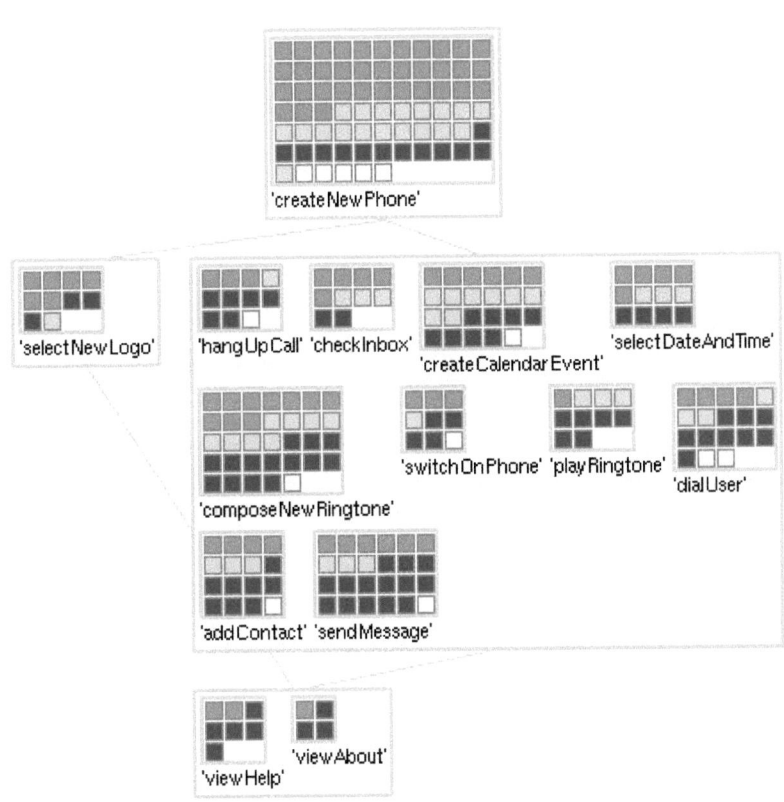

Figure 8.5: Team Collaboration view from the PhoneSimulator-1 System. The small squares represent classes (colored by owner), the medium rectangles represent features and the large rectangle represent teams of developers who collaborated to develop the features.

CHAPTER 8. EXTRACTING DEVELOPER ROLES WITH FEATURE ANALYSIS

was responsible for the creation of images used by the application and classes that manipulated these images. Thus, the green developer *touches* only two packages of the system. Once the first iteration of the system was completed, the developers adopted a *user-story* or *feature* development strategy. In other words, the responsibility for developing new features (*e.g., playRingTone*) was typically assigned to one or two developers. They confirmed our finding that the *blue* developer was responsible for developing the *playRingTone* feature (Figure 8.3 (p.133)).

8.6.3 PhoneSimulator-2

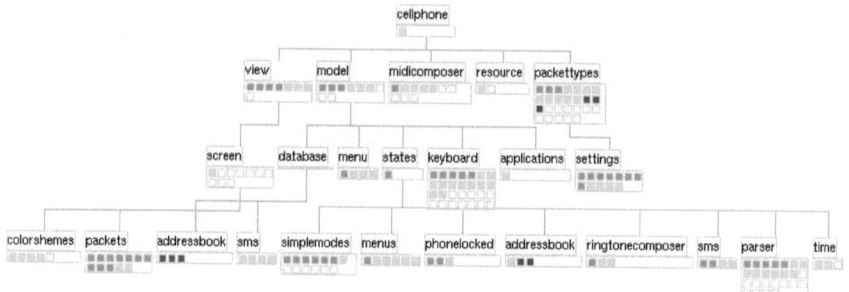

Figure 8.6: Package Owner (PhoneSimulator-2)

This system consists of 196 classes and 25 packages and was developed by 4 developers. We traced 10 features and obtained a 68% coverage of classes.

Figure 8.6 (p.138) shows the package owner view of the system for PhoneSimulator-2. From this view, we detect 5 packages where only the *cyan* developer is active. However, these packages contain only very few classes. Although the team consisted of 4 developers, the visualization reveals that only three of the developers actually own classes.

Our visualizations reveal that the *cyan* developer and the *red* developer are the key developers of this system. The *blue* developer is exclusively responsible for the package model::database::addressbook.

Which developers or groups of developers are responsible for which features? Figure 8.7 (p.139) shows the team feature view of the system. We see that the *cyan* and *red* developers are responsible for all of the features that we traced. We also see that the blue user shares responsibility for the *addContact* and *newCellphone* features. This feature is related to the addressbook subsystem of the application, for which the blue developer is solely responsible.

8.6. CASE STUDY 1: STUDENT TEAM PROJECTS

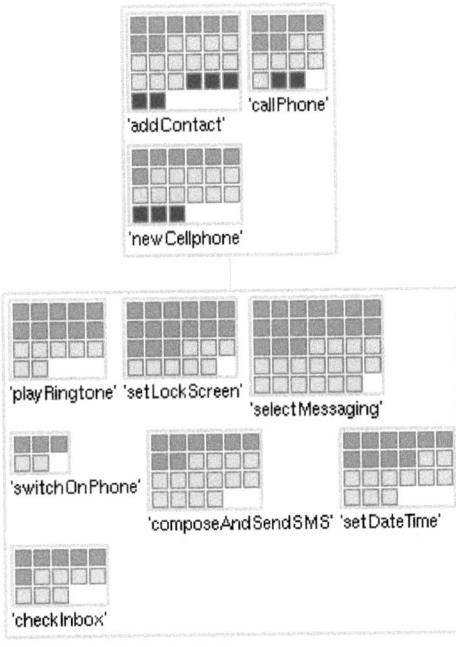

Figure 8.7: Developer Collaborations (PhoneSimulator-2)

CHAPTER 8. EXTRACTING DEVELOPER ROLES WITH FEATURE ANALYSIS

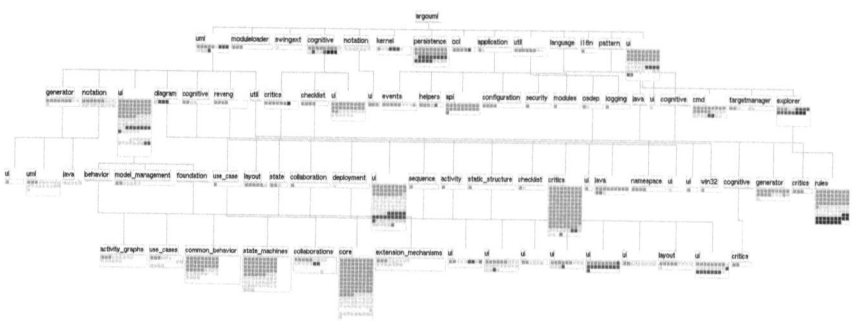

Figure 8.8: Package Hierarchy View of the argoUML system showing classes colored by owner

Do developers develop features or functional blocks? We detect that there are structural divisions of responsibilites (*e.g.*, the addressbook package). However, the developers seem to be working in pairs to develop individual packages. From our visual analysis of the *package hierarchy* and *team collaboration* views, we see that the main developer (cyan) is clearly the developer with most responsibility from a structural and features perspective of the system. Discussions with students of the second team confirmed our findings.

8.7 Case Study 2: ArgoUML Case Study

To test the scalability of our technique, we applied it to ArgoUML, an open source UML modeling application implemented in Java. We chose ArgoUML because: (1) we have access to developer knowledge in the documentation of ArgoUML to validate our results, (2) it is open source and we have access to the CVS repository to obtain the information we need to calculate our ownership measurement of files, and (3) it has been used by us in Chapter 4 (p.43), and by other researchers as a reverse engineering case study.

We focus on the core of the application, (*i.e.*, we exclude library classes and plugin features). We parsed the source code and obtained a model consisting of 2075 classes. To narrow the scope of our investigation we filtered out the classes in the library org.tigris that provide GUI classes and Java library classes. This resulted in 1501 classes.

We exercised 11 features by interacting with the user interface and traced each feature individually. We achieved a coverage of 58% of the classes.

Figure 8.8 (p.140) shows a package owner view of the system. There are 83 packages in total. 13

8.7. CASE STUDY 2: ARGOUML CASE STUDY

packages are owned solely by the *red* developer and four packages owned soley by the *cyan* developer. The remaining 66 packages are owned predominantly by the *red* developer. Thus, our analysis reveals that a subsystem is predominantly developed by one developer. There is structural division of responsibilities between the *red* and *cyan* developers on a package boundary.

Which developers or groups of developers are responsible for which features? We identified 11 teams of collaborating developers, shown in Figure 8.9 (p.142). Each team is responsible for one or two features. There is only one feature *browsecritique* where only one developer (*cyan*) is responsible for all classes of a feature. For all other features, we see that three or more developers are responsible for the classes of that feature.

From Figure 8.9 (p.142) we see that the *red* developer is predominantly responsible (*i.e.,* owns 80% of the classes) for the *generateCodeforClass* feature. Figure 8.10 (p.143) shows this feature in the context of a package hierarchy view of the system. The *feature-specific* classes crosscut 9 of the packages of ArgoUML.

Figure 8.9 (p.142) also reveals that the *red* developer is also predominantly responsible (*i.e.,* owns 65% of the classes) for the *startup* feature. Figure 8.11 (p.143) shows this feature in the context of the package hierarchy of the system. The *feature-specific* classes crosscut 37 of the packages of ArgoUML. The startup feature is responsible for initializing the application.

Our analysis also reveals that the *cyan* developer is also predominantly responsible for the importXMI and exportXMI features (*i.e.,* owns 50% of the classes). In both cases *feature-specific* classes crosscut the same 5 packages of ArgoUML.

Do developers develop features or functional blocks? We detect both structural and feature divisions of responsibilities. Of the 10 distinct developers we detect by applying our ownership measurement, our visual analysis reveals that there are two main developers (*red* and *cyan*). We verified that these two developers correspond to the main developers of ArgoUML. We detect that the *red* developer is responsible for most of the classes in the system and owns most of the packages. He is predominately responsible for most (80%) of the features we traced. The *cyan* developer's responsibilities correspond to both package and feature boundaries. Our results show that in the case of ArgoUML, it is difficult to deduce whether a developer strategy aligns with a structural or a feature perspective, as the responsibilitiy for classes of the application is dominated by two main developers. Despite this, our results reveal the existence of both development strategies.

CHAPTER 8. EXTRACTING DEVELOPER ROLES WITH FEATURE ANALYSIS

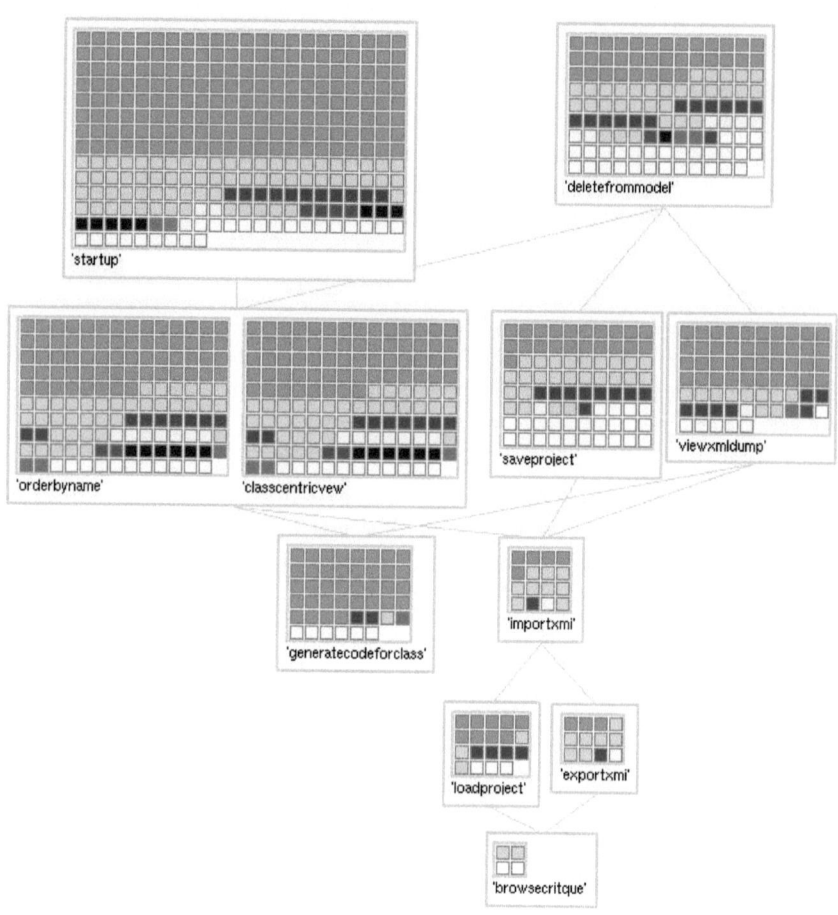

Figure 8.9: Team Collaboration of ArgoUML showing relationships between Teams

8.7. CASE STUDY 2: ARGOUML CASE STUDY

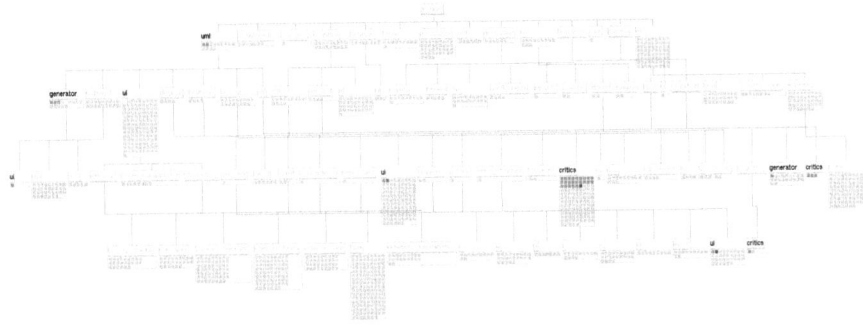

Figure 8.10: ArgoUML Generate Code For Class Feature

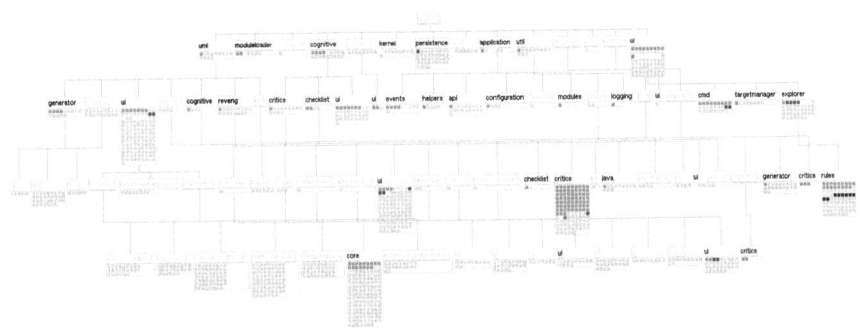

Figure 8.11: ArgoUML Startup Feature

8.8 Discussion

The Ownership Measurement. We chose to use an ownership measurement calculated by analyzing CVS log data. This solution is therefore coupled to the CVS tool. However, we have encapsulated the repository dependent code, thus minimizing the required effort to adapt our solution to another repository (*e.g.,* Subversion or Clearcase) if required.

Our validation revealed a flaw in our ownership measurement. In discussion with developers of PhoneSumulator-1 we discovered that the *red* developer appears to own a large proportion of the classes. This is an incorrect conclusion as the *red* developer restructured a large proportion of the classes in response to an automatic style checker flagging long methods. As a result of this editing, our ownership calculation assigns him as owner of these classes. Thus, the ownership measurement does not reveal who really developed the code in this case.

Classes without owners. Our ownership of classes is based on the assumption that there is a one-to-one relationship between classes and files. This is not true in the case of the Java case studies we chose. A file may contain more than one class, or there may be inner classes. To tackle this problem, we would need to model a file entity and by statically analyzing the files we could extract the one-to-many relationship between a file and classes.

Team definition. For this analysis, we extracted our definition of a team from the ownership information of feature-specific classes of features. There are alternative ways to define a team based on structural collaborations. We plan to investigate the definition of teams based on extracting the developer collaborations in more detail in the future. Our visualization of a package hierarchy of a system reveals that developers tend to develop a system from a package perspective. The feature teams reveal how developers collaborate when implementing code that is specific to one feature. In our case studies, we see that one or two developers were responsible for implementing a feature.

The Roles of Software Developers. Our technique focuses exclusively on software development activities. It excludes activities such as configuration management, creation of resources (*e.g.,* image files), build and release management. These are all relevant activities within a development project. Thus, the picture we obtain of a developer is incomplete.

8.9 Related Work

Researchers in the field of reverse engineering and system comprehension are becoming aware of the importance of analyzing the role of the developer and exploiting new sources of data such as source code repositories to understand software systems [Gîrba *et al.*, 2005a; Hassan and Holt, 2004;

8.9. RELATED WORK

Lethbridge et al., 2005; Wu et al., 2004]. Our main focus with this work is to define a reverse-engineering approach that exploits developer information of a system's features.

Lethbridge et al. define a taxonomy of data collection techniques to obtain information about the roles of software engineers during the development of a project [Lethbridge et al., 2005]. Their work highlights the growing awareness of this source of information in the field of reverse engineering and system comprehension.

Eick et al. used data generated from a change management system to better understand how communication occurs in a globally distributed software development [Eick et al., 2001]. They used several modeling techniques to understand the relationship between the modification request interval and other variables including the number of people involved, the size of the change, and the distributed nature of the group, working on the change.

Xiaomin Wu et al. describe a tool to visualize [Wu et al., 2004] the change log information to provide an overview of the active places in the system as well as of the author activities. They display measurements like the number of times an author changed a file, or the date of the last commit.

Chuah and Eick proposed three visualizations for comparing and correlating different evolution information like the number of lines added, the errors recorded between versions, number of people working etc. [Chuah and Eick, 1998].

Zimmerman et al. aimed to provide a mechanism to warn developers about the correlation of changes between functions. The authors placed their analysis at the level of entities in the meta-model (*e.g.,* methods) [Zimmermann et al., 2004]. The same authors defined a measure of coupling based on co-changes [Zimmermann et al., 2003].

Anvik et al. [Anvik et al., 2006] describe a semi-automatic technique to assign bug reports to developers. They base their analysis on data extracted from the bug repository of a software development project and use a machine learning algorithm to support the assignment of bugs to the appropriate developer. One major contribution of their work is that they identify the problem of tracing the correct developer to address a given bug report.

Canfora et al. [Canfora and Cerulo, 2006] also consider the problem of assigning change requests to developers of open source projects. They design an approach to assign change requests to developers based on analyzing the previous assignment history of the change requests.

The work of Anvik et al. and Canfora et al. identifies a motivation for our technique of associating developers to features.

Our main focus was to define a reverse engineering approach that considers the roles of developers in the context of both static and dynamic views of the system.

8.10 Summary

In this chapter, our goal was to analyze the roles of developers from both a structural and a feature perspective of a system. We extended Dynamix with developer information. We establish the relationships between classes and developers and exploit the existing relationships expressed in our model to associate the features to individual developers or teams of developers. In particular we addressed the questions:

1. *Which groups of developers are responsible for which features?* We exploited our feature perspective to identify teams of developers responsible for features. We define a team collaboration based on a partial ordering of teams, and we reveal which developers and teams of developers are responsible for which features.

2. *Do developers develop features or do they develop functional blocks?* Our visualizations of a package hierarchy showing owners of classes reveal which developers are responsible for which classes. This view shows structural groupings of classes as packages. Our analysis of student projects revealed that in these cases, the developers distributed responsibility according to package boundaries. Different developers implement specialized functionalities such as XML handling or database interaction. The boundaries of model-view-controller are also split between different developers. We also discovered, that for some features, a developer strategy reflecting feature boundaries was adopted when new features were added.

The main contributions of our approach are:

— We identify a novel way of analyzing roles of developers with respect to features of a system.

— We describe a technique to extract and visualize static and dynamic views of relationships between developers and structural packages and feature views.

— We extract and model collaborations between developers and teams of developers based on their ownerships of classes of features.

— We define Developer and Team entities for the Dynamix meta-model.

Chapter 9

Lessons Learned: a Retrospective

In this chapter, we take a step back to examine how we addressed the problem of exploiting feature knowledge in reverse engineering. When we started our analysis work, our review of the state-of-the-art revealed that although several researchers had addressed the problem of locating the parts of source code that implemented features, the notion of a feature in a reverse engineering and system comprehension context had not yet been fully exploited. Our primary focus was to take up this challenge. We recognized that by establishing the links between domain knowledge abstractions (*i.e.*, features) and the implemented system, we could exploit these links in reverse engineering analysis, thus supporting system comprehension throughout a system's life-cycle.

In this dissertation, we described our feature-centric analysis and our Dynamix meta-model. In this chapter we present some of the challenges we tackled along the way. We review both our high level analysis decisions and low level technology decisions.

Structure of the chapter. In the next section we take a look at the definitions and underlying mechanisms of our work. In Section 9.2 (p.150) we discuss our research focus and our choice of experiments. We look in detail at some of the aspects of our feature-centric analysis in Section 9.3 (p.151), and we summarize in Section 9.4 (p.152).

9.1 Definition and Mechanisms

Researchers who undertake feature analysis are faced with the following issues:

Feature Definition. One of the first choices we were faced with was to define a *feature*. Our definition was influenced on the one hand, by *Feature Identification* approaches, and on the

CHAPTER 9. LESSONS LEARNED: A RETROSPECTIVE

other hand, by our research goal of exploiting domain knowledge in reverse engineering. We adopted the definition of a feature as a unit of observable behavior triggered by the user [Eisenbarth *et al.*, 2003]. However, our approach does not exclude other definitions. For example, non-observable activities of a system such as house-keeping tasks can also be described as features.

One-to-One Mapping between Features and Traces. For the experiments described in this dissertation, we assume a one-to-one mapping between feature-traces and features. This is a simplification of reality, as the execution path of a feature varies depending on the combination of user inputs when it is triggered. Some researchers [Eisenbarth *et al.*, 2003], define a many-to-many relationship between traces and features, so that they can capture multiple execution paths through a feature. However, extending our representation of a feature in Dynamix to model multiple execution paths would require only a minor extension to express a many-to-one relationship between feature traces and features.

Multi-Threaded Applications. For our experimentation and feature definition, our model does not currently take multi-threading into consideration. Once again extending our representation of a feature in Dynamix to incorporate multiple threads of execution is would require only a minor extension to express a many-to-one relationship between threads and features.

Similar Features. Our feature-centric analysis revealed that certain features were very similar and perhaps could be considered as variations of the same canonical feature (*e.g.*, addPage, copyPage of our SmallWiki case study). The recent work of Kothari *et al.* addresses this by identifying that software systems are characterized by a set of canonical features [Kothari *et al.*, 2006]. In their approach, they treat system behavior as a distinct feature only when it is significantly different from a set of features that have been already traced.

Tracing. When tracing an application, we needed to make the decision about what type of behavioral data we should capture. For our first experiments, we traced applications at the level of message sends (*i.e.*, activations). However for our hot spot analysis approach described in Chapter 7 (p.109), we performed a more fine-grained analysis of the runtime behavior, so it was essential that the traces we captured contained information about the sender and receiver instance information so that we could associate activations with objects. We did not perform experiments that required tracing at the level of state accesses. However, Dynamix could easily be extended to include this information. Furthermore, we identify that this level of detail would be useful for correlating static measurements (*e.g.*, lines of code) and dynamic analysis measurements (*e.g.*, statements executed).

Trace Collection. The means of instrumenting an application is language dependent. To obtain traces from SmallWiki and Moose applications, we use a code instrumenting technique for Smalltalk based on method wrappers [Brant *et al.*, 1998]. In a previous experiment with Java

9.1. DEFINITION AND MECHANISMS

applications [Kuhn et al., 2005b], we used the *Ejp (Extensible Java Profiler)* [Vauclair, 2003] based on the Java Virtual Machine Profiler Interface (JVMPI). Finally, for a later experiment we developed a profiler, which we call *J-WireTap* which is built on the Jip profiler, so that we could control the data collected by the tracer and use a format so that we could load the trace into our **DynaMoose** tool for analysis. We used *J-WireTap* for our ArgoUML and Phone-Simulator case studies [Greevy et al., 2007]. For our Pier experiment, we used the Object Flow Tracer Tool for Squeak [Lienhard et al., 2006]. As long as the traces obtained from the system under analysis contain message send events and instance information, our approach will work for any object oriented language. We discuss the challenges of extracting traces for dynamic analysis in more detail in another work [Denker et al., 2006].

Recall. A limitation of our approach is that it is difficult to calculate precison and recall for our results. This is due to the nature of feature analysis. We perform feature analysis to discover which source artefacts are relevant to a feature. It is the well-known fact that dynamic analysis is not exhaustive, as all possible paths of execution are not exercised [Ball, 1999]. Therefore, an analysis of features always has to be understood in the context of the actual execution. While this is a difficulty, at the same time it is a key characteristic as running a feature can be related directly to internal program behavior.

Selective Instrumentation. For some of our experiments, we performed a selective instrumentation of a system to limit the amount of dynamic information generated; we use our knowledge of an application to determine what is relevant for a particular feature. Our instrumentation only included classes from the namespace or packages of the application under investigation and excluded library calls. This resulted in incomplete traces, but was sufficient to focus on the parts of the code that have been implemented specifically for the application. In the Moose case study described in Chapter 5 (p.67)), we did not instrument every Moose namespace as we have a good knowledge of the application and omitted the parts which we already knew were irrelevant for the features we investigated.

Distinct Traces or Marked Traces. In our early experiments, we extracted individual traces to represent the features. Our analysis focused on the relationships between features and the source artefacts (classes and methods). However, when we considered analyzing the runtime behavioral entities (objects) we realized that one trace of multiple features was more complete than single traces, as we preserve information about how features share usage of objects at runtime. This information is essential for analyzing runtime relationships between features.

CHAPTER 9. LESSONS LEARNED: A RETROSPECTIVE

9.2 Focus of Analysis

Choice of Case Study. For our early experiments we focused on SmallWiki and Moose as we had direct access to developer knowledge to validate our results. In particular, for our evolution experiments [Greevy and Ducasse, 2005b; Greevy *et al.*, 2006a], we needed access to multiple versions. For later experiments, in particular the experiment where we analyze team work of developers with respect to features [Greevy *et al.*, 2007], we needed to experiment with a system that had been developed in a team. Moreover, as we mine CVS repository data, we needed access to an application's project repository.

Choice of Experiments. One of our initial research goals was to study the evolvability of object-oriented systems. A key focus in this dissertation was on the analysis of how features evolve and how feature knowledge helps interpret changes.

A Collaborative Environment. We emphasize the value of a collaborative reverse engineering and reengineering environment. This enables researchers to share underlying mechanisms and results and to profit from the synergies and commonalities of each others work. We outline our environment in Appendix C (p.167). By making the Dynamix meta-model and tool environment accessible, we open up the possibility for other researchers to adopt our model and build on it for their own particular research goals.

Visualizations. A key aspect of our analysis is the use of visualizations. Most of our visualizations are simple graphs or distribution map-like visual representations of compact feature views [Ducasse *et al.*, 2006a], built using the Mondrian tool [Meyer *et al.*, 2006]. These visualizations are interactive, thus providing the scope to analyze results at different levels of detail [M.-A. D. Storey and Michaud, 2001]. In our visual feature hot spot analysis [Greevy *et al.*, 2006b], we adopted a 3D approach that is based on a 3D extension to CodeCrawler. Following this direction, we quickly realized that 3D visualization for software engineering is a controversial topic. Despite this, we believe that there is a lot of scope for further work in 3D visualization of dynamic behavior.

Validation. The validation of our techniques relies on developer knowledge. In a reverse engineering context, developer knowledge is invaluable to confirm and interpret the results of our experiments. However, to validate the general usefulness of the techniques for a software engineer in a development environment, we believe there is a lot of scope to perform empirical studies of a quantitative and qualitative nature. Such experiments are essential to assess how software engineers perceive a features perspective in the context of their work.

9.3 Aspects of Feature Analysis

Many of the topics we discuss here are as a result of our experience with applying feature-centric analysis on the case studies.

On the Stability of Feature Affinity. Our Feature Affinity measurement provides a means of interpreting the role of a class based on the results of exercising a set of features. This measurement is dependent on the number of features exercised and the type of features traced. If two features with similar functionality are executed, classes that are specific to these features will be assigned the Feature Affinity level *low group*. In our evolution experiments (Chapter 5 (p.67), Chapter 6 (p.87)), we chose to exercise the same set of features for each version. Thus, we expect that Feature Affinity levels of a source artefact under these circumstances should remain the same. Our technique detected changes due to modifications in the code and thus supports the software engineer in interpreting the changes in the context of the features that have been exercised.

On Levels of Granularity of Feature Views and Scalability. In many of our experiments, we selected classes as a unit of granularity. For a more coarse-grained overview of a system features, for example when considering large systems, we could select a package as the unit of granularity. During our experimentation with the SmallWiki case study in Chapter 6 (p.87), analysis of the system's structural models revealed that the number of packages increased from 13 to 43 in the main development track. We were interested to see which features were now using functionality of the new packages. Thus we extracted feature views as groups of packages and applied history measurements to compute additions in the number of characterized packages participating in a feature. Our results revealed that 7 of the new packages were referenced by the *components* feature. Thus, by analyzing feature views of packages we obtained a coarse-grained view of which features are affected by the addition of new packages in the system and what type of functionality is provided by the packages (*i.e.,* single feature, low group, high group or infrastructural).

In the same way, we obtained a more fine-grained analysis by extracting feature views as sets of methods. We applied our measurements to reveal how a feature view changes with respect to its participating methods. The problem of scalability may be addressed by adopting an iterative approach to feature definition and by selecting a more coarse-grained feature view.

On Coverage. Our feature analysis approach does not achieve 100% coverage of the system. For the purpose of feature location, complete coverage of a system is not necessary [Wilde and Scully, 1995]. Wilde and Scully's *Software Reconnaissance* technique, and other approaches based on this technique, do not locate all the code associated with a feature, but provide good starting points for the software maintainer to understand the implementation of a feature

[Wilde and Scully, 1995].

An Iterative Approach. It is by performing feature analysis in the first place that we determine which features are related to source artefacts and how similar they are. Thus, obtaining the best feature definition for an analysis is based on the analysis itself. This clearly suggests an iterative approach to feature definition based on the findings of feature analysis.

9.4 Summary

In this chapter we have outlined the lessons we have learned with respect to undertaking feature-centric reverse engineering. We summarized the definitions and mechanisms we adopted, and our reasons for the descisions we made. We reiterated the focus of our analysis. Finally we highlighted and discussed aspects of feature analysis and variations.

Chapter 10

Conclusions

To fully exploit features in reverse engineering, we need to treat features as primary units of analysis. We identified the research goals of this dissertation as follows: (1) to enrich reverse engineering analysis techniques that extract structural views of a system with semantic knowledge about roles of source artefacts in features of a system, and (2) to reason about a system in terms of features themselves and relationships between features.

Our solution is a feature-centric analysis that extracts complementary, feature-enriched views of a system. We extract and model features as explicit entities and reason about a system in terms of these entities. We describe Dynamix, a meta-model that expresses the execution entities of feature behavior and their relationships. Furthermore our meta-model expresses the relationships between the execution entities and a structural model of source code. A key element of our analysis is to combine static and dynamic views of a system.

We have validated our work by applying our approach on software systems of varying size and complexity. To highlight the language independence of our approach, we selected case studies implemented in different object-oriented languages (VisualWorks Smalltalk, Squeak and Java).

CHAPTER 10. CONCLUSIONS

We have presented several feature-enriched, reverse engineering analyses:

Three perspectives of feature centric analysis. We applied feature centric analysis on two software systems, Pier (implemented in Squeak), and ArgoUML (implemented in Java):

— *Feature Perspective.* We reasoned about a system in terms of its features. The level of granularity chosen for our experiments was the class. We presented an interactive visualization of compact feature views to show the distribution of classes over the features. Our Feature Affinity measurement showed relevance of classes in the context of compact feature views. We distinguished between classes specific to one feature, a small group of features, a large group of features, or all of the features we traced. Our case studies showed that this perspective successfully identified classes relevant to a feature. Our approach presents a software engineer a means to understand a system in terms of its features.

— *Structural Perspective* We focussed on source artefacts enriched with semantic knowledge about their roles in features. When a source artefact (*e.g.*, a class) needs to be modified, a software engineer is aware that a change to an *infrastructural* class may affect many of the features of the system. Similarly, if a class is assigned a *single feature* value, it represents a good starting point for understanding a particular feature.

— *Feature Relationship Perspective.* We highlighted the role of feature relationships in system comprehension. We defined static relationships based on the degree of overlap of source artefacts. We introduced a taxonomy to describe relationships (*i.e.*, when two features share a high proportion of the source artefacts, we say that they are *tightly related*). We also described dynamic relationships of features, based on the number of instances that are accessed by one feature, but created by other features. We used graph visualizations to depict these dependencies.

Evolution: A Structural Perspective. We show how our feature-centric analysis enriches an evolution analysis of a system. Our approach combines both *history analysis* and *version analysis* techniques. We defined history measurements to measure how the roles of classes change with respect to the features of a system over a series of versions (*i.e.*, we analyzed the effect of time on the Feature Affinity property of classes). Our experiments revealed that this perspective highlighted places in the code that had changed. The feature context of the changes supported the interpretation of the changes.

Evolution: A Feature Perspective. Once again our approach combined a history-centric and version-centric analysis. We defined *history measurements* [Gîrba *et al.*, 2005b] to measure how features of a system change over a series of versions. We validated our approach by applying it to a problem where the development efforts of parallel development tracks needed to be reconciled. We showed that our features perspective successfully provided insights into the extent and intent of changes. Our feature view visualizations reveal candidate conflicting changes and duplicated effort.

Object-oriented dynamic information. With this analysis, we exploited object-oriented dynamic data such as object-instantiation and message sends between instances to understand runtime behavior of features and visualize features in 3D to detect *feature hotspots* (*i.e.,* areas of intense activity in features). We demonstrated the expressiveness of Dynamix to consider a more fine-grained representation of a feature than a compact feature view. We addressed the problem of large amounts of data by adopting a visual analysis approach.

Developer roles. We apply feature analysis to extract developer roles with respect to features. Our features perspective of a system introduces a novel way of considering the roles of developers in the implementation of a system.

10.1 Other Feature-Centric Research

We briefly outline other feature-centric research we have been involved in. This work is not covered in this dissertation:

Semantic analysis. Kuhn et al. developed an approach to detect similarities between features by applying semantic analysis to execution traces [Kuhn et al., 2005b]. With this technique we identified similar features using the feature traces to represent documents and method calls to represent the terms of the documents.

Features as Signal Traces. Kuhn and Greevy describe a novel representation of the *feature traces* in terms of a time series as a means of representing large amounts of data. We exploited some of the time series analysis toolkit to compare features and to establish relationships between features. We used our Feature Affinity measurement to extract parts of the traces that represent unique patterns of execution (*i.e.,* single feature) and common patterns [Kuhn and Greevy, 2006a; Kuhn and Greevy, 2006b].

Object Flow Analysis. Lienhard et al. analyzed the fine-grained dynamic relationships between features based on tracking object aliasing [Lienhard et al., 2007a; Lienhard et al., 2007b]. We extracted feature dependencies and associated context with the dependencies.

A Features Perspective in IDEs. Röthlisberger et al. [Röthlisberger et al., 2007] defined an extension to the IDE to provide an integrated a feature browser. The goal of a feature perspective is to support system maintenance by providing views of the methods that are exercised by a feature. In an ongoing work, they also empirically analysed the advantages of the feature browser for users. They also collected data on the user's subjective opinion of feature views enriched with our *featurecharacterization* measurement.

Higher Abstractions for Dynamic Analysis. In this work, Denker *et al.* argued for the need to adopt a higher level view of a software system, when considering abstracting runtime information [Denker *et al.*, 2006]. We identified the need to define an intermediate *behavioral* layer that provides access to reified runtime entities, so that developers of dynamic analysis techniques do not have to focus on low-level language specific details.

J-WireTap. We built an interactive Java profiler for extracting feature traces from Java applications and imported them for feature-centric analysis into our *DynaMoose* dynamic and feature analysis tool. We describe our analysis environment in more detail in Appendix C (p.167)

10.2 Future Work

Having defined a feature-centric analysis and a meta-model to represent feature entities and their relationships, we identify scope of further work in this area. We have established a foundation and defined a vocabulary. By doing so, we open new perspectives that lead to many ideas for further research. We list a few of the directions:

— *Fine-grained Analysis of Feature Traces.* Many of the analysis techniques, apart from the feature hot spot analysis technique described in Chapter 7 (p.109), manipulated a compact feature view as a representation of a feature. There is scope to perform a more fine-grained comparison of feature traces by considering of dynamic data such as sequence of execution of events or frequency of execution, or variations in messages due to parameters.

— *Feature Definition.* Execution paths are affected by inputs. Thus, we need to consider many-to-one and one-to-many relationships between traces and features. Thus, Dynamix could be adaped to express a more complex feature entity.

— *Units of Functionality.* Our analysis techniques revealed recurring patterns of execution within the execution traces of features. For example with the SmallWiki and Pier applications, we identified the recurring patterns of HTTP request response functionality and page rendering functionality. We identify the need to define abstractions to represent component functionalities of a feature that represent a smaller unit of granularity.

— *Feature Relationships.* We analyzed the relationships between features based on shared usage of source artefacts and shared object instances. We identify the scope to continue on this research direction, as feature relationships of a system's problem domain are crucial for understanding the business rules and constraints of a system. Often, in the case of legacy systems, the only reliable source of information regarding the business rules are in the application itself. However, as this information is not explicit in the source code, these constraints may be difficult to locate and interpret. Moreover, we identify scope to consider a temporal perspective of changing relationships between features over time.

— *Combining Dynamic and Static Metrics.* We identified as a result of our evolution analysis techniques that features provide semantic context for changes. However, we believe that there is scope to extend our feature-centric perspectives to incorporate static measurements. In the case of our evolution analysis approaches, we could correlate changes in static and dynamic views of a system.

— *Exploiting System Tests.* Some researchers have used test cases to exercise features of a system [Licata et al., 2003; Eisenberg and De Volder, 2005]. The problem with this is that many test cases are unit tests and do not exercise domain concepts, rather low-level developer concerns. In a previous work, we proposed a semi-automatic technique to compose unit tests into higher level tests [Gaelli et al., 2005; Gaelli, 2006]. We believe that a higher-level *feature* test should be an integral part of a software development life-cycle. To achieve this a framework similar to the xUnit Framework providing some means to compose unit tests would support the creation of feature tests [Beck and Gamma, 1998]. Furthermore, feature tests would formally establish the links between features specified at requirements analysis, and over the life-cycle of a system and a system source code. The goal of feature tests would be to provide the basis for generating execution traces that are treated as feature traces for feature-centric analysis.

— *Feature Analysis Integrated in the Development Environment.* We believe that reverse engineering techniques should be readily and easily accessible to the software engineer during the development lifecycle of a system. An iterative approach to software development may mean that even within the development life-cycle, the problem of understanding earlier iterations is an issue. A software engineer may be required to understand earlier iterations and identify where refactorings may be required to allow the addition of new features.

— *Feature Modeling.* This field of research focuses on the requirements phase of a system. We identify the need to exploit the terminology of Feature Modeling in a reverse engineering context. We need to bridge the gap between feature modeling and feature-centric reverse engineering.

Appendix A

Definitions

For general terms:

Reverse engineering is the process of analyzing a subject system to create representations of the system at a higher level of abstraction. [Chikofsky and Cross II, 1990]

An *entity* is something that has separate and distinct existence in objective or conceptual reality [Soanes, 2001].

For model, meta-model and measurement we use the following definitions:

A *model* is a simplification of a system built with an intended goal in mind. The model should be able to answer questions in place of the actual system [Bézivin and Gerbé, 2001].

A *meta-model* is a specification model for a class of systems under study where each system under study in the class is itself a valid model expressed in a certain modeling language [Seidewitz, 2003].

A *measurement* is a mapping from the empirical world to the formal, relational world. Consequently, a measure is the number assigned to an entity by this mapping to characterize an attribute [Fenton and Pfleeger, 1996].

For features we use the following definitions:

A *feature* is a realized functional requirement of a system. A feature is an observable unit of behavior of a system triggered by the user [Eisenbarth *et al.*, 2003].

There are many definitions for the word feature. The most appropriate definition in our context in the Websters Dictionary is:

a prominent part or characteristic

Feature interaction is a situation in which system behavior does not as a whole satisfy each of its component features individually [Gibson, 1997].

A *feature trace* is a sequence of runtime events (*e.g.,* object creation/deletion, method invocation) that describes the dynamic behavior of a feature.

A *Feature Affinity* describes the degree of usage of a source entity by the features of the feature model. The OCL definition is provided in Chapter 3, Figure 3.3 (p.32).

A *feature view* is a grouping of source entities (*e.g.,* Packages, Classes, Methods, Instances) abstracted from a feature trace. The compact feature view used in the dissertation represents one type of *feature view*. It describes a tuple of sets of source entities, each set contains source entities with the same Feature Affinity level. The OCL definition is provided in Chapter 3, Figure 3.5 (p.35).

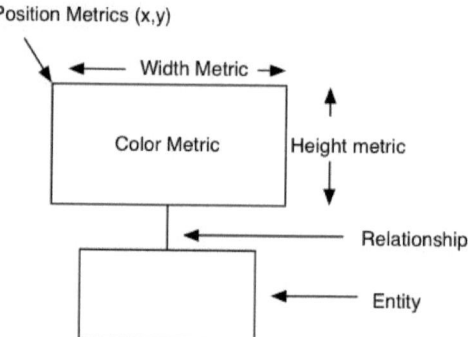

Figure A.1: The principle of polymetric views

Our visualizations are based on polymetric views:

A *polymetric view* [Lanza and Ducasse, 2003] is a graph-based visualization of static code or runtime behavior enriched with up to five software metrics. The nodes represent structural or dynamic entities of a system and the edges represent relationships between the node entities. The visualization is enriched with metrics by adapting the node size, color and position of nodes and edges to reflect numeric values. For example, the higher the value of the metric, the larger the node.

As a polymetric view combines software visualization with software metrics, it eliminates the need to interpret large metric tables. After learning the visual language of polymetric views one gets a fast overview about the software system, its entities and relationships.

A *dendrogram* a branching diagram representing a hierarchy of categories based on degree of similarity or number of shared characteristics especially in biological taxonomy. Figure A.2 (p.161) is a simple dendrogram diagram showing how it clusters 3 features based on a distance value.

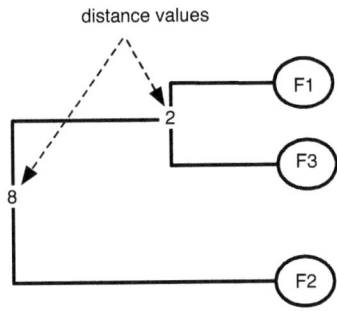

Figure A.2: A Simple Dendrogram showing two Feature Clusters

We compute the order of the feature views in a visualization using a *dendogram seriation algoritm*. It builds a dendrogram of clusters of features based on a distance measurement. We use our *featureSimilarity* measurement (see Figure 3.7 (p.38)) to determine how the clusters of features are computed. The leaves of the dendogram determine the order of feature views in our visualization.

The Webster's dictionary defnes *seriation* as the arrangement of a collection of artefacts in a series.

Transitive Reduction.

We express the transitive property in predicate logic as follows:
Let R be a relation between to vertices of a graph. Let X be the set of all vertices.

$$\forall a, b, c \in X, aRb \land bRc \rightarrow aRc \tag{A.1}$$

The *transitive reduction* of a graph is its minimal representation. Given a binary relation R over a set X is transitive if it holds for all a, b, and c in X, that if a is related to b and b is related to c then

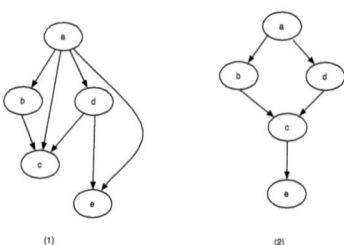

Figure A.3: Applying Transitive Reduction to a Simple Graph.

a is related to c. With transitive reduction we do not represent the edge of the transitive relation, as we assume the transitive property holds. Figure A.3 (p.162) shows two graphs (1) and (2). Graph (2) shows the result of applying transitive reduction to Graph (1).

Appendix B

Dynamix: Summary and Variations

B.1 Introduction

We provide an overview of our Dynamix meta-model and the extensions proposed in this dissertation unified in one diagram.

We also show variations to modeling features to incorporate modeling some of the variations identified in Chapter 9 (p.147), namely multi-threading applications and many-to-one relationships between features and feature traces.

B.2 Dynamix and Extensions

In Figure B.1 (p.164) we provide an overview of our Dynamix a summary of the extensions to Dynamix.

B.3 Dynamix Variations

We describe extensions to the Dynamix meta-model described in this dissertation to encompass two variations: (1) many-to-one relationships between features and traces, and (2) multi-threaded

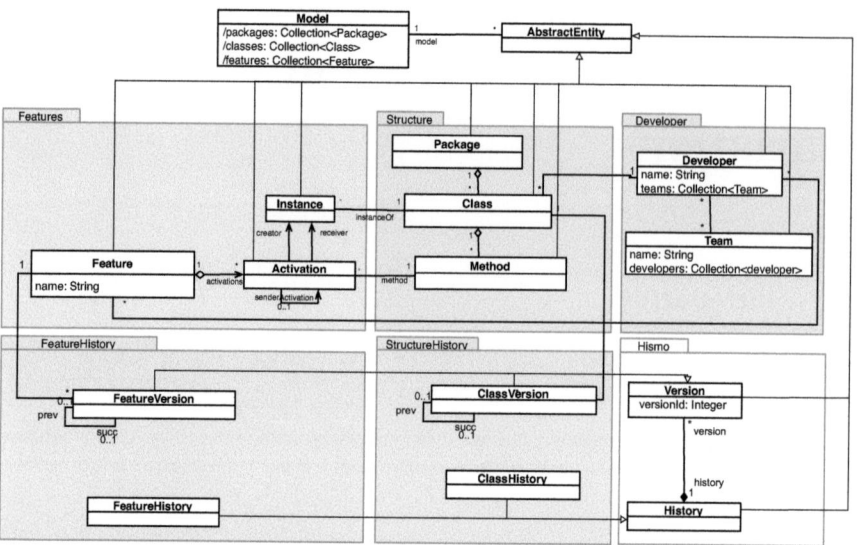

Figure B.1: The Dynamix meta-model showing the main Entities of the Feature, Structure, FeatureHistory, StructureHistory and Developer Packages

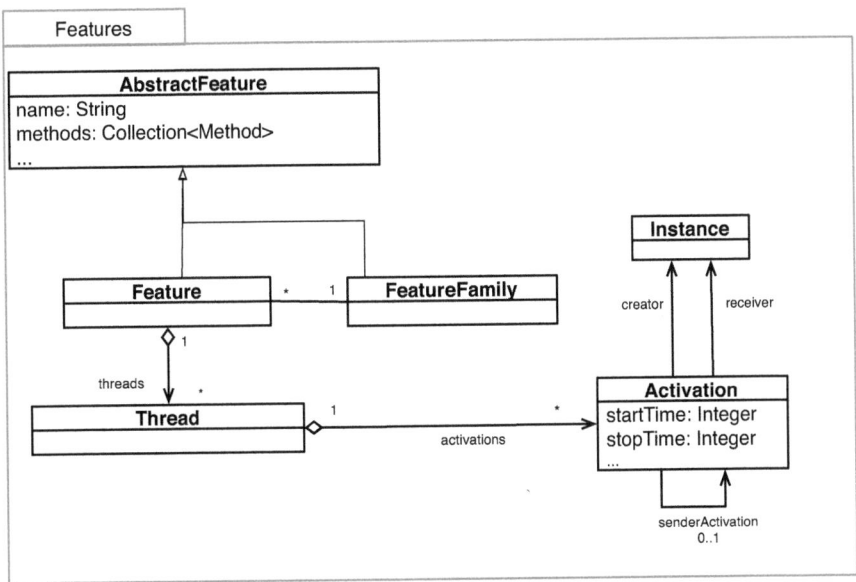

Figure B.2: Features Package of Dynamix showing Entities to model Multi-Threading (Thread) and One-to-Many Relationships (FeatureTrace) between Features and Execution Paths.

applications.

AbstractFeature. This provides a common interface to manipulate *Feature* entities or *FeatureFamily* entities.

FeatureFamily. The Dynamix model described in this dissertation restricts the definition of a feature to one path of execution. It defines a one-to-one mapping between features and traces. However, as discussed in Chapter 9 (p.147), the execution path of a feature may vary depending on the combination of user inputs entered when invoking a feature. In Figure B.2 (p.165) we show the *FeatureFamily* entity as having a one-to-many relationship with the *Feature* entity of our original Dynamix model. In this case the *FeatureFamily* entity allows us to collectively manipulate one or more *Feature* entities and also retains its ability to to collectively manipulate all the *Activations* that correspond to the events of the execution trace of a feature..

Thread. To cope with multi-threaded applications, we extend our model with a *Thread* entity to model one thread of execution in a parallel application. Figure B.2 (p.165) shows the *Thread* entity our model. Each *FeatureTrace* entitiy consist of one or more threads of execution of a feature trace. The *Thread* entity maintains a list (as an ordered collection) of *Activations* modeling the method events of the thread. As with our original **Dynamix** model, the *Activations* maintain a reference to their sender *Activation*. In this way we preserve the order of execution of events in an execution thread.

Appendix C

DynaMoose: Trace Extraction, Meta-Modelling and Feature Analysis

In this chapter we describe *DynaMoose*, the tool we built to implement our Dynamix meta-model and the various feature-centric analysis techniques described in this dissertation. *DynaMoose* exploits the generic infrastructure of Moose [Ducasse *et al.*, 2005a; Nierstrasz *et al.*, 2005], a reverse engineering and reengineering environment.

In Chapter 3 (p.25) we introduced our Dynamix meta-model which expresses feature execution entities, their relationships to each other, and to structural entities of source code. Dynamix underlies the various feature-centric analysis techniques presented in this dissertation. A primary goal of our work was to show how our Dynamix meta-model supports feature-centric analysis from many different, complementary perspectives.

We demonstrated in Chapter 3 (p.25) that Dynamix not only supports the *Feature Affinity* measurement defined in this work, but also accommodates metrics from other *Feature Identification* techniques such as the Software Reconnaissance approach [Wilde and Scully, 1995] and *dedication* and *concentration* metrics proposed by Wong *et al.* [Wong *et al.*, 2000].

Extensibility is an important aspect of Dynamix. In Chapter 5 (p.67) and Chapter 6 (p.87) we demonstrated the extensibility of Dynamix to support evolution analysis of multiple versions of a system, and in Chapter 8 (p.127)), we demonstrated extensions to our model to incorporate mining source code repository data to correlate developers with the static and dynamic entities of Dynamix.

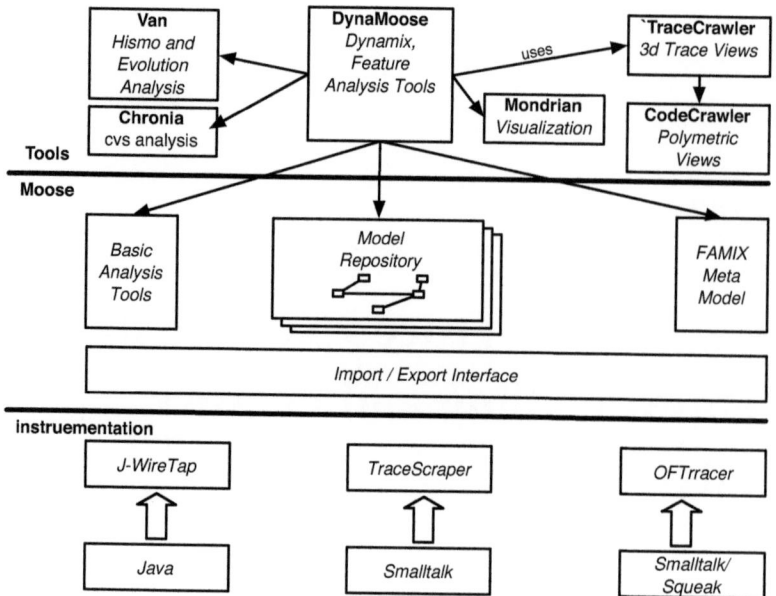

Figure C.1: DynaMoose, Moose and the Instrumentation Layer.

Structure of the Chapter. In the next section (Section C.1 (p.168)) we provide an overview of *DynaMoose* in the context of the overall architecture of Moose. In Section C.2 (p.169) we outline the tools we use to extract feature traces from different object-oriented applications. Then in Section C.3 (p.170) we briefly describe the tools we used to perform our feature-centric analysis.

C.1 Architectural Overview

Figure C.1 (p.168) shows the position of *DynaMoose* in the overall architecture of Moose. Different analysis tools and components of Moose are represented by a rectangles. The edges between the rectangles and DynaMoose indicate that DynaMoose interfaces or uses the features of these tools or components to support feature analysis. The default meta-model of Moose is FAMIX, a language independent meta-model [Demeyer et al., 2001]. Moose has a repository that can store multiple models providing the necessary infrastructure for holding and managing multiple versions.

At the core of *DynaMoose* is the implementation of Dynamix. In our implementation, Dynamix is built on top of FAMIX [Demeyer *et al.*, 2001] and is MOF 2.0 compliant.

Dynamix extends the meta-model with the notion of features. When *DynaMoose* is loaded in Moose, then Moose is *feature aware* (*i.e.,* the entire environment is capable of manipulating features).

C.2 Extracting Traces of Features

One of the fundamental task of dynamic analysis is to obtain and manipulate runtime traces of a system's behavior. Typically, dynamic analysis involves intrumenting the program under investigation to record its runtime behavior. Detailed knowledge of the target programming language or virtual machine is required to implement dynamic analysis tools. Our focus was on obtaining feature traces.

— We built *J-Wiretap* to extract traces from Java applications. *J-WireTap* is built on the *JIP* (Java Interactive Profiler) [jip,] and the JavaAssist library[1]. The *JIP* profiler is based on the JVMTI interface and provides control to turn on and off profiling at runtime. With this tool we generate one trace containing marked features (*i.e.,* we mark the start and end of the individual traces). With our *J-WireTap* tool, we export the feature traces to a MSE format[2], which describes Dynamix execution entities (Features, Activations and Instances). We used the *J-WireTap* for the ArgoUML experiments described in Chapter 4 (p.43) and Chapter 8 (p.127).

— We built *TraceScraper* to perform code instrumentation for Smalltalk based on the method wrappers tool of Brant *et al.*. [Brant *et al.*, 1998]. *TraceScraper* runs feature exercising scripts and captures individual traces of the executions. The traces are modeled as Dynamix entites. We used *TraceScraper* for our experiments described in Chapter 5 (p.67) and Chapter 6 (p.87).

— For our experiments with Pier (Chapter 3 (p.25)) we used the Object-Flow Tracer [Lienhard *et al.*, 2006]. The Object Flow Tracer is implemented for the Squeak environment. It adopts an orthogonal view of runtime behavior by capturing not only the message sends, but also how object references are passed around a system at runtime. When analyzing the dynamic relationships between features, as described in Chapter 3 (p.25), we focused on how instances were accessed between features.

---

[1] http://www.jboss.com/products/javassist
[2] http://smallwiki.unibe.ch/moose/mseformat/

C.3 Using the Tools of the Moose Reengineering Environment

We built our *DynaMoose* analysis tool to integrate and use other tools of the Moose reengineering environment. In this section we outline which Moose tools we used and for which analysis technique.

C.3.1 Visualizing Features and Feature-enriched Structural Views

One key element of the approaches we describe is visualization. We implemented two main types of visualizations, based on two distinct software tools:

— *CodeCrawler* is a visualization tool implementing polymetric views [Lanza and Ducasse, 2003; Ducasse and Lanza, 2005]. It is based on a graph notion where the nodes and edges in the graph represent entities in a model. The view of dynamic data presented in Chapter 2, Figure 2.1 (p.13) is an example of a polymetric view.

— *TraceCrawler* [Wysseier, 2005] interprets the trace information provided by TraceScraper and controls the visualization. It processes execution traces in the Moose model and represents the events of the trace as 3D visualizations. The visualization is created by CCJun [Wysseier, 2004] which is an extension of CodeCrawler [Lanza, 2003] and based on the 3D framework Jun.

Our 3D visualizations provide an overview of the entire collection of data that is represented. This can often be difficult to interpret in the case of large systems with a large number of classes. Therefore the interactive capabilities of our visualization are integral to the discussion of our analysis approach.

— *Mondrian* [Meyer, 2006] provides basic building blocks to allow declarative scripting to express visualizations based on an underlying model. We made extensive use of Mondrian visualizations in this dissertation. For example, we represent our compact feature views (Chapter 3 (p.25)) and the variations we used to represent changes to features over a series of versions (Chapter 6 (p.87)) with simple mondrian visualizations. Our Mondrian visualizations are polymetric representations as we map metrics (*e.g.,* Feature Affinity) to the nodes and edges of the graph visualizations we use.

Mondrian visualizations are also interactive. We can query the nodes to obtain more fine-grained details about the underlying entity which it represents (*e.g.,* class name or source code).

C.3.2 Evolution Analysis

Van, the version analysis tool of Moose, supports the analysis of multiple versions of software systems [Gîrba, 2005]. We exploited the history and version analysis capabiliities of Van by extending our Dynamix meta-model with *History* and *Version* entities for both structural (*e.g.,* Class) and execution (*e.g.,* Feature) entities. In *DynaMoose* we implemented extensions to *Van* to manipulate *History* and *Version* entities and to define *feature-centric* history and version properties.

C.3.3 Developer Analysis

Chronia is an implementation of a CVS protocol to allow direct connectivity to CVS repositories [Seeberger, 2006]. Our developer analysis technique described in Chapter 8 (p.127) uses *Chronia* to extract developer data from a CVS repository and model the resulting data in Moose. In our approach, we establish relationships between the repository data extracted by *Chronia* and Dynamix so that we associate developers with features.

C.4 Summary

We provided a brief overview of the tool environment of our feature-centric analysis techniques. In particular, we explained the visualization tools and their role in the analysis techniques described in this dissertation. We highlighted which Moose tool was used in each of the analysis techniques.

Bibliography

[Antoniol and Guéhéneuc, 2005] Giuliano Antoniol and Yann-Gaël Guéhéneuc. Feature identification: a novel approach and a case study. In *Proceedings IEEE International Conference on Software Maintenance (ICSM 2005)*, pages 357–366, Los Alamitos CA, September 2005. IEEE Computer Society Press.

[Anvik *et al.*, 2006] John Anvik, Lyndon Hiew, and Gail C. Murphy. Who should fix this bug? In *Proceedings of the 2006 ACM Conference on Software Engineering*, 2006.

[Ball, 1999] Thomas Ball. The concept of dynamic analysis. In *Proceedings European Software Engineering Conference and ACM SIGSOFT International Symposium on the Foundations of Software Engineering (ESEC/FSC 1999)*, number 1687 in LNCS, pages 216–234, Heidelberg, sep 1999. Springer Verlag.

[Basili, 1997] Victor Basili. Evolving and packaging reading technologies. *Journal Systems and Software*, 38(1):3–12, 1997.

[Beck and Gamma, 1998] Kent Beck and Erich Gamma. Test infected: Programmers love writing tests. *Java Report*, 3(7):51–56, 1998.

[Bézivin and Gerbé, 2001] Jean Bézivin and Olivier Gerbé. Towards a precise definition of the OMG/MDA framework. In *Proceedings Automated Software Engineering (ASE 2001)*, pages 273–282, Los Alamitos CA, 2001. IEEE Computer Society.

[Biggerstaff and Perlis, 1989] T.J. Biggerstaff and A.J. Perlis. *Software Reusability Volume I: Concepts and Models*, volume I. ACM Press & Addison Wesley, Reading, Mass., 1989.

[Biggerstaff *et al.*, 1993] Ted J. Biggerstaff, Bharat G. Mittbander, and Dallas Webster. The concept assignment problem in program understanding. In *Proceedings of the 15th international conference on Software Engineering (ICSE 1993)*. IEEE Computer, 1993.

[Brant et al., 1998] John Brant, Brian Foote, Ralph Johnson, and Don Roberts. Wrappers to the rescue. In *Proceedings European Conference on Object Oriented Programming (ECOOP 1998)*, volume 1445 of *LNCS*, pages 396–417. Springer-Verlag, 1998.

[Briffault and Ducasse, 2001] Xavier Briffault and Stéphane Ducasse. *Squeak*. Eyrolles, Paris, November 2001.

[Canfora and Cerulo, 2006] Gerardo Canfora and Luigi Cerulo. Supporting change request assignment in open source development. In *Proceedings of 2006 ACM Symposium on Applied Computing*, pages 1767–1772. ACM, ACM Society Press, 2006.

[Chen and Rajlich, 2000] Kunrong Chen and Václav Rajlich. Case study of feature location using dependence graph. In *Proceedings IEEE International Conference on Software Maintenance (ICSM)*, pages 241–249. IEEE Computer Society Press, 2000.

[Chikofsky and Cross II, 1990] Elliot Chikofsky and James Cross II. Reverse engineering and design recovery: A taxonomy. *IEEE Software*, 7(1):13–17, January 1990.

[Chuah and Eick, 1998] Mei C. Chuah and Stephen G. Eick. Information rich glyphs for software management data. *IEEE Computer Graphics and Applications*, 18(4):24–29, July 1998.

[Conway, 1968] Melvin E. Conway. How do committees invent? *Datamation*, 14(4):28–31, April 1968.

[de Bono, 1990] Edward de Bono. *Simplicity*. Penguin Books Ltd, 1990.

[De Pauw et al., 1993] Wim De Pauw, Richard Helm, Doug Kimelman, and John Vlissides. Visualizing the behavior of object-oriented systems. In *Proceedings OOPSLA '93*, pages 326–337, October 1993.

[De Pauw et al., 2006] Wim De Pauw, Sophia Krasikov, and John Morar. Execution patterns for visualizing web services. In *Proceedings ACM International Conference on Software Visualization (SoftVis 2006)*, New York NY, September 2006. ACM Press.

[Deissenboeck and Ratiu, 2006] Florian Deissenboeck and Daniel Ratiu. A unified meta-model for concept-based reverse engineering. In *Proceedings of the 3rd International Workshop on Metamodels, Schemas, Grammars and Ontologies (ATEM'06)*, 2006.

[Demeyer et al., 2000] Serge Demeyer, Stéphane Ducasse, and Oscar Nierstrasz. Finding refactorings via change metrics. In *Proceedings of 15th International Conference on Object-Oriented Programming, Systems, Languages, and Applications (OOPSLA '00)*, pages 166–178, New York NY, 2000. ACM Press. Also appeared in ACM SIGPLAN Notices 35 (10).

[Demeyer et al., 2001] Serge Demeyer, Sander Tichelaar, and Stéphane Ducasse. FAMIX 2.1 — The FAMOOS Information Exchange Model. Technical report, University of Bern, 2001.

[Demeyer et al., 2002] Serge Demeyer, Stéphane Ducasse, and Oscar Nierstrasz. *Object-Oriented Reengineering Patterns*. Morgan Kaufmann, 2002.

[Demeyer et al., 2003] Serge Demeyer, Stéphane Ducasse, Kim Mens, Adrian Trifu, and Rajesh Vasa. Report of the ECOOP'03 workshop on object-oriented reengineering, 2003.

[Denker et al., 2006] Marcus Denker, Orla Greevy, and Michele Lanza. Higher abstractions for dynamic analysis. In *2nd International Workshop on Program Comprehension through Dynamic Analysis (PCODA 2006)*, pages 32–38, 2006.

[Ducasse and Lanza, 2005] Stéphane Ducasse and Michele Lanza. The class blueprint: Visually supporting the understanding of classes. *Transactions on Software Engineering (TSE)*, 31(1):75–90, January 2005.

[Ducasse et al., 2004] Stéphane Ducasse, Michele Lanza, and Roland Bertuli. High-level polymetric views of condensed run-time information. In *Proceedings of 8th European Conference on Software Maintenance and Reengineering (CSMR'04)*, pages 309–318, Los Alamitos CA, 2004. IEEE Computer Society Press.

[Ducasse et al., 2005a] Stéphane Ducasse, Tudor Gîrba, Michele Lanza, and Serge Demeyer. Moose: a collaborative and extensible reengineering environment. In *Tools for Software Maintenance and Reengineering*, RCOST / Software Technology Series, pages 55–71. Franco Angeli, Milano, 2005.

[Ducasse et al., 2005b] Stéphane Ducasse, Lukas Renggli, and Roel Wuyts. Smallwiki—a meta-described collaborative content management system. In *Proceedings ACM International Symposium on Wikis (WikiSym'05)*, pages 75–82, New York, NY, USA, 2005. ACM Computer Society.

[Ducasse et al., 2006a] Stéphane Ducasse, Tudor Gîrba, and Adrian Kuhn. Distribution map. In *Proceedings of 22nd IEEE International Conference on Software Maintenance (ICSM '06)*, pages 203–212, Los Alamitos CA, 2006. IEEE Computer Society.

[Ducasse et al., 2006b] Stéphane Ducasse, Tudor Gîrba, and Roel Wuyts. Object-oriented legacy system trace-based logic testing. In *Proceedings of 10th European Conference on Software Maintenance and Reengineering (CSMR'06)*, pages 35–44. IEEE Computer Society Press, 2006.

[Dunsmore et al., 2000] Alastair Dunsmore, Marc Roper, and Murray Wood. Object-oriented inspection in the face of delocalisation. In *Proceedings of ICSE '00 (22nd International Conference on Software Engineering)*, pages 467–476. ACM Press, 2000.

[Ebraert et al., 2006] P. Ebraert, T. D'Hondt, Y. Vandewoude, and Y. Berbers. User-centric dynamic evolution. In *Proceedings, ERCIM 2006*, 2006.

[Eick et al., 2001] Stephen Eick, Todd Graves, Alan Karr, J. Marron, and Audris Mockus. Does code decay? assessing the evidence from change management data. *IEEE Transactions on Software Engineering*, 27(1):1–12, 2001.

[Eisenbarth et al., 2003] Thomas Eisenbarth, Rainer Koschke, and Daniel Simon. Locating features in source code. *IEEE Computer*, 29(3):210–224, March 2003.

[Eisenberg and De Volder, 2005] Andrew Eisenberg and Kris De Volder. Dynamic feature traces: Finding features in unfamiliar code. In *Proceedings IEEE International Conference on Software Maintenance (ICSM 2004)*, pages 337–346, Los Alamitos CA, September 2005. IEEE Computer Society Press.

[Ernst et al., 1999] Michael D. Ernst, Jake Cockrell, William G. Griswold, and David Notkin. Dynamically discovering likely program invariants to support program evolution. In *Proceedings of ICSE '99*, May 1999.

[Fenton and Pfleeger, 1996] Norman Fenton and Shari Lawrence Pfleeger. *Software Metrics: A Rigorous and Practical Approach*. International Thomson Computer Press, London, UK, second edition, 1996.

[Fischer and Gall, 2004] Michael Fischer and Harald Gall. Visualizing feature evolution of large-scale software based on problem and modification report data. *Journal of Software Maintenance and Evolution: Research and Practice*, 16(6):385–403, 2004.

[Fischer et al., 2003] Michael Fischer, Martin Pinzger, and Harald Gall. Analyzing and relating bug report data for feature tracking. In *Proceedings IEEE Working Conference on Reverse Engineering (WCRE 2003)*, pages 90–99, Los Alamitos CA, November 2003. IEEE Computer Society Press.

[Fowler et al., 1999] Martin Fowler, Kent Beck, John Brant, William Opdyke, and Don Roberts. *Refactoring: Improving the Design of Existing Code*. Addison Wesley, 1999.

[Fowler, 2003] Martin Fowler. *UML Distilled*. Addison Wesley, 2003.

[Gaelli et al., 2005] Markus Gaelli, Orla Greevy, and Oscar Nierstrasz. Composing unit tests. In *Proceedings of SPLiT 2006 (2nd International Workshop on Software Product Line Testing)*, September 2005.

[Gaelli, 2006] Markus Gaelli. *Modeling Examples to Test and Understand Software*. PhD thesis, University of Berne, November 2006.

[Gall et al., 1998] Harald Gall, Karin Hajek, and Mehdi Jazayeri. Detection of logical coupling based on product release history. In *Proceedings International Conference on Software Maintenance (ICSM '98)*, pages 190–198, Los Alamitos CA, 1998. IEEE Computer Society Press.

[Gibson, 1997] Paul Gibson. Feature requirements models: Understanding interactions. In *Feature Interactions in Telecommunication Networks*, pages 46–60. IOS Press, 1997.

[Gîrba and Ducasse, 2006] Tudor Gîrba and Stéphane Ducasse. Modeling history to analyze software evolution. *Journal of Software Maintenance: Research and Practice (JSME)*, 18:207–236, 2006.

[Gîrba and Lanza, 2004] Tudor Gîrba and Michele Lanza. Visualizing and characterizing the evolution of class hierarchies, 2004.

[Gîrba et al., 2005a] Tudor Gîrba, Adrian Kuhn, Mauricio Seeberger, and Stéphane Ducasse. How developers drive software evolution. In *Proceedings of International Workshop on Principles of Software Evolution (IWPSE 2005)*, pages 113–122. IEEE Computer Society Press, 2005.

[Gîrba et al., 2005b] Tudor Gîrba, Michele Lanza, and Stéphane Ducasse. Characterizing the evolution of class hierarchies. In *Proceedings of 9th European Conference on Software Maintenance and Reengineering (CSMR'05)*, pages 2–11, Los Alamitos CA, 2005. IEEE Computer Society.

[Gîrba, 2005] Tudor Gîrba. *Modeling History to Understand Software Evolution*. PhD thesis, University of Berne, Berne, November 2005.

[Gold and Mohan, 2003] Nicolas Gold and Andrew Mohan. A framework for understanding conceptual changes in evolving source code. In *Proceedings of International Conference on Software Maintenance 2003 (ICSM 2003)*, pages 432–439, September 2003.

[Greevy and Ducasse, 2005a] Orla Greevy and Stéphane Ducasse. Characterizing the functional roles of classes and methods by analyzing feature traces. In *Proceedings of WOOR 2005 (6th International Workshop on Object-Oriented Reengineering)*, July 2005.

[Greevy and Ducasse, 2005b] Orla Greevy and Stéphane Ducasse. Correlating features and code using a compact two-sided trace analysis approach. In *Proceedings of 9th European Conference on Software Maintenance and Reengineering (CSMR'05)*, pages 314–323, Los Alamitos CA, 2005. IEEE Computer Society.

[Greevy et al., 2005a] Orla Greevy, Stéphane Ducasse, and Tudor Gîrba. Analyzing feature traces to incorporate the semantics of change in software evolution analysis. In *Proceedings of 21st IEEE International Conference on Software Maintenance (ICSM'05)*, pages 347–356, Los Alamitos, September 2005. IEEE Computer Society.

[Greevy et al., 2005b] Orla Greevy, Michele Lanza, and Christoph Wysseier. Visualizing feature interaction in 3-D. In *Proceedings of VISSOFT 2005 (3th IEEE International Workshop on Visualizing Software for Understanding)*, pages 114–119, September 2005.

[Greevy et al., 2006a] Orla Greevy, Stéphane Ducasse, and Tudor Gîrba. Analyzing software evolution through feature views. *Journal of Software Maintenance and Evolution: Research and Practice (JSME)*, 18(6):425–456, 2006.

[Greevy et al., 2006b] Orla Greevy, Michele Lanza, and Christoph Wysseier. Visualizing live software systems in 3D. In *Proceedings of SoftVis 2006 (ACM Symposium on Software Visualization)*, September 2006.

[Greevy et al., 2007] Orla Greevy, Tudor Gîrba, and Stéphane Ducasse. How developers develop features. In *Proceedings of 11th European Conference on Software Maintenance and Reengineering (CSMR 2007)*, pages 256–274, Los Alamitos CA, 2007. IEEE Computer Society.

[Hamou-Lhadj and Lethbridge, 2004] A. Hamou-Lhadj and T. Lethbridge. A survey of trace exploration tools and techniques. In *Proceedings IBM Centers for Advanced Studies Conferences (CASON 2004)*, pages 42–55, Indianapolis IN, 2004. IBM Press.

[Hamou-Lhadj et al., 2005] A. Hamou-Lhadj, E. Braun, D. Amyot, and T. Lethbridge. Recovering behavioral design models from execution traces. In *Proceedings IEEE European Conference on Software Maintenance and Reengineering (CSMR 2005)*, pages 112–121, Los Alamitos CA, 2005. IEEE Computer Society Press.

[Hassan and Holt, 2004] Ahmed Hassan and Richard Holt. Predicting change propagation in software systems. In *Proceedings 20th IEEE International Conference on Software Maintenance (ICSM'04)*, pages 284–293, Los Alamitos CA, September 2004. IEEE Computer Society Press.

[Hsi and Potts, 2000] Idris Hsi and Colin Potts. Studying the evolution and enhancement of software features. In *Proceedings IEEE International Conference on Software Maintenance (ICSM 2000)*, pages 143–151, New York NY, 2000. IEEE Computer Society Press.

[Hunt and McIlroy, 1976] James Hunt and Douglas McIlroy. An algorithm for differential file comparison. Technical Report CSTR 41, Bell Laboratories, Murray Hill NJ, 1976.

[Jerding and Rugaber, 1997] Dean Jerding and Spencer Rugaber. Using visualization for architectural localization and extraction. In Ira Baxter, Alex Quilici, and Chris Verhoef, editors, *Proceedings of WCRE '97 (4th Working Conference on Reverse Engineering)*, pages 56–65. IEEE Computer Society Press, 1997.

[Jerding et al., 1996] Dean Jerding, John Stasko, and Thomas Ball. Visualizing message patterns in object-oriented program executions. Technical Report GIT-GVU-96-15, Georgia Institute of Technology, May 1996.

[Jerding et al., 1997] Dean J. Jerding, John T. Stasko, and Thomas Ball. Visualizing interactions in program executions. In *Proceedings of ICSE '97*, pages 360–370, 1997.

[jip,] Java interactive profiler. http://sourceforge.net/projects/jiprof.

[Kang et al., 2002] K.C. Kang, Jaejoon Lee, and Patrick Donohoe. Feature-oriented product line engineering. *IEEE Software*, 2002.

[Kleyn and Gingrich, 1988] Michael F. Kleyn and Paul C. Gingrich. GraphTrace — understanding object-oriented systems using concurrently animated views. In *Proceedings OOPSLA '88 (International Conference on Object-Oriented Programming Systems, Languages, and Applications*, volume 23, pages 191–205. ACM Press, November 1988.

[Korel and Rilling, 1997] Bogdan Korel and Jurgen Rilling. Dynamic program slicing in understanding of program execution. In *5th International Workshop on Program Comprehension (WPC '97)*, pages 80–85, 1997.

[Koschke and Quante, 2005] Rainer Koschke and Jochen Quante. On dynamic feature location. *International Conference on Automated Software Engineering, 2005*, pages 86–95, 2005.

[Kothari et al., 2006] Jay Kothari, Trip Denton, Spiros Mancoridis, and Ali Shokoufandeh. On computing the canonical features of software systems. In *13th IEEE Working Conference on Reverse Engineering (WCRE 2006)*, October 2006.

[Krajewski, 2003] Jacek Krajewski. QCR - A methodology for software evolution analysis. Master's thesis, Information Systems Institute, Distributed Systems Group, Technical University of Vienna, April 2003.

[Kuhn and Greevy, 2006a] Adrian Kuhn and Orla Greevy. Exploiting the analogy between traces and signal processing. In *Proceedings IEEE International Conference on Software Maintainance (ICSM 2006)*, Los Alamitos CA, September 2006. IEEE Computer Society Press.

[Kuhn and Greevy, 2006b] Adrian Kuhn and Orla Greevy. Summarizing traces as signals in time. In *Proceedings IEEE Workshop on Program Comprehension through Dynamic Analysis (PCODA 2006)*, pages 01–06, Los Alamitos CA, October 2006. IEEE Computer Society Press.

[Kuhn et al., 2005a] Adrian Kuhn, Stéphane Ducasse, and Tudor Gîrba. Enriching reverse engineering with semantic clustering. In *Proceedings of 12th Working Conference on Reverse Engineering (WCRE'05)*, pages 113–122, Los Alamitos CA, November 2005. IEEE Computer Society Press.

[Kuhn et al., 2005b] Adrian Kuhn, Orla Greevy, and Tudor Gîrba. Applying semantic analysis to feature execution traces. In *Proceedings IEEE Workshop on Program Comprehension through Dynamic Analysis (PCODA 2005)*, pages 48–53, Los Alamitos CA, November 2005. IEEE Computer Society Press.

[Kyo C.Kang et al., 1990] Sholom G. Cohen Kyo C.Kang, James A. Hess, William E. Novak, and A. Spencer Peterson. Feature oriented design analysis (foda) feasibility study. Technical Report CMU/SEI-90-TR-21-ESD-90/TR-222, iSoftware Engineering Institute, Carnegie Mellon University, Pittsburgh, PA, 1990.

[Lange and Nakamura, 1995a] Danny Lange and Yuichi Nakamura. Interactive visualization of design patterns can help in framework understanding. In *Proceedings ACM International Conference on Object-Oriented Programming Systems, Languages and Applications (OOPSLA 1995)*, pages 342–357, New York NY, 1995. ACM Press.

[Lange and Nakamura, 1995b] D.B. Lange and Y. Nakamura. Object-oriented program tracing and visualization. Research Report RT0111, IBM Research, Tokyo Research Laboratory, 1995.

[Lanza and Ducasse, 2002] Michele Lanza and Stéphane Ducasse. Understanding software evolution using a combination of software visualization and software metrics. In *Proceedings of Langages et Modèles à Objets (LMO'02)*, pages 135–149, Paris, 2002. Lavoisier.

[Lanza and Ducasse, 2003] Michele Lanza and Stéphane Ducasse. Polymetric views—a lightweight visual approach to reverse engineering. *Transactions on Software Engineering (TSE)*, 29(9):782–795, September 2003.

[Lanza, 2003] Michele Lanza. Codecrawler — lessons learned in building a software visualization tool. In *Proceedings of CSMR 2003*, pages 409–418. IEEE Press, 2003.

[Lehman *et al.*, 1997] Manny Lehman, Dewayne Perry, Juan Ramil, Wladyslaw Turski, and Paul Wernick. Metrics and laws of software evolution–the nineties view. In *Proceedings IEEE International Software Metrics Symposium (METRICS'97)*, pages 20–32, Los Alamitos CA, 1997. IEEE Computer Society Press.

[Lethbridge *et al.*, 2005] Timothy C. Lethbridge, Susan Elliot Sim, and Janice Singer. Studying software engineers: Data collection techniques for software field studies. *Empirical Software Engineering, Springer Science and Business Media, Inc., The Netherlands*, 10(3):311–341, July 2005.

[Licata *et al.*, 2003] D. Licata, C.D. Harris, and S. Krishnamurthi. The feature signatures of evolving programs. In *Proceedings IEEE International Conference on Automated Software Engineering*, pages 281–285, Los Alamitos CA, October 2003. IEEE Computer Society Press.

[Lienhard *et al.*, 2006] Adrian Lienhard, Stéphane Ducasse, Tudor Gîrba, and Oscar Nierstrasz. Capturing how objects flow at runtime. In *Proceedings International Workshop on Program Comprehension through Dynamic Analysis (PCODA 2006)*, pages 39–43, 2006.

[Lienhard *et al.*, 2007a] Adrian Lienhard, Orla Greevy, and Oscar Nierstrasz. Tracking objects to detect feature dependencies. In *Proceedings International Conference on Program Comprehension (ICPC 2007)*, 2007. to appear.

[Lienhard *et al.*, 2007b] Adrian Lienhard, Adrian Kuhn, and Orla Greevy. Feature dependency browser – a case-study for rapid prototyping of visualizations for mondrian. In *Proceedings IEEE International Workshop on Visualizing Software for Understanding (Vissoft 2007)*, 2007.

[M.-A. D. Storey and Michaud, 2001] C. Best M.-A. D. Storey and J. Michaud. SHriMP Views: An interactive and customizable environment for software exploration. In *Proceedings of International Workshop on Program Comprehension (IWPC '2001)*, 2001.

[Maletic et al., 2002] Jonathan I. Maletic, Andrian Marcus, and Michael Collard. A task oriented view of software visualization. In *Proceedings of the 1st Workshop on Visualizing Software for Understanding and Analysis (VISSOFT 2002)*, pages 32–40. IEEE, June 2002.

[Marcus et al., 2003] Andrian Marcus, Louis Feng, and Jonathan I. Maletic. 3d representations for software visualization. In *Proceedings of the ACM Symposium on Software Visualization*, pages 27–ff. IEEE, 2003.

[Marcus et al., 2004] Andrian Marcus, Andrey Sergeyev, Vaclav Rajlich, and Jonathan Maletic. An information retrieval approach to concept location in source code. In *Proceedings of the 11th Working Conference on Reverse Engineering (WCRE 2004)*, pages 214–223, November 2004.

[Mehta and Heineman, 2002] Alok Mehta and George Heineman. Evolving legacy systems features using regression test cases and components. In *Proceedings ACM International Workshop on Principles of Software Evolution*, pages 190–193, New York NY, 2002. ACM Press.

[Meyer et al., 2006] Michael Meyer, Tudor Gîrba, and Mircea Lungu. Mondrian: An agile visualization framework. In *ACM Symposium on Software Visualization (SoftVis 2006)*, pages 135–144, New York, NY, USA, 2006. ACM Press.

[Meyer, 2006] Michael Meyer. Scripting interactive visualizations. Master's thesis, University of Bern, November 2006.

[Morris et al., 2003] Steven Morris, Benyam Asnake, and Gary Yen. Dendrogram seriation using simulated annealing. *Information Visualization*, 2(2):95–104, 2003.

[Nagpurkar and Krintz, 2006] Priya Nagpurkar and Chandra Krintz. Phase-based visualization and analysis of java programs. In *Elsevier Science of Computer Programming, Special issue on Princples of programming in Java*, volume 59,Number 1-2, pages 131–164, January 2006.

[Nierstrasz and Ducasse, 2004] Oscar Nierstrasz and Stéphane Ducasse. Moose–a language-independent reengineering environment. *European Research Consortim for Informatics and Mathematics (ERCIM) News*, 58:24–25, July 2004.

[Nierstrasz et al., 2005] Oscar Nierstrasz, Stéphane Ducasse, and Tudor Gîrba. The story of Moose: an agile reengineering environment. In *Proceedings of the European Software Engineering Conference (ESEC/FSE 2005)*, pages 1–10, New York NY, 2005. ACM Press. Invited paper.

[Price et al., 1993] Blaine A. Price, Ronald M. Baecker, and Ian S. Small. A principled taxonomy of software visualization. *Journal of Visual Languages and Computing*, 4(3):211–266, 1993.

[Rajlich and Gosavi, 2002] Václav Rajlich and Prashant Gosavi. A case study of unanticipated incremental change. In *18th International Conference on Software Maintenance (ICSM 2002), Maintaining Distributed Heterogeneous Systems, 3-6 October 2002, Montreal, Quebec, Canada.* IEEE Computer Society, 2002.

[Reiss, 2003] Steven P. Reiss. Visualizing Java in action. In *Proceedings of SoftVis 2003 (ACM Symposium on Software Visualization)*, pages 57–66, 2003.

[Renggli, 2003] Lukas Renggli. SmallWiki: Collaborative content management. Informatikprojekt, University of Bern, 2003. http://smallwiki.unibe.ch/smallwiki.

[Richner and Ducasse, 1999] Tamar Richner and Stéphane Ducasse. Recovering high-level views of object-oriented applications from static and dynamic information. In Hongji Yang and Lee White, editors, *Proceedings of 15th IEEE International Conference on Software Maintenance (ICSM'99)*, pages 13–22, Los Alamitos CA, September 1999. IEEE Computer Society Press.

[Richner and Ducasse, 2002] Tamar Richner and Stéphane Ducasse. Using dynamic information for the iterative recovery of collaborations and roles. In *Proceedings of 18th IEEE International Conference on Software Maintenance (ICSM'02)*, page 34, Los Alamitos CA, October 2002. IEEE Computer Society.

[Richner, 2002] Tamar Richner. *Recovering Behavioral Design Views: a Query-Based Approach.* PhD thesis, University of Berne, May 2002.

[Riebisch, 2003] Matthias Riebisch. *Towards a More Precise Definition of Feature Models*, pages 64–76. BooksOnDemand Publ. Co. Norderstedt, 2003.

[Robillard and Murphy, 2002] Martin P. Robillard and Gail C. Murphy. Concern graphs: finding and describing concerns using structural program dependencies. In *ICSE'02: Proceedings of the 24th International Conference on Software Engineering*, pages 406–416, New York, NY, USA, 2002. ACM Press.

[Röthlisberger *et al.*, 2007] David Röthlisberger, Orla Greevy, and Adrian Lienhard. Supporting software maintenance with interactive feature driven browsing. In *Proceedings IEEE International Workshop on Visualizing Software for Understanding (Vissoft 2007) (tool demonstration)*, 2007.

[Salah and Mancoridis, 2004] Maher Salah and Spiros Mancoridis. A hierarchy of dynamic software views: from object-interactions to feature-interacions. In *Proceedings IEEE International Conference on Software Maintenance (ICSM 2004)*, pages 72–81, Los Alamitos CA, 2004. IEEE Computer Society Press.

[Seeberger, 2006] Mauricio Seeberger. How developers drive software evolution. Master's thesis, University of Bern, January 2006.

[Seidewitz, 2003] Ed Seidewitz. What models mean. *IEEE Software*, 20(5):26–32, September 2003.

[Soanes, 2001] Catherine Soanes, editor. *Oxford Dictionary of Current English*. Oxford University Press, July 2001.

[Stasko *et al.*, 1998] John T. Stasko, John Domingue, Marc H. Brown, and Blaine A. Price, editors. *Software Visualization — Programming as a Multimedia Experience*. The MIT Press, 1998.

[Stroulia and Systä, 2002] E. Stroulia and T. Systä. Dynamic analysis for reverse engineering and program understanding. *SIGAPP. Applied Computing Review*, 10(1):8–17, 2002.

[Čubranić and Murphy, 2003] Davor Čubranić and Gail Murphy. Hipikat: Recommending pertinent software development artifacts. In *Proceedings 25th International Conference on Software Engineering (ICSE 2003)*, pages 408–418, New York NY, 2003. ACM Press.

[Vauclair, 2003] Sebastien Vauclair. Extensible Java profiler. Master's thesis, Ecole Polytechnique Fédérale de Lausanne, 2003. http://ejp.sourceforge.net.

[Vion-Dury and Santana, 1994] Jean-Yves Vion-Dury and Miguel Santana. Virtual images: Interactive visualization of distributed object-oriented systems. In ACM Press, editor, *Proceedings of OOPSLA 1994*, pages 65–84, 1994.

[Walker *et al.*, 1998] Robert J. Walker, Gail C. Murphy, Bjorn Freeman-Benson, Darin Wright, Darin Swanson, and Jeremy Isaak. Visualizing dynamic software system information through high-level models. In *Proceedings OOPSLA '98*, pages 271–283. ACM, October 1998.

[Wilde and Huitt, 1992] Norman Wilde and Ross Huitt. Maintenance support for object-oriented programs. *IEEE Transactions on Software Engineering*, SE-18(12):1038–1044, December 1992.

[Wilde and Scully, 1995] Norman Wilde and Michael Scully. Software reconnaisance: Mapping program features to code. *Software Maintenance: Research and Practice*, 7(1):49–62, 1995.

[Wong *et al.*, 2000] Eric Wong, Swapna Gokhale, and Joseph Horgan. Quantifying the closeness between program components and features. *Journal of Systems and Software*, 54(2):87–98, 2000.

[Wu *et al.*, 2004] Xiaomin Wu, Adam Murray, Margaret-Anne Storey, and Rob Lintern. A reverse engineering approach to support software maintenance: Version control knowledge extraction. In *Proceedings of 11th Working Conference on Reverse Engineering (WCRE 2004)*, pages 90–99, Los Alamitos CA, November 2004. IEEE Computer Society Press.

[Wysseier, 2004] Christoph Wysseier. CCJun – polymetric views in three-dimensional space. Informatikprojekt, University of Berne, June 2004.

[Wysseier, 2005] Christoph Wysseier. Interactive 3-D visualization of feature-traces. Master's thesis, University of Berne, Switzerland, November 2005.

[Xing and Stroulia, 2004] Zhenchang Xing and Eleni Stroulia. Understanding class evolution in object-oriented software. In *Proceedings 12th IEEE International Workshop on Program Comprehension (IWPC'04)*, pages 34–43, Los Alamitos CA, 2004. IEEE Computer Society Press.

[Zaidman and Demeyer, 2004] A. Zaidman and S. Demeyer. Managing trace data volume through a heuristic clustering process based on event execution frequency. In *Proceedings IEEE European Conference on Software Maintenance and Reengineering (CSMR 2004)*, pages 329–338, Los Alamitos CA, March 2004. IEEE Computer Society Press.

[Zaidman and Demeyer, 2005] A. Zaidman and S. Demeyer. Mining argouml with dynamic analysis to establish a set of key classes for program comprehension. In *Proceedings of the 5th International Workshop on Reverse Engineering (WOOR 2005)*, 2005.

[Zaidman et al., 2005] A. Zaidman, T. Calders, S. Demeyer, and J. Paredaens. Applying webmining techniques to execution traces to support the program comprehension process. In *Proceedings IEEE European Conference on Software Maintenance and Reengineering (CSMR 2005)*, pages 134–142, Los Alamitos CA, 2005. IEEE Computer Society Press.

[Zenger, 2002] Matthias Zenger. Type-safe prototype-based component evolution. In *Proceedings ECOOP 2002*, volume 2374 of *LNCS*, pages 470–497, Malaga, Spain, June 2002. Springer Verlag.

[Zimmermann et al., 2003] Thomas Zimmermann, Stephan Diehl, and Andreas Zeller. How history justifies system architecture (or not). In *6th International Workshop on Principles of Software Evolution (IWPSE 2003)*, pages 73–83, Los Alamitos CA, 2003. IEEE Computer Society Press.

[Zimmermann et al., 2004] Thomas Zimmermann, Peter Weißgerber, Stephan Diehl, and Andreas Zeller. Mining version histories to guide software changes. In *26th International Conference on Software Engineering (ICSE 2004)*, pages 563–572, Los Alamitos CA, 2004. IEEE Computer Society Press.

Die VDM Verlagsservicegesellschaft sucht für wissenschaftliche Verlage abgeschlossene und herausragende

Dissertationen, Habilitationen, Diplomarbeiten, Master Theses, Magisterarbeiten usw.

für die kostenlose Publikation als Fachbuch.

Sie verfügen über eine Arbeit, die hohen inhaltlichen und formalen Ansprüchen genügt, und haben Interesse an einer honorarvergüteten Publikation?

Dann senden Sie bitte erste Informationen über sich und Ihre Arbeit per Email an *info@vdm-vsg.de*.

Sie erhalten kurzfristig unser Feedback!

VDM Verlagsservicegesellschaft mbH
Dudweiler Landstr. 99　　　　　　Telefon +49 681 3720 174
D - 66123 Saarbrücken　　　　　　Fax　　　+49 681 3720 1749

www.vdm-vsg.de

Die VDM Verlagsservicegesellschaft mbH vertritt

Printed by Books on Demand GmbH, Norderstedt / Germany